Working with Mindfulness

Praise for *Working with Mindfulness*

'The delightfully accessible style of this book reveals profound and transformative truths. It will guide you in direct mindfulness practices, while also skilfully addressing important areas such as ethics at work and scientific evidence for mindfulness. Michael and Josie manage to inspire without intimidating, and to teach without preaching, in their guide for waking up at work.'

**Martin Aylward, Founding Teacher,
MindfulnessTrainingInstitute.com**

'Practical, engaging, and fun to read, this book is a comprehensive guide to the benefits of mindfulness at work.'

Ruth Baer, Professor of Psychology, University of Kentucky

'Perfectly shows how busy workers can easily use mindfulness skills, in order to improve their health and productivity. Mindfulness can sometimes seem otherworldly, but this book shows how people can easily use and apply these key skills without interrupting the demands of their daily lives.'

**Frank W. Bond, Ph.D., Professor of Psychology and Management,
Director of the Institute of Management Studies,
Goldsmiths, University of London**

'*Working with Mindfulness* is a practical guide for working people about how to reduce individual stress by doing a number of simple exercises while at work. It is well written, simple to follow and can make a difference to you and your colleagues to cope with pressures of the modern workplace.'

**Professor Sir Cary Cooper, Manchester Business School,
University of Manchester**

'Excellent book with extensive information and practical guidance to help you clearly learn and understand how to use mindfulness at work.'

JP Dallmann, International Banker and Author, Specialist in Business and People Transformation, Leadership and Innovation, VCC UK

'*Working with Mindfulness* is an engaging and practical guide to reducing stress, transcending setbacks and enhancing performance at work. With more than 50 mindfulness exercises, it's a perfect introduction to a more fulfilling way of working.'

Arianna Huffington, Editor-in-Chief of The Huffington Post and Author of *The Sleep Revolution*

'Mindfulness and compassion can help us create better lives and more creative and collaborative workplaces. This fun and intensely pragmatic book shows us how.'

Russell Kolts, Ph.D. Professor of Psychology, Eastern Washington University and Author of *Living with an Open Heart*

'*Working with Mindfulness* is a wonderfully pragmatic book full of down-to-earth-easy-to-use ways to bring the power of mindfulness into the workplace. If every business got this book and used it, the world would be a much better place.'

Kevin L. Polk, Ph.D., Clinical Psychologist and ACT Matrix Trainer, The Psychological Flexibility Group

'Full of fresh, no-nonsense advice. If you care about the health, wellbeing and happiness of your team and are passionate about increasing their loyalty, confidence and success you can't afford to not to read this book. I learnt so much.'

Gina Ritchie, Buying Director, Liberty Ltd

'Combining the burgeoning evidence base from mindfulness research with cutting edge insights from contextual behavioural science, (ACT) this book will convince both boardroom strategist and beleaguered workplace warrior – especially when they engage with the copious suggestions for personal practice – that mindfulness at work addresses both bottom lines: productivity and well-being.'

Martin Wilks, Chartered Psychologist, Mindfulness Teacher and Peer-Reviewed ACT Trainer

'An excellent practical guide to managing stress in the workplace and beyond.'

Martin Zetter, former Senior Economist, Macfarlanes

Working with Mindfulness

Keeping calm and focused to get the job done

DR MICHAEL SINCLAIR AND JOSIE SEYDEL

Harlow, England • London • New York • Boston • San Francisco • Toronto • Sydney
Auckland • Singapore • Hong Kong • Tokyo • Seoul • Taipei • New Delhi
Cape Town • São Paulo • Mexico City • Madrid • Amsterdam • Munich • Paris • Milan

Pearson Education Limited
Edinburgh Gate
Harlow CM20 2JE
United Kingdom
Tel: +44 (0)1279 623623
Web: www.pearson.com/uk

First published 2016 (print and electronic)

ISBN: 978-1-292-09832-6 (print)
      978-1-292-09833-3 (PDF)
      978-1-292-09835-7 (ePub)

British Library Cataloguing-in-Publication Data
A catalogue record for the print edition is available from the British Library

Library of Congress Cataloging-in-Publication Data
Names: Sinclair, Michael (Michael I.), author. | Seydel, Josie, author.
Title: Working with mindfulness : keeping calm and composed to get the job
    done / Dr. Michael Sinclair and Josie Seydel.
Description: Harlow, England ; New York : Pearson, 2016. | Includes
    bibliographical references and index.
Identifiers: LCCN 2016000852 (print) | LCCN 2016008694 (ebook) | ISBN
    9781292098326 (pbk.) | ISBN 9781292098357 (ebook)
Subjects: LCSH: Job stress. | Mindfulness (Psychology) | Stress management.
Classification: LCC HF5548.85 .S564 2016 (print) | LCC HF5548.85 (ebook) |
    DDC 650.1—dc23
LC record available at http://lccn.loc.gov/2016000852

10 9 8 7 6 5 4 3 2 1
20 19 18 17 16

Cartoons by Stu McLellan
Cover design by Two Associates
Print edition typeset in 10 and ITC Giovanni Std by SPi Global
Print edition printed in Great Britain by Henry Ling Ltd, at the Dorset Press, Dorchester, Dorset

NOTE THAT ANY PAGE CROSS REFERENCES REFER TO THE PRINT EDITION

Contents

About the authors

Dr Michael Sinclair is a Consultant Counselling Psychologist and the Clinical Director of City Psychology Group (CPG) in London, UK He is an Associate Fellow of the British Psychological Society, a Registered Practitioner Psychologist with the Health and Care Professions Council as well as a Chartered Scientist, registered with the Science Council, UK He has provided the highest quality psychological interventions, including therapy and coaching, to individuals, couples, families, groups and teams for over 16 years. He acts as the consultant to a growing number of corporate human resources and occupational health departments based in the City of London as well as internationally, assisting with employees' stress management and productivity, and provides corporate training to leadership teams and key executives working across a range of industries within both the private and public sector. With his approach firmly rooted in contextual behavioural science, he has expertise in delivering a range of evidenced-based mindfulness interventions and has been trained in the USA by the pioneers of the mindfulness-based approach, Acceptance and Commitment Therapy (ACT). He has been dedicated to his own mindfulness practice for over 10 years. He regularly provides mindfulness workshops to both corporate as well as large public audiences and is actively involved in teaching mindfulness to psychologists as well as other health professionals. He has published a range of self-help books as well as academic papers on his research and practice. He appears frequently in the media where he provides commentary on psychological health and mindfulness in the workplace as well as in life more generally.

Josie Seydel is a Chartered Counselling Psychologist, registered with the Health and Care Professions Council, an Associate Fellow of the British Psychological Society and a Certified Mindfulness Teacher (with The Mindfulness Training Institute). She has been practising meditation since 1986. She has extensive experience providing effective mindfulness-based psychological therapy to corporate executives and assisting occupational health departments in managing workplace stress. Her other areas of specialist clinical practice include working with eating disorders, adolescents, self-harm and suicide. She has experience designing and delivering innovative, engaging and high-quality mindfulness workshops to public audiences as well as regularly facilitating mindfulness practice groups. Along with her work as a Clinical Associate at City Psychology Group, she also runs a thriving private practice in Devon, UK.

Authors' acknowledgements

We would like to thank our dear friends and family as well as our closest colleagues for their patience and encouragement while we have been writing this book. We are also sincerely grateful to all those whom we have ever had the pleasure to meet and serve in our work; without our connection with each and every one of you, this book would not have been possible. Thank you also to Eloise Cook at Pearson for all her hard work and support and to Stuart McLellan (www.stumclellan.co.uk) for the delightful illustrations.

Also, thank you to all those hard workers out there who read this book; we sincerely hope you experience the benefits of mindfulness in your work and life.

Publisher's acknowledgements

We are grateful to the following for permission to reproduce copyright material:

Text

'The Worst Day Ever?' by Chanie Gorkin, page 144; Extract on page 157 from The Telegraph (2009, March 31). Men Spend More Time Gossiping than Women, http://www.telegraph.co.uk/news/uknews/5082866/Men-spend-more-time-gossiping-than-women-poll-finds.html, © Copyright of Telegraph Media Group Limited 2015, © Telegraph Media Group Limited 2009; Quote on page 257 from Papero, D. Anxiety and Organisations, www.bowentheory.com/anxietyandorganizationspapero.htm, The Bowen Center; Extract on page 298 from MAPPG. Mindful Nation UK (2015, October 20, from themindfulnessinitiative.org.uk), http://themindfulnessinitiative.org.uk/images/reports/Mindfulness-APPG-Report_Mindful-Nation-UK_Oct2015.pdf, The Mindfulness Initiative

Picture Credits

The publisher would like to thank the following for their kind permission to reproduce their photograph:

Alamy Images: INTERFOTO /125

All other images © Pearson Education

Introduction

Hi! We are so glad that you have chosen to read this book and hope you have also enjoyed reading *Mindfulness for Busy People* (Pearson) and if not or you haven't yet read it, then WHY NOT? Well, seriously, it is absolutely excellent of course, but perhaps you were hoping for something a little more specific regarding one of the most stressful areas in our lives – work? And here it is. So how are you doing? How is work going? Let's see:

▶ Feeling overstretched?

▶ Underpaid?

▶ Like, no one really gets just how much work you have to do?

▶ Feeling burnt out?

▶ Unfulfilled?

▶ Overwhelmed?

▶ Lacking motivation? Maybe confidence?

▶ Can't seem to focus?

▶ Haven't got enough creativity to get the job done?

▶ Want to jump-start your colleagues/team/yourself into more action?

▶ Wondering how you can make your business a success?

Well, whether you answered *yes* or even *no* to any or all of these questions, welcome and we hope that this book will offer you a solution to these or any other work-related dilemmas that you may be facing. We could continue to run off a list of all the thousands of possible reasons that may have motivated you to pick this book up but in the spirit of breaking an old habit and trying something new, we're not going to do that. The fact is that you are reading this now, and that's enough. We both thank you and sincerely hope that you find what you seek and that this book inspires you in the deepening of your inquiry.

> **❝The fact is that you are reading this now, and that's enough.❞**

As Practitioner Psychologists working in the heart of London's square mile, we have introduced mindfulness to thousands of people and hundreds of teams and businesses all of whose working lives have improved dramatically as a consequence, whether that's because they've come to experience less stress, more confidence and creativity, improved focus and productivity, better relationships with colleagues and effective team dynamics or an overall healthier and more meaningful and fulfilling culture and environment within which to work (or all of the above). Let's face it, mindfulness is everywhere these days, it's been really hard to miss the headlines. More and more about its multitude of benefits, particularly for our work and working lives, is now being researched, written and talked about at an increasingly rapid rate. So just in case you have been living underneath a rock in some faraway land for the last few years, or maybe finding it hard to keep up with all the latest breaking news and research, or you just simply want a clear, no-nonsense and concise practical guide of what mindfulness has to offer you and your work, we chose to write this book. So here it is.

We hope that in reading this book you'll come to:

▶ Understand what mindfulness is, how to practise it and how it's relevant to your work.

▶ Improve your resilience and effectiveness in today's modern, fast-paced workplace.

▶ Increase your productivity, performance and efficiency at work.

▶ Enhance your creativity, decision-making, problem-solving, delegating, prioritising and time-management skills.

▶ Ensure your working relationships with colleagues and businesses are healthy, wholesome and the most productive that they can be.

▶ Improve your well-being, and ability to reduce and manage stress in your workplace.

▶ Develop greater care, compassion and connection with yourself and colleagues.

▶ Understand how applying mindfulness to your working environment can help you and your business to remain healthy and thrive.

About this book

This book has been written as a pragmatic, down-to-earth and quick introduction to using mindfulness at work. It is a practical book, intended to help you reduce stress and improve your day-to-day focus and effectiveness in the workplace. It may also help you begin to cultivate a healthier and more meaningful and rewarding environment within which to work (if that is what you also choose to do) for yourself, your team and the greater good of your organisation as a whole.

Instead of offering a specific mindfulness programme for you to follow, this book has attempted to provide a broad overview of the most salient insights and developments around the application of mindfulness at work, drawing on the tradition of mindfulness as well as on more modern scientifically proven mindfulness-based approaches to psychological change. Should you want to learn more about mindfulness, there are also other more in-depth books on the subject, some of which we have listed within the 'Recommended reading' section at the end of this book.

How to use this book

To help you practise mindfulness while you're on the job, throughout your working day, there are over 50 practical mindfulness-based exercises included throughout the book. You will find a range of these exercises, entitled 'Mindful on the job', which do not require any extra time out of your working day, embarrassing postures or degrees in philosophy in order to practise them; each one is clearly marked with a symbol as indicated on the next page. These types of mindfulness practices are designed to help you cope and/or perform better in typical work-related situations. They have not been written as a plan or programme for you to follow in any particular order over a set number of days or weeks. Instead, they are designed so that you can use any one of them, as and when you want to in the context of relevant work-related scenarios. That being said, in order for you to benefit from them the most, we would advise that you practise ALL of them as often and as regularly as you can, even at times when you feel that you may be coping and/or performing well. In order to really benefit from mindfulness (and especially for the longer term), you will need to keep practising it, as often as possible. There is also a chart entitled 'Quick Reference Guide to Keeping Mindful on the Job' included in Chapter 8 which we hope will provide you with a useful overview to the mindfulness practices included in this book and which particular work-related scenarios each one is most useful for.

There are audio recordings that accompany this book too. These guided mindfulness practices can be downloaded for free from the following website: www.pearson-books.com/mindfulnesswork

The particular practices that are accompanied by an audio guide are indicated in the book with the following symbol:

The book also includes a number of 'Work in progress' exercises which again are clearly marked with their own unique symbol (this symbol is indicated below too). These specific types of exercises are designed to help you learn more about the underlying principles of mindfulness that we're keen to get across to you. They will crop up throughout the book at relevant points to stimulate your further thought and reflection on the specific mindfulness-related concepts that you're reading about.

Please feel free to adapt any of the exercises to suit you or your working environment better, and also please feel free to share your experiences with colleagues.

Types of exercises with corresponding symbols

Mindful on the job   *Work in progress*

You will find case studies and experiential excerpts highlighted through-out the text which have been adapted from real-life scenarios of our work with our clients as well as from our own lives and work. Each chapter also contains summaries of current research under the title, 'Proven in science, smart for business'. In addition, towards the end of each chapter you will find a list of bulleted summary points called 'Mindfulness top tips to go' including what we think are the essential take-away messages from each chapter. Following each chapter you'll see a 'Useful resources' section which includes links and references to extra external sources which you may want to explore. Please note that all names and identifying markers have been removed from the case study material within this book to protect the confidentiality of our clients.

A few further notes before you read on ...

First and foremost, this book is intended to be a practical and experi-ential guide to help you to practise mindfulness for yourself in the con-text of your work. The reason for this is that as psychologists we know that our learning is greatly enhanced through our experience and also, as you'll soon discover (if you don't know already), in order to benefit from mindfulness you do need to practise it. Alongside all these exercises, however, you will also find lots of information, research and facts on the practice and principles of mindfulness generally, and on mindfulness at work specifically. We will also describe mindfulness practice and its applications in detail in each relevant section of the book, so that your knowledge can evolve alongside your practical experiences. We are really keen for you to experience mindfulness for yourself for the reasons given above but also in this way you won't need to take our word for it (or anybody else's); you will see the benefits unfolding in a way that makes sense through your very own direct experience.

We love words and debates – it is our work after all! However, we also know that language is all too often the problem, not always the solution, so we will be encouraging you to actually experience what we're on about, as best as we/you can. Trying to describe mindfulness can become a bit like trying to explain the colour 'green'; there are loads of technical definitions and many, many metaphors (we like those, so watch out for them!), but the best way to really understand and learn about it is to try it out for yourself.

We have been really excited about writing this book and being able once again to demonstrate how mindfulness is incredibly relevant and applicable to our modern lives. Most people think that this ancient practice (over 2,500 years old) is all about sitting crossed-legged on a cushion in a temple, in some faraway mystical land, chanting for hours to monotone sounds, and not at all relevant for the realities of our day-to-day modern lives. However, we hope to show you once again that mindfulness does have its place in our modern world (more so than ever!) and specifically in our work too, and with purposeful efforts to practise it our work and working lives can dramatically improve.

"Mindfulness is incredibly relevant and applicable to our modern lives."

We hope that in reading this book and trying out ALL the exercises included in it, you will begin to notice how the real mindfulness practice is not so much about sitting meditating for hours on end, but more in how we actually conduct ourselves at work, day to day, moment by moment while we're on the job. It's all well and good to sit somewhere quiet, close your eyes and breathe but when we bring this practice to life in our work, in real time, say while sitting in a meeting, responding to incessant emails, managing multiple demands, or interacting with colleagues, now that is where the fun really begins! Although some of the exercises included in this book may seem a little odd or silly at first, and even though your mind may want to judge them so, we do encourage you to *never mind your mind* and take your time to try them out nonetheless, as best and as often as you can to ensure that you get the full experience. Please do take your time as you work your way through this book. We hope you enjoy it and that it makes a real difference to you and your work!

Using mindfulness at work

In this first chapter you will discover:

▶ How this book can address some of the daily challenges you face at work.

▶ An overview of how businesses are now using mindfulness to address some of these very same challenges.

▶ How practising and benefiting from mindfulness at work doesn't have to get in the way of your day-to-day job.

▶ An overview of what mindfulness is and your first taste (in this book anyway) of practising it.

It's hard not to recognise how the reality of work has changed dramatically over the last few decades. We now find ourselves working in ever more challenging, complex and ambiguous times. Workers and employers alike are all looking for ways to help them cope with change, uncertainty and the accelerating rate at which we work. Advancements in technology and the culture of incessant email communication mean that being at work no longer simply means being physically present at the office. We are now connected to one another in a way that we have never been before, 24 hours a day, 7 days a week, go, go, go! This is all taking its toll on our resilience and none of this looks as if it is likely to slow down, any time soon. Understandably, this all brings into question our human capacity to continue to cope with it all. People are turning to mindfulness as a way to de-stress and deal with this 24-hour communication culture; they're searching for an antidote to overwhelming and excessive workloads, all the constant doing, rushing around, thinking and struggling, and in doing so are also discovering that mindfulness offers our work and working lives so much more besides.

More and more of the corporate executives, managers and business leaders that we teach mindfulness to, are recognising the positive impact that mindfulness can have on their business in terms of productivity and more profitable decision-making. These days we are all being asked to work and perform at peak levels and succeed in an increasingly interconnected, demanding and rapidly changing global environment. Old and habitual ways of operating within a highly competitive market no longer seem to serve us so well, and our clients have reported how mindfulness has helped them to adapt and become more open and flexible while developing new ways of listening and responding to colleagues and clients and also innovating with more skill and a rejuvenated sense of equanimity. Furthermore, in our work delivering mindfulness training for teams we're continuously told how collaboration and teamwork are greatly enhanced within a more compassionate environment following the team's practice of mindfulness, which has often become a 'must-do' for many of them at the start of any team meeting and/or working day ahead.

So what is all the fuss about? Well, before you continue to read on we thought you might like to take a mindful moment right now to experience a short taster of mindfulness straight away. Before you read any further, take a moment or two now to try the following exercise.

Exercise 1.1: Mindful on the job

Your starter for ten

We know we haven't given you a lot of detail on what mindfulness is as yet. But just so that you get a flavour right away and see just how accessible mindfulness is (remember our goal is to provide you with as much experience of mindfulness as possible while you read this book), follow these ten steps right now to help you see just how mindfulness has the potential to offer up a moment of peace in among the daily chaos. You might like to continue to use this as your 'must do' at the start of a busy day (and at any other points in-between). So rather than starting your day in the usual way (like running through your 'to-do list'), why not break an old habit and start it with this exercise instead. Go on, give it a try right now:

1 Just take a moment to think through all you have already done today.
2 Now consider all that you still 'have' to do.
3 Next notice the environment around you (colours, sounds, etc.).
4 Notice any sensations in the body (tension, stiffness, twitchiness, etc.).
5 Notice how you are feeling (overwhelmed, fired up, impatient, etc.).
6 Now take a moment to consider just the moment you are in.
7 Just for this moment put aside what has happened already and what is yet to happen and allow yourself to experience 'just this'.
8 Give yourself ten seconds (you can just guess if you like) just to sit or stand where you are and not do anything else right now.
9 Just notice your experiences (sounds, sights, sensations, feelings, thoughts), as they naturally come and go, rise and fall; there is no need to follow any of them.
10 When you are ready you can now choose to jump back into the rush of your day.

Whatever your experience of doing this exercise was, maybe a sense of peace, stillness or calm or even frustration, confusion or boredom (or all of the above), any is absolutely fine. Just notice and welcome that too. There's no need to try hard to work any of this out; all will be revealed and make more sense soon. So for now, let's continue on.

Booming business

You've probably already heard that more and more businesses are recognising the benefits of mindfulness. Often and most mentioned is Google which has implemented its own internal mindfulness programme (called 'Search Inside Yourself') for employees since 2007. General Mills also invests in mindfulness, as well as other large corporations such as Yahoo, Apple and Unilever. The list really does go on (and on!). There are a rapidly growing number of companies encouraging their employees to practise mindfulness and, when reviewing some of the research findings specifically related to reductions in business costs, it is easy to understand why.

❝More and more businesses are recognising the benefits of mindfulness. ❞

Proven in science, smart for business

▶ One particular study[1] by Duke University analysed the savings made at Aetna Health Insurance in 2012 after CEO Mark Bertolini made yoga, meditation and wellness programmes available to his then 49,000 employees. At that time 3,500 employees signed up for the mindfulness and yoga programmes. This is already quite impressive, just because the likelihood of our grannies and grandpas ever having even heard of these things at our age would have been highly unlikely. However, more remarkable still is that overall it was found that there was a 7 per cent drop in health-care costs, and among those that participated in the mindfulness programme there was a 36 per cent decrease in perceived stress levels and an increase of 62 minutes of productivity each week. Yes, you read that right – each week! Even those wanting to dismiss mindfulness and yoga as hippy-dippy-doo-dah nonsense would struggle to argue with these encouraging results. ➤

But one study alone looks a little sad, so how about this:

▶ Following a seven-week mindfulness course at General Mills there was a 60 per cent increase in the numbers of staff who reported that they were now taking time each day to optimise personal productivity, and a 50 per cent rise in reports from staff stating that following their mindfulness training they now make time to eliminate tasks with limited productivity value. Of the senior executives who took the seven-week course, 80 per cent reported an improvement in their ability to make productive decisions while 89 per cent reported how they felt that they had become better listeners.

Let's continue with our 'top five' listed success stories:

1 It is widely documented that Vermont-based Green Mountain Coffee Roasters includes mindfulness meditation as part of its offerings to its employees and it is worth noting that this company has also delivered double-digit net sales growth for the past 27 consecutive quarters.

2 & 3 eBay and Huffington Post ensure that mindfulness meditation rooms are available on site for their employees across all their offices. And it's no great surprise that UK-based firms are quickly following suit too.

4 Transport for London (TFL), introduced mindfulness training to its workforce as part of its stress-management strategy following a review in 2003 which highlighted that mental health difficulties were one of the most significant health problems affecting its employees. Following the implementation of their stress-management programmes, TFL reported that absenteeism caused by stress, anxiety and depression dropped by 71 per cent. Eighty-four per cent of participants said they were 'relating to others better'; 82 per cent increased the amount of exercise they did; 77 per cent improved their diet or tackled drinking and/or smoking problems; and 54 per cent improved their sleeping patterns following the mindfulness training they received.

5 Intel is another company that has been offering mindfulness training to its employees since 2012. A nine-week programme called Awake@ Intel has just recently been rolled out to its 100,000 employees working across 63 countries. An initial evaluation of this programme showed some promising results. On average, the 1,500 employees that have participated in the programme so far reported a two-point decrease (on a 10-point scale) in their experience of stress and feeling overwhelmed, a three-point increase in overall happiness

and well-being, and a two-point increase in having new ideas and insights, mental clarity, creativity, the ability to focus, the quality of relationships at work and the level of engagement in meetings, projects and collaboration efforts. Considering these results it is really no surprise that the firm is now backing the roll-out of this programme to its global workforce.

There are a whole bunch of other firms who have also now jumped on the bandwagon and begun to implement mindfulness training for their staff. Among the growing number of blue-chip businesses, companies and public bodies encouraging their employees to take up mindfulness practice at work, this side of the pond are: Bank of England, NPower, The Department of Health, Innocent, the NHS, Virgin, BP in Canary Wharf (who have a meditation room on-site), Goldman Sachs (who offer their employees use of in-house meditation pods), Credit Suisse, KPMG, Barclay's, PriceWaterhouseCoopers and Deloitte. This ancient practice is now seeping into Parliament too where over a hundred MPs, peers and parliamentary staff have also had their very own kick-starter taste of weekly mindfulness sessions. (Please see 'Useful resources' for some links and documents listing these and other companies who are using mindfulness.)

Yes, mindfulness is becoming increasingly popular and a very hot topic and the interest from organisations continues to grow. And this doesn't seem to be just another fad. One main reason for this is that over the past decade more and more scientific evidence is emerging that speaks to the multitude of benefits that mindfulness practice can bring. Understandably, companies can find it hard to ignore the hard scientific facts, and, with this growing body of research comes also a growing confidence around the positive effects of mindfulness, for both the individual employee and consequently the organisation as a whole.

Countless CEOs, business leaders and MPs are openly talking about mindfulness, their experiences and its benefits. We are lucky enough to hear feedback on a daily basis in our practice from our corporate clients as well as having our own on-going personal experience, but for those of you who do not yet know much about mindfulness, or are curious to hear about what some of the individuals and groups behind all the lists, data and research have to say, here are a few examples:

'Stress-reduction and mindfulness don't just make us happier and healthier, they're a proven competitive advantage for any business that wants one.'

Arianna Huffington, Co-Founder and Editor in Chief, *The Huffington Post*
(Taken from huffpost.com; please see 'Useful resources' section
for link to full blog post)

'… That compassion to ourselves, to everyone around us – our colleagues – customers, that's what the training of mindfulness is really about.'

**Janice Marturano, Deputy General Counsel, General Mills, Founder &
Executive Director, Institute of Mindful Leadership
(See a video of Janice Marturano speaking about mindful leadership
listed in the 'Useful resources' section)**

'[mindfulness] Meditation is the best thing I have ever done to calm myself and separate from the 24/7, connected world. By centering into myself, I can focus my attention on the important things, develop an inner sense of well-being, and gain clarity in making decisions. My most creative ideas come from meditating, and meditation has built resilience to deal with difficult times. No doubt it has helped me become a better leader.'

**Bill George, Professor of Management Practice, Harvard Business School,
Former CEO of Medtronic & Goldman Sachs Board Member
(Taken from huffpost.com; please see 'Useful resources' section
for link to full blog post)**

'We find that mindfulness is a transformative practice, leading to a deeper understanding of how to respond to situations wisely. We believe that government should widen access to mindfulness training in key public services [health, education, workplaces, criminal justice system], where it has the potential to be an effective low-cost intervention with a wide range of benefits.'

**Mindfulness All-Party Parliamentary Group (MAPPG) (Taken from
oxfordmindfulness.org; please see 'Useful resources' section for link to the
Interim Report of the MAPPG)**

For employers, the improvement of mental health and an associated, increased ability to manage stress and enhance resilience easily translates into reduced absenteeism and higher productivity among its workforce. Among the other work-related benefits of mindfulness are enhanced emotional intelligence (that is, a greater awareness and improved regulation of emotions), improved decision-making and strategic-thinking abilities, and a heightened ability to focus and work creatively. With all these benefits it's hardly surprising that organisations are beginning to weave this simple practice and set of principles into their company culture and the psyche of their employees, as quick as they can and in a number of ways. The implementation of mindfulness in the workplace can commonly take many forms, some of which may include:

▶ offering mindfulness-based stress prevention and management training programmes as part of larger health, well-being and wellness initiatives;

▶ providing mindfulness-based psychological therapy interventions for distressed employees;

▶ incorporating it into management and leadership development programmes, often in the form of training on emotional intelligence, self-management and resilience, communication skills, team effectiveness and performance, managing stress in others, creativity, well-being and strategic thinking;

▶ using it to inform executive mentoring and coaching practice;

▶ weaving it into corporate social responsibility policies;

▶ setting aside time and space (and dedicated facilities) within the work environment and during the working day to specifically engage with mindfulness practice.

As you continue to develop your own understanding of mindfulness, and start to experience its benefits for yourself, you may want to present this, together with the evidence from some of the studies listed throughout this book to support a case for investment in further training in mindfulness as part of your own workplace's continued well-being, learning and development programmes.

So what exactly is mindfulness?

Mindfulness is a term that specifically refers to practices, techniques and theory derived from Buddhist meditative practices and was traditionally part of a broad spiritual path. The concepts of mindfulness have been secularised over the past 40 or so years and it is not necessary to entertain any particular spiritual outlook in order to practise or benefit. That said, the principles of mindfulness – in essence the intentional, purposeful focusing of attention on the 'here and now' in an open and accepting way – brings up many observations of life 'just as it is' which may lead you to consider our reality quite differently and at times this shift in perspective can be, well, put quite frankly, absolutely mind-blowing (in a good way).

'The unexamined life is not worth living.'

Socrates

Before we natter on with more definitions and descriptions of mindfulness and explanations of how it might be relevant to you and your work, we thought it probably best to begin in the simplest way, by inviting you to try the following exercise right now so you can start to experience for yourself what it's all about …

Exercise 1.2: Work in progress

It's all about discriminating (in a very PC way, of course)

You can do this exercise with any object that you have in reach right now (we usually hand people a marker pen, so if you have one to hand then great); it can be anything at all that you can hold in your hand: a pen, mobile phone, watch from your wrist, maybe an apple, a sweet, piece of gum or other piece of food that can sit in your hand comfortably or even this book you're reading right now, whether in a hard copy or your Kindle itself. For the rest of the exercise we are going to refer to this object as 'X'.

We're going to invite you do two mini 'experiencing' exercises with X; the first one involves experiencing X with your five senses. Then when we've done that, we're going to invite you to experience X in your mind. So grab X now and hold it in your hand/s. Ready? OK.

1 First we invite you to experience X with your sight. Take your time to gaze and look upon X carefully. Notice what you see. Its shape, colours, markings, the space around X (do this for at least 10 seconds or so before you move on to step 2).

2 Now, we invite you to experience X with your touch. Notice the weight of X in your hand, acknowledge the temperature of X: is it cool, warm maybe? Run your fingers around X and really notice the texture, lumps, bumps, markings (again take your time).

3 Next, experience X with your sense of smell. Hold it up to your nose and take a few whiffs (if you don't feel comfortable to do this, that's ok; just acknowledge the absence of any smell from X).

4 Now (this may sound weird, but) we encourage you to experience X with your sense of taste – take a lick. (We know, YUK! Again, if you don't feel comfortable, just notice the absence of taste.)

5 Finally, it's time to listen to X. Notice what sounds X makes – nothing noticeable? Great, then just notice and acknowledge the absence of sound – or you might like to give X a flick or tap with your finger – ah, we have noise!

Right, now, put X down to one side and close your eyes (if you don't feel comfortable doing that, then rest your gaze on a still object or spot in front of you and droop your eyelids slightly). We're now going to experience X through our mind. Ooooo! Ready?

▶ Bring X to mind, and try to remember and imagine what it looks, feels, smells, tastes and sounds like. Don't rush this part; take your time to bring these senses to life in your mind, one at a time (do this for at least 10 seconds or so).

So, to end this exercise, we want you to answer two quick questions:

1 Did you *notice* any difference in the two types of experiencing (five senses versus in the mind)?

2 Whether you answered *yes* or *no*, take a moment now to reflect on WHO is it exactly that is *noticing* whether there is a difference?

Well, who is it that notices the difference?

That's right, it's YOU!

So, there you have it; you have the ability to be aware, notice and therefore discriminate between being present, in the 'here and now' (i.e. five senses experiencing) versus being caught up in your mind (i.e. experiencing X mentally). That's what it takes to practise mindfulness (the ability to *notice* where your attention is: either focused on the here and now or lost and caught up in your mind). If you can notice that difference, then we're good to go (if you didn't, that's absolutely fine too, just take your time to try the exercise again, you'll get it soon enough). By the way, this exercise forms part of 'The Matrix', which is a model designed to understand and engender *psychological flexibility*. It has been developed from the excellent work of Dr Kevin Polk and if you want to find out more about this model and his work you might like to follow the relevant link listed in the 'Useful resources' section at the end of this chapter.

From an exercise like the one above we come to realise that there is in fact a larger, more spacious part of the mind, a wider perspective, which can notice whether we are either focused on our present moment experience or caught up in distraction and mental experience. This wider perspective is *awareness* and that is what mindfulness is: *awareness of what is, just how it is, right now, just in this moment.* Implicit in this kind of awareness is *acceptance,* no judgement or evaluation, just openness and curiosity to how our life and experience is unfolding moment to moment. It is from awareness such as this that we have more clarity of mind and can then make choices: for instance, we can choose to bring our attention away from distracting thoughts about the past or the future or how life should be, and return it back to observing our experience, just as it is, in that present moment.

Most of the time our attention is not where we want it to be and mindfulness training is all about purposefully maintaining a present, moment-by-moment awareness of our thoughts, feelings, bodily sensations and the surrounding environment as best we can. We may choose to use our sensory experience (the breath or bodily sensations, for example) as a focal point in our mindfulness training, to return our wandering mind to, again and again without judgement or any expectation that our attention should stay focused on any one thing/sensation, in any given moment.

Mindfulness training is like training a muscle in the gym, where we might engage in repetitive exercise to increase muscle mass and strength; in mindfulness training we train the mind to stay where we want it to be, by remaining aware and returning our attention to a focal point, again and again. To extend the analogy further, just like going to the gym we also need to take care not to overwork (over-effort), to be gentle with ourselves, compassionate towards our inevitable struggles, busy minds and challenging emotional states. This requires a caring attitude, which can also be practised, so that we are able to meet ourselves more fully in mindfulness. Mindfulness training is not only about focused-attention training (more on what mindfulness isn't below). Although our attention and focus is likely to improve by noticing where our mind is, so too will our capacity for patience, kindness and compassion as we continuously bring our attention away from distraction back to a chosen focal point with the utmost acceptance and care.

Furthermore, just like training in the gym, there will be times when our interest wanes or wanders, and so to maintain our passion and to enhance the benefits of practice we also need to keep an attitude of curiosity, as Jon Kabat-Zinn (a very well established secular mindfulness teacher) says: 'When you pay attention to boredom it gets unbelievably interesting' (more on this in Chapter 6). Curiosity keeps mindfulness fresh, joyful and creative and allows us to see and appreciate the infinite subtleties of life. The beauty to recognise about mindfulness training is that we don't actually have to go to a gym but can instead choose to do our mindfulness training anywhere, even on the job, while we are at work, or wherever we are and in whatever we may be doing.

What mindfulness isn't

We have previously given a rundown of some of the common myths and untruths about mindfulness and what it isn't about (Sinclair and Seydel, 2013, p. 10); however, we thought it might be useful to have a recap of some of the most common misconceptions here once again and to clear these up straight away. Here are our top four reminders on what mindfulness isn't:

Mindfulness is NOT ...

1. ... about escaping work, relaxing, missing out or being lazy (when you could be doing something more productive!)

This is the most common concern and misunderstanding that we often hear from our busy and high-achieving corporate clients. The truth is that mindfulness is not passive in any sense; it is about training the mind, and as we've said already, much in the same way that we might train our bodies at the gym. Just like a physical workout, mindfulness training takes practice, energy and effort (although usually there's less sweating involved). Mindfulness training involves a transformation of the mind from an unconscious, impulsive state of reactivity to a state of awareness and more effective responsiveness. Furthermore, mindfulness is about facing the reality of our working life head-on, seeing it just how it is, the good as well as the bad, being honest with ourselves and recognising how we truly operate and function as a person. With mindfulness training you will begin to understand yourself with more accuracy and clarity and feel more in control of yourself and your actions. You might also be pleased to know that mindfulness doesn't mean that we simply have to accept or 'put up' with everything and never make important changes or take action when our needs are not being met. Instead it gives us clarity of mind and skills of self-regulation to act effectively in ways that truly matter to us in our work.

2. ... about sitting around crossed-legged, meditating for hours on end

Although finding a quiet place to sit down and meditate is a great way to practise, cultivate and reinforce the qualities and principles of mindfulness (read here: present moment focus, non-judgemental awareness, open curiosity, acceptance and compassion), it is not the only way to do it or what mindfulness is per se. Mindfulness is really about how you go about your life and carry yourself through your working day, moment by moment, bringing these qualities with you. Mindfulness can be practised in many ways, in any moment and in whatever we may be doing, like while talking to a colleague, sat in a meeting, delivering a presentation, using your phone, walking around the office or eating your lunch at your desk. Although some of the practices in this book will encourage you to close your eyes and focus on your breath, we do hope that you'll soon realise that the real mindfulness practice is how we choose to conduct ourselves in every moment throughout our busy working day.

3. ... about clearing the mind of thoughts

Despite popular beliefs (and hopes!), mindfulness is not about eliminating, changing, or suppressing our troublesome thoughts and worries about work. Trying to do that will just lead to more upsetting thoughts and frustration; it's impossible, the thoughts will just rebound (don't think about all the unanswered emails in your inbox)! Likewise, it's not about problem-solving or analysing our thoughts away. Mindfulness is about bringing awareness to our thoughts, noticing them and in doing just that we may find that the mind begins to settle and clear all of its own accord. It's inevitable that you will become distracted by thoughts while you practise mindfulness, and it is important to remember that this is a natural and human phenomenon and just what to expect; distraction is not a sign of failure but something to also be aware and mindful of (read here: notice distractions with non-judgemental awareness, acceptance and compassion). When we bring these qualities to noticing that our mind is distracted in this way, bam(!), we are back in the present moment, practising mindfulness once again.

4. ... a sure-fire, quick-fix solution to all your work-related problems

Mindfulness will bring many benefits, relief and effective solutions to many of your work-related dilemmas; however, it is certainly not a panacea. Mindfulness practice is all about cultivating awareness – which is implicitly non-judgemental and accepting (no other agenda, just that) – yet from this a multitude of benefits will no doubt arise for you and your working life generally, simply as a fortunate by-product of your regular practice. Although it is natural to want more of these benefits (like feeling calmer, less stressed, more level headed, energised, productive and creative on the job), it is important not to become too preoccupied or attached to them as that is bound to backfire and get in the way of your practice and you actually realising them for yourself. Wanting a specific outcome or wishing things were different is only human, so bringing mindful attention to that 'natural wanting' itself too will help to lessen disappointment and frustration when times feel bleak and/or you don't get what you want. Working life is tough and stressful and mindfulness cannot change that. It can, however, help you to cope and perform better in the face of the inevitable daily stress, hardship, challenges and struggles that your work is bound to continue to present to you. It is important to remember also that there are many other effective ways to deal with challenges at work (like prioritising items on your agenda to make the most of your time or going for a run on your lunch break to de-stress); mindfulness is all-inclusive, so it is OK to use these strategies too alongside your regular practice.

More about mindfulness for work ...

At the most basic level mindfulness comes as a highly effective form of stress-reduction: a relatively simple set of techniques for helping you get through the working day with a little more ease and grace. However, as you start to become more aware of what is really going on in your working life (not just the panics, daydreams and yearnings about what *might* be) through these simple-to-learn techniques, you will find that a whole range of benefits will become increasingly available to you. Instead of becoming caught in distracting, irrelevant or time-wasting struggles, mindfulness helps the development of more meaningful, clear and focused decision-making. As the use of mindfulness too increases our discernment, we can step back from habitual reactivity, urges and impulses and instead have more clarity of mind, a sharpened focus of attention and the capacity to engage with level-headed creative and fresh approaches in the workplace. These can then also be implemented conscientiously, effectively and in ways which enhance our working environment both in terms of our individual well-being and productivity and in the development of a thriving, healthy business.

We hope that this is all sounding as great to you as it does to us. No doubt, by now you're just itching to find out more and get started on practising mindfulness some more yourself. So, enough of the blab (for now); let's keep keeping this real. Here is a classic to get you started:

Exercise 1.3: Mindful on the job 🎧

Mindfulness of breathing

We can't rabbit on enough about this practice. This is the most useful practice of all as it has the wonderful benefit of always being accessible. Whether travelling to and from work, sat at your desk, in a meeting or while public speaking, your breath is always there too. There are simply no excuses (although you are bound to think of loads anyway) unless you have actually kicked the oxygen habit, and then hopefully work-related worries will all be over anyway (but as we have no data on this, we do **not** recommend this form of stress-reduction).

1 Begin by noticing your body now either sitting, standing, walking, lying down or however it is on this earth at this very moment.

2 You do not need to adjust yourself or your breathing in any special way, or refrain from doing this. Just notice yourself exactly as you are. Whatever thoughts, sensations or emotions arise, they are the ones you want, just exactly as they are.

3 As you become aware of your body, notice the breath being breathed by the body.

4 Notice the physical sensations of one inhalation and one exhalation wherever you notice these most strongly (i.e.: the tip of the nose, over the lips, the back of the throat, the stomach, the rib cage – it doesn't matter which; just allow one or more of these sensations to take centre stage in your attention).

5 Track each in-breath from its entry point into the body (i.e. tip of the nose, flowing over the lips), as it travels on its journey, down the back of the throat, filling the lungs, and the stomach.

6 Track each out-breath as it makes its outward journey along the same route up and back out of the body.

7 Thoughts, other sensations, urges or emotions may arise: this is natural; there is no need to hook into these, push them away or act on them in any way. Simply notice that this happens (it's absolutely fine and normal) and be as attentive to the breath as you can be. From each distraction simply return again and again to noticing and tracking the breath. You need do nothing else. Just watch one breath at a time, just for now.

8 Repeat the above from anything between once to hundreds of times a day (we do recommend that you keep this practice going at least once a day – even for a few minutes or so).

What effect does this have?

You may already have observed a multitude of things in this practice, such as many distracting thoughts, a sense of calm, questions about 'getting it right/wrong', physical sensations, noises, boredom, frustration, curiosity. Bet that either you can think of several more or we haven't even mentioned the ones relevant to you. Mindfulness can be likened to putting a microscope on your usual experience and seeing deeply into the minutiae of the mind's constant activity. Often our normal response is to try and interfere with this – 'Oh, I don't like that grubby thought about the guy in accounts, I'll try to shove that away', or the like. We start to see the mind struggling and squirming away in the Petri dish of our life (see, told you we liked metaphors), generally not looking too pretty.

We can begin to see our tendencies to judge ourselves (NOT calm enough/good enough/mindful enough), our desire to be other than we are (better/richer/quieter) or elsewhere (Barbados/home/pub); basically we usually are struggling for anything other than this moment and this sets us up for perpetual dissatisfaction as life unfolds in a series of not-quite-right moments – bah humbug! The 'good' stuff doesn't last; it isn't enough, or is too expensive, health-damaging or difficult to sustain. Our world can shrink to one of lack. Work can look like: not enough pay, not enough appreciation, not enough time, energy or fulfilment. Our strategies for pushing all these depressing thoughts and emotions away are themselves exhausting and generally unsustainable, and our sad trick is usually then to label ourselves as failures or lacking in some way too, or the world as unfair or unforgiving and then it is time to lie on the floor in a puddle and weep . . .

OR . . . We use mindfulness to observe, like through the microscope, and we just watch. The squirmy thoughts and irritating little emotions stop wriggling about quite so much when we stop prodding them. When we keep our 'hands off', so to speak, they usually tend to still a bit and then we find, weirdest of weird, that we might begin to feel a bit . . . calm (we know, weird, right?). Even if those thoughts and emotions, backaches and odd air-conditioning noises are still being quite active, we realise that we don't need to do anything with them, not for this moment anyway, and then, another weird thing is that we might notice a sense of . . . spaciousness – ah, freedom at last!

Before you drift off on a cloud of cosmic bliss, let's just bring it back to earth. We need calmness and spaciousness on this planet and probably more so in an office near you! So the practicality of spending a few moments watching your breath is enormously beneficial as you will reduce your levels of stress and increase your mental clarity and all the benefits that may come from that, just by using this simple practice, which doesn't have to take long at all, and, do you know what else too? Julie sitting across the desk doesn't have to even know that you're doing it (unless you want to tell her, of course). If you did not find these particular qualities in your brief foray into mindfulness, then leave the concern alone (we said 'hands off!') and just notice where you struggle and what arises for you out of this; it will give you clues as to the habitual operating of your mind and that this particular way of thinking/being is quite pernicious. Frequently thoughts can look like: 'mindfulness is not for me', 'I'm not good at this', 'this book is cr*p'. The last one is a downright lie, but otherwise hold these thoughts lightly, the best you can, like a butterfly in the palm of your hand, and allow yourself time to develop a new skill; it takes practice, and there is much, much more to come.

'The simple process of focusing on the breath in a relaxed manner, in a way that teaches you to regulate your emotions by raising one's awareness of mental processes as they're happening, is like working out a bicep, but you are doing it to your brain.'

Fadel Zeidan, PhD, University of North Carolina

Josie: I have been a practitioner of mindfulness meditation, as part of my Buddhist practice, since the age of 18. I'm 38 at the time of writing. Sometimes the last 20 years makes me feel embarrassed that I have practised mindfulness for so long and still burn the toast, shout at the kids and can't park the car very well. I feel my inner critic telling me all the while 'well, that's not very mindful is it?', 'If only your clients/ readers/mother could see you now!' The difference, I suppose, is that I know this critic rather well and am pretty skilled at telling it to take a flying leap. If I listened to my critic, I wouldn't do anything, let alone put myself out there to dare to write a book about mindfulness – 'Ha! Who do you think you are?' When I read some of the bad reviews on Amazon (far in the minority, but my inner critic only pays attention to the comments that make it feel real, which is the bad stuff), I cried. I believed for those moments that I must not be quite good enough, that I shouldn't even feel sad, because having written all about 'mindfulness' ('yeah, like you're some kind of expert, Josie!'), I should be over all this ego-trippy, caring what others say about you stuff. Then I sat and breathed, I followed each in-breath and each out-breath ➤

and my critic shut up for a bit. After 20 years, I know the goodness of my practice. I know my own fragile humanity and I see that in the faces of those all around me too. Mindfulness helps me to remember and to feel connected no matter what.

So my critic pops up, says 'you're no good', I say 'no thanks, not today', have a breath and continue with my work.

We thought it might be a good time to share some of what the science tells us about the benefits of mindfulness in the workplace. So let's get some hard facts down to begin to support all this. There is a fast growing evidence base for the multitude of positive effects that mindfulness can bring to our work and working life and we will continue to share some more of this research with you throughout the book. Here are just a few notes before we start to take a look at some of this research:

1 The benefits of mindfulness at work are also corroborated by an exciting and growing number of studies into particular workplace interventions which include mindfulness as a key element of bringing about psychological and behavioural change. Acceptance and Commitment Training (ACTraining) is one such mindfulness-based intervention which we will refer to now and again and that has shown promising results for both improving job-task performance and reducing stress within the workplace. ACTraining (which is based on the six core processes of Acceptance and Commitment Therapy or ACT, originally developed by the University of Nevada Psychologist, Professor Steven C. Hayes and colleagues) supports the development of workers' *psychological flexibility* (more about psychological flexibility in Chapter 6), which involves the practice of a range of mindfulness exercises and techniques as well as many others. First and foremost we want to note that ACT is embedded in the science of human behaviour, language and cognition. Other than mindfulness there are a number of other salient processes and principles at its core, yet it does recognise the centrality of mindfulness in helping workers to more effectively manage thoughts and feelings so that they can ultimately take more committed action towards valued workplace goals.

2 We have collected together a number of studies that demonstrate the efficacy of mindfulness, either generally or specifically, for our work.

Although the mindfulness interventions or programmes under investigation in these studies may differ in some way from one another, we have not always highlighted which specific one is being used but we do assure you that the 'active ingredient' (mindfulness) is always there and its qualities the same. For example, Mindfulness-Based Stress Reduction (MBSR) and Mindfulness-Based Cognitive Therapy (MBCT) are two very similar eight-week mindfulness courses that are commonly used in the studies mentioned in this book. There is in fact a huge crossover in the content and delivery of these programmes and the mindfulness component is essentially identical in both so we did not feel that within the scope of this book it was always necessary to specify which is being used in each particular study mentioned.

3 We have picked and included some of the juiciest research for you so that you can add a greater sense of confidence to your own explorations as you develop your mindfulness skills at work. It is also extremely useful to understand and share the findings of relevant mindfulness research if you ever have to justify using mindfulness, as some folks are far more inclined to listen to the viewpoint of Professor Clever-Cloggs than to you (unless by weird coincidence you also happen to be Professor Clever-Cloggs). If you wish to make a proposal for including mindfulness programmes, training and implementation at work, you may want to refer to this and the other research related sections in this book and wave them under the noses of your colleagues.

4 PS: just in case you don't know, a control group is a group which receives no change in their normal conditions (i.e. no mindfulness, medications, relaxation exercises, etc.). This is so that any group with a change (i.e. mindfulness, medications, relaxation exercises, etc.) can be compared to a baseline group. Any quantitative research without a control group is considered by some as quite meaningless. A control group picked at random (randomised control groups/trials) from the participants is usually even better as there will have been no intentional or unintentional biasing towards certain factors in the study (such as men or women, for example). For statistical purposes it is usually important that any research has a sample group of at least 30 participants in order for the results to be considered relevant for the general population (but this does not mean that studies with fewer are irrelevant; they may simply be quite specific to that particular population – e.g. Vietnamese factory workers – or they could just be preliminary findings).

So now that's all cleared up, take a look at this:

Proven in science, smart for business

Decreasing burnout

Mindfulness as a form of stress reduction has been widely researched and documented and more of this research is now focusing on the relationship between mindfulness and work-related stress specifically. In a recent study[2], researchers at Ohio State University found that a workplace mindfulness-based intervention significantly reduced stress levels among staff working at an intensive care unit: as highly stressful an environment as any we can imagine. Participants were randomly assigned to either an eight-week mindfulness-based intervention or a control group with no mindfulness training. The saliva (nice) of participants from both groups was tested before and after the intervention, and, while there was no change in the control group, a significant decrease in the levels of salivary α-amylase (an index of sympathetic activation of the nervous system — also known as the 'fight or flight' response) was measured in the group that received mindfulness training. Although the levels of stress did not change before and after the mindfulness intervention, the staff's response to stress did change. Work-related stress cannot always or easily be eliminated, but this study shows that mindfulness can help people cope with work-related stress and its harmful effects in highly stressful work environments. One of the researchers concludes that a 'mindfulness-based intervention in the workplace could decrease stress levels and the risk of burnout'.

Burnout in corporate finance

In another study[3] the researchers set out to determine the relationship between burnout, job satisfaction, social support and mindfulness within a corporate organisation. A total of 209 employees working in a financial corporate environment participated in the study. Of the variables measured, mindfulness (as the one intrapersonal strategy) came just second to job satisfaction as the most significant predictor of burnout. The researchers conclude that 'mindfulness may in the long run provide organisations with a valuable tool to manage high burnout levels of employees within the workplace'.

Stress management and exhaustion

Reducing stress, exhaustion and burnout easily translates to financial savings for a business, and the good news is that mindfulness-based interventions can help with all that, as also confirmed by these two studies. In one study[4] the researchers were interested to explore the effects of ACTraining for stress management

➤

among employees working in a large media organisation. A total of 90 employees participated in this study and were allocated either to an ACTraining group, an Innovation Promotion Program (that aimed to help employees change perceived stressful events at work), or a wait-list group (control). After three half-day sessions of the intervention groups, the participants from the ACTraining showed significantly lower levels of psychological distress than those in the innovation training and wait-list control groups. ACT also resulted in improvements in innovation potential. Consistent with ACT's theory of change, the improvements in mental health and innovation found among the ACT participants were explained by increases in (mindfulness-based) psychological flexibility. In another study[5] a similar three-half-day ACTraining intervention was found to bring about a significant decrease in emotional exhaustion among a group of government workers as compared to a control group.

Competence even in chaos

It's all well and good to know that mindfulness can help reduce stress and even prevent burnout on the job (which is of course excellent news) but what about helping us with a typically frantic and demanding work environment? Well, one study[6] set out to investigate just that and specifically if and how mindfulness could actually help employees cope while working within such a chaotic environment. A total of 98 restaurant waiters took part in this study and their managers were asked to rate them in terms of their individual job performance. Those measured to have higher mindfulness scores were also rated as having a better job performance. Interestingly, workplace mindfulness contributed to job performance, irrespective of how engaged the waiters were on the job. This research suggests that mindfulness enhances cognitive resources to help people attend to a range of tasks even if they are less engaged with the job. This is one of the first studies that shows how mindfulness can enhance cognitive performance even in a rapidly changing and highly demanding work environment.

Pretty impressive stuff, hey (well, we think so anyway)? And this really is just a taste of the huge body of scientific research that is out there already and also still being done on mindfulness and specifically mindfulness at work. We have loads more great studies and interesting facts to share with you in each relevant chapter, as the book unfolds. But for now, at this early stage we'd also like to turn your attention to some of the larger issues and debates relating to mindfulness and our work.

Being in the moment and achieving goals

'By operating "mindfully" and making critical adjustments in a timely manner, business organisations are better able to manage the unexpected in a challenging, highly competitive environment.'

Karl Weick, University of Michigan's Ross School of Business

One commonly raised concern about mindfulness and business is that mindfulness and competitive business are at odds with one another. Mindfulness encourages present-focused awareness and attention to the 'here and now'. Competitive business is focused on outcomes, predictions, goals and future based events. How can the practice of 'letting go' of judgements and thoughts and refocusing continually on 'the moment' help us to make sensible discriminations, decisions and plans to put these into action effectively? Is it even possible to be mindful and achieve a profit and reach goals or objectives?

Michael: So here's the thing. As I sit writing this book, getting it ready for publication (eek!) my mind is giving me some very compelling thoughts indeed, like 'Yeah right, who you kidding? What makes you think you can do it?' Now, buying into these thoughts is all too easily done and exactly what I'd tend to do, especially at stressful times when I'm running on autopilot, with deadlines looming. My other instinctive and habitual response to these thoughts is to try to shut them up, maybe by thinking of something else altogether or arguing back in some way – but this just feels like I'm caught up in a game of tug-of-war with a school bully who's determined to win and see me come crashing, face first to the ground. Either way, it's all too time-consuming and stressful – a real show stopper! So, sorry folks, no more writing today. But writing this book, raising awareness of psychology, helping others and making the most out of this fortunate opportunity is what really matters to me; that's what I really care about and what I want my professional life to be about – so what else can I do? How am I supposed to get the job done despite these pesky thoughts trying their best to hinder my progress? Well, my experience tells me that there is another way, yes sireee; although over ten years of dedicated mindfulness practice doesn't stop those troublesome thoughts demanding my attention, it DOES offer me another route to success. I have a choice here – let the bully win or simply drop the rope and carry on regardless. Awareness, and simply acknowledging those troublesome thoughts

➤

---

as they naturally arise with exquisite present moment-to-moment focus frees up the time, energy and mental space to continue – and hey presto, here's another paragraph for you all to read, unless you've already keeled over in boredom, that is (ah, there's that bully again!)?

Exercise 1.4: Work in progress

Deciding how we choose

Consider the next item on your agenda for the day, perhaps a phone call to a client, a meeting with colleagues or a report to write. Let's just take a moment before you complete this task to consider what moves you to engage in this activity, what motivates you. Ask yourself:

1 What is motivating me to do this task? For example:
   (a) Fear of not doing it (i.e. anxiety, fear of failure, being reprimanded, shame, job security, etc.)
   (b) Desire to get something (i.e. excitement, praise, recognition, money, sense of self-worth, etc.)
   (c) Automatic pilot (i.e. hadn't thought about any of this – it's just what I do!)
   (d) Something else not mentioned
   (e) Nothing comes to mind

2 What sensations arise in the body as I think about the task? For example:
   (a) Stiffness in the shoulders
   (b) Tightness/butterflies in the belly
   (c) Stillness
   (d) Something else
   (e) Nothing

3 Just for now, what's there if I don't look to the answers to Questions 1 and 2 of this exercise (i.e: my habitual, knee-jerk responses) for my motivation? For example:

(a) Purpose/Meaning/Satisfaction

(b) Liberation

(c) Fear/Disorientation

(d) Numbness/Blankness/Nothing

(e) Don't know

4 Where in the body do I feel these emotions/sensations? For example:

(a) Head, tension

(b) Hands, tingling

(c) Legs, restless

(d) Whole body, still, relaxed

(e) No sensations seem to arise

5 To a greater or lesser extent can I now notice both habitual motivation (Questions 1 and 2) and an absence of or alternative kind of motivation to engage in the task (Questions 3 and 4)?

6 Do I now still choose to complete the task?

Yes – Mindfulness has not hindered your ability to make decisions, in fact now you may even have some sense of a space for actively *choosing* to complete your task. You may even have a new way of seeing motivation when released from a habitual response. You are gaining insight into the nature of yourself and your relationship with work, and continued investigation with mindfulness practice will help you understand this process further; read on and keep practising.

Maybe – With an awareness of your struggle to engage in the task right now, see equally, a new awareness of another aspect of this moment's reflection which requires you to do what is necessary and needed in this moment. You can still complete the task even if you feel averse to doing it. This is because you can mindfully recognise that other factors seem more important than your reluctance to engage, and as such you can still choose to do the task. If you feel strongly that the task is not necessary or needed (right now), leave the task undone; it is not necessary or needed (in this moment at least)!

Don't know – How often do we allow ourselves not to know what we want? See if you can just allow this for a while, maybe something will change, maybe not, but you may be able to give yourself enough space to find out rather than simply reacting habitually. If not knowing becomes intolerable, then either look to the chapter on how to

'Maintain peak performance' (Chapter 6) or just repeat Exercise 1.3 from earlier on in this chapter, another time or two; don't get too hung up on getting it 'right' and if you must you can still do the task not knowing if you want to do it (because this is probably what you've already been doing for so long anyway)!

No – Mindfulness has aided you in making a decision not to complete this task (right now or maybe ever). You have clarity that this task is not serving you or aligning with your personal or work-related values and what really matters to you most right now (there's more on 'values' to come, in Chapter 6) in this moment.

Take a moment to reflect for yourself if this brief process has enabled you to understand mindfulness as a tool for making sensible, clear and considered decisions. For instance, if a task could wait, but normally you would push on and skip lunch out of habitual impatience and anxiety (maybe you noticed in a tension in your back), this time you recognise the impatience and back pain, and see that if you don't look to impatience for motivation you actually feel disengaged and have sensations of hunger, knowing that this task could actually wait (no urgent necessity or need) – then off you trot for lunch, coming back later refreshed and with increased energy for the task. And then you take a look at an article on how skipping lunch is actually detrimental to your overall performance on the job (take a look at the article from City A.M. listed in the 'Useful resources' section at the end of this chapter) to reinforce your new behaviour. Perhaps you are making the same choice you would've made if you just fired on 'automatic', but this time you have considered your motivation rather than just being reactive. This present-based focusing (which can be cultivated through regular mindfulness practice) can take no more than a few seconds and yet may be just enough to start a radical (and helpful) shift in how you *choose* to engage with your work. You may even develop a new passion and thirst for work as you look beneath your habitual responses and see something else there which offers you a choice and clarity in how you respond to your working day.

"Mindfulness can greatly enhance your decision-making abilities at work."

We hope that this book will show you how mindfulness can greatly enhance your decision-making abilities at work, improving your productivity and overall performance. Making decisions while on the job can be an arduous and at times frenetic task. Our fear of making the wrong decision means that we can put off making them for some time. Conversely, feeling under pressure means that at other times decisions can be made rather carelessly in the heat of the moment and we may regret knee-jerk responses later on. Mindfulness can help us along the way throughout the whole decision-making process, from identifying when a decision needs to be made, what decision actually needs to be made, acting on it, to appraising it. Here are three further ways that mindfulness can really improve your decision-making and performance while on the job:

1. Identifying when and what to decide

When the heat is on and we feel under pressure, our decision-making can be very poor. We may make quick and rash decisions, sometimes conforming to social pressure without any real consideration of how any decision links to our own personal objectives or values (again there's more on values in Chapter 6, later on). Mindfulness can help us to pause and reflect, to consider whether a decision actually needs to be made now and if so what the best course of action actually is, based on what matters most to us at that given time. This way we can be sure that we will be comfortable with the decision we make later on and that the decision we end up making is meaningful and doesn't take us away from our goals and objectives. Practising mindfulness strengthens our ability to retain focus and clarity around the dilemma/s at hand, helping us to weed out irrelevant information, meaning that we are less likely to rely on stereotypes in our decision-making and more likely to base our decisions on relevant and useful information.

2. Acting on decisions

Mindfulness helps us to gain some distance from our thoughts and emotions, which can often serve as obstacles to effective decision-making and taking purposeful action. All decisions will be accompanied with a degree of uncertainty, and mindfulness can help us to manage our fear of the unknown and increase our confidence and tolerance in the face of uncertainty (more of this in Chapter 3), meaning we are less likely to procrastinate around putting our considered decisions into action.

3. Appraising and learning from our decisions

Reflecting on our decisions (not just the ones that work out well!) is a crucial feature of the decision-making process that many of us tend to forget about. Mindfulness keeps us self-aware, meaning that we are more likely to consider the effectiveness of our decisions and learn from them, helping us to continue to improve our decision-making competencies in the longer term. Listening to feedback is not easy (more on this in Chapter 5), especially in the cut-throat reality of the corporate world. Mindfulness helps us to open up to negative feedback and use it proactively.

Arguably, making decisions mindfully may appear to take more time, but the care and attention given to each stage of the decision-making process may in fact save you time and lead to you making more effective decisions in the long run.

We do hope to show you that it is our focus on the present which actually frees us up to making the best possible choices about our future and in achieving our goals in ways which can maximise their success. What is actually required is a radical paradigm shift within ourselves to consider that there are alternative ways of operating which may be more beneficial to ourselves and our workforce than those which we may have previously been trying to utilise. Small changes in our perspective, such as when using Exercise 1.4 above, can have larger ramifications for our motivation and engagement with our workload, our teams, colleagues and our business as a whole. We can begin to see more clearly into the kinds of ways we habitually operate and then look beyond those to something new, which is not necessarily so driven, self-critical and ultimately damaging to our quality of work, our well-being or our company dynamics. For many years now, despite the boom of business in the Western world and developing countries, the motto has been aggressive business. But business paradigms are changing. For example, in the 1960s Nike's mission statement was 'Crush Adidas'. In the 1980s it was 'Crush Reebok'. Nike's current mission statement is 'To bring inspiration and innovation to every athlete in the world.'

Mindfulness calls us to explore this and challenges concepts which many of us are tiring of, such as the 'dog eat dog' mentality, which create so much stress, unsustainability and ultimately are bad for business (more on this in Chapter 7). We do not need to lose our 'edge' or eradicate competition, but actually hone these with cool clarity rather than aggressive reactivity. When we understand the exponential growth of work-related stress, depression or anxiety in the workplace (estimated in the UK in 2014/15 by the Labour Force Survey and reported by the Health and Safety Executive) to be 440,000 out of a total of 1,200,000 cases for all work-related illnesses, and how work-related stress accounts for 43 per cent of all working days lost due to ill health, and we can also see the emerging research on the effectiveness of mindfulness in the workplace, we cannot ignore that a shift is both timely and needed.

Indeed, the change in the ethos of business is already alive and kicking. This book has been commissioned, written and published because mindfulness has something to offer the business community and there is a thirst for that among the global workforce. First Direct, HMP service, The US Military, Nike, Monsanto (to name just a few more!) are investing their precious time and resources into mindfulness training programmes because they are showing results which benefit their employees, without whom there would be no business.

Mercenary mindfulness business

The other side of the coin regarding mindfulness's role in business comes from a debate within and between Buddhist communities and practitioners for whom mindfulness is part of a broader spiritual practice which also involves ethics, compassion and community. Many large corporations with interests which sometimes conflict with local community and environmental concerns or issues of social welfare, use mindfulness, but not necessarily in an apparently ethical, compassionate or community-minded way. So are competition, individualism and profit-making at odds with mindfulness?

The main argument here is that businesses are using mindfulness not for the purpose it was originally intended (read here: to awaken people from delusion, animosity, selfishness and greed). Instead it is used as a watered-down quick-fix technique to become less stressed, more focused and productive in the hope of generating greater profit, and in doing so there is the danger of actually reinforcing and even exacerbating *mindlessness* and the exact distasteful human qualities (such as the greed that seems to fuel boom and bust) that mindfulness was initially intended to heal. It is all well and good should executives become more productive and better focused as a by-product of their mindfulness practice, but are their intentions to practise aligned with social ethics and genuinely held beliefs around the goodness of wise action for the enhancement of compassion and social harmony? Is their practice in the service of promoting human flourishing and the well-being of all others or just their own? It is further criticised that in a rush to secure greater profits via the reduction in stress and enhancement of cognitive prowess among their workforces, businesses are simply plastering over the wounds inflicted upon their employees while not acknowledging (but instead concealing) the real underlying cultural problems and causes of stress within their organisations. Further, as a decontextualised offering, easily and neatly packaged into wellness programmes, mindfulness may appear strikingly attractive to organisations as it conveniently passes the buck on to the individual employee: i.e. a way of providing Joe in compliance with a new self-help tool to manage his personal stress, rather than acknowledging and reforming the dysfunctional systems at a cultural and organisational level.

However, even with all this said, another question occurs to us: is mindfulness even possible without compassion, community mindedness and ethics? Well, we'd say, basically, no, it isn't. Mindfulness is *awakeness*, seeing things as they are. When our self-esteem and self-worth are attached to particular outcomes, such as achieving a certain goal or status, a sense of pressure, anxiety and tension is naturally activated. This clouds our vision and contact with our heart's deepest desires. We can misinterpret this anxiety as something motivating; however, it can also be viewed as craving. The distinction is one that can arise from awakeness and then there is choice – whether to take prosocial, or unwholesome less socially harmonious action. Mindfulness practice cannot and will not eradicate the egocentric tendencies that exist in each of us but it can and does awaken us to notice these, and the very shackles that bind us tightly to them. From this awakened state we are then able to more freely choose personal actions that are aligned with what truly matters most to us, our colleagues, workforces and the welfare of society at large.

The debate about secular mindfulness is ongoing and complex, and often highly personal. We, as authors, offer you mindfulness in the same spirit that we practise as psychologists. That is, that we hope that you will use these skills, which we have developed through our own experience and practice, helping many others and ourselves, to alleviate suffering. If this suffering is alleviated through stress reduction, higher company profits or making deeply compassionate ethical choices, then welcome. Although we care deeply and hold some concerns about the secularisation of mindfulness and particularly how traditional Buddhist ideals may be lost in translation (more on this in Chapter 8), you can also hear that we don't share the same level of scepticism held by the critics of the corporate mindfulness movement. Although it is early days and arguably there is not yet any hard proof as to the deeper or lasting wholesome impact that mindfulness may have on corporate working culture, we do nonetheless hold faith that in time a positive transformation will occur. We need this faith and there is also great value in patience while continuing to observe what unfolds moment by moment. For now, we would like to restate that in our own work with organisations and businesses, we have heard from self-report and witnessed first-hand how mindfulness training and ongoing practice has given rise to a more natural compassion towards the colleagues, superiors, customers, the wider organisation and even the competitors of the executives, managers and senior leaders that we've trained. This compassion has extended beyond the confines of the corporate world to wider society and specifically to those less fortunate. We also want to note the growing scientific evidence that supports the fact that mindfulness actually does train compassion and acts of altruism. And here's some of it below, for you to consider yourself.

Proven in science, smart for business

Mindfulness trains compassion

One study[7] found a significant difference in displays of compassionate behaviour among participants (with little or no prior training in mindfulness practice) who had been assigned to either an eight-week mindfulness meditation course or an eight-week mindfulness and compassion meditating course or a waiting list control (no mindfulness or compassion meditation whatsoever). The researchers found that only 15 per cent of the participants from the control group demonstrated compassionate responses to a person in pain, while 50 per cent of participants from the meditation groups did. There was also no difference between the two meditation groups, indicating that mindfulness practice even without an explicit focus on compassion still significantly increases compassionate behaviour.

In another study[8] researchers were keen to test the impact of their Compassion Cultivation Training (CCT) program which was developed at Stanford University's Centre for Compassion and Altruism Research and Education. CCT programs are now becoming of greater interest within corporate organisations and there is some exciting research being carried out as we write this (more about this in Chapter 5). Anyway, for now, the results of this study which included a community sample of 100 adults randomly assigned to either a CCT group or a wait-list (control) group showed that the amount of formal mindfulness practised as part of the CCT was significantly associated with increased compassion for others.

We're not here, writing this book to change the world, nor to bring down large corporations or end global suffering in the widest sense, once and for all (as if we'd be so arrogant)! We write this book in our professional capacity, in the service of helping others to alleviate their suffering, others whose lives we may be fortunate to touch, as best we can and if that gives rise to a natural, wider, larger (or even organisational) transformation, then so be it. We are hopeful that as mindfulness continues to alleviate stress, more space is created from within which the human and inherent prosocial qualities and drives (which we believe we each hold) of kindness, compassion, openness, acceptance and goodwill can and will then more naturally flow.

We will see the themes discussed in this chapter of the book emerging and recurring periodically throughout the rest of the book as they are so central to mindfulness and business. But for now, simply consider that by engaging with mindfulness you are becoming part of a new wave of creative and intelligent individuals who are helping their businesses to be more successful.

Below is a list of some of the most salient action points that you might like to take away from this chapter.

Mindfulness top tips to go

▶ Begin practising the exercises in this chapter on a daily basis (you might like to set a reminder on your mobile phone or desktop computer to help you along in forming this new habit).

▶ Find places and times to practise mindfulness that work well for you (e.g. on the train to and from work, before a meeting, in your lunch break, at your desk, with other colleagues, etc.).

▶ Remember that even a few minutes of mindfulness practice are enough to start feeling the benefits and free up habitual, stressful thinking patterns.

▶ Consider how mindfulness provides you with a greater capacity to make better decisions on the job and how it can enhance your focus, productivity and efficiency (more on this in the next chapter).

▶ Mindfulness training is accessible at any moment by focusing on 'just this here and now experience'; focus on the five senses (notice what you see, hear, smell, taste and/or feel as you touch,). Paying attention to these experiences in any and all activities you may do will orient you to the present moment and out of being compulsively caught up in unhelpful mental processes (such as distracting thoughts).

▶ Remember to use your breath also as it is always easily available as a focal point for mindfulness practice.

So, we've come to the end of this first chapter. How are you doing? Sold? If you aren't yet totally convinced, that is absolutely fine. A degree of scepticism will keep you inquiring and investigating as long as you are open-minded enough to give this a try. If you are not willing to invest some more energy and attention to trying mindfulness as a tool for yourself and/or your work/business, then neither are you in a valid position to knock it. But since you have chosen to even entertain looking at this book, then we think you might already be willing! Hopefully your questions and queries will become enlivened and enriched through this particular book which we hope will also engage you in the dynamic debates occurring about mindfulness and business.

Useful resources

▶ Adams, J. (2011, May). *Mindfulnet organization: The business case for mindfulness – companies who have adopted mindfulness practices* [Mindfulnet.org]. Retrieved from: http://www.themindfulbrain.net/uploads/8/7/5/2/8752798/the_business_case_for_mindfulness_in_the_workplace.pdf

▶ George, B. (2015, July 27). *The power of mindful leadership* [The Huffington Post Blog]. Retrieved from: http://www.huffingtonpost.com/bill-george/the-power-of-mindful-lead_b_7878482.html

▶ Huffington, A. (2013, March 18). *Mindfulness, meditation, wellness and their connection to corporate America's bottom line* [The Huffington Post Blog]. Retrieved from: http://www.huffingtonpost.com/arianna-huffington/corporate-wellness_b_2903222.html

▶ Marturano, J. [Institute for Mindful Leadership]. (2014, January 27). *How to be a mindful leader* [video file]. Retrieved from: https://www.youtube.com/watch?v=ZsaZjFS0aAU

▶ Mindfulness All-Party Parliamentary Group (January 2015). *Mindful Nation UK: Interim report of the Mindfulness All-Party Parliamentary Group (MAPPG)* [oxfordmindfulness.org]. Retrieved from: http://www.oxfordmindfulness.org/wp-content/uploads/mindful-nation-uk-interim-report-of-the-mindfulness-all-party-parliamentary-group-january-2015.pdf

▶ Morris, J. (2015, January 6). *Bupa: Workers who skip lunch risk harming their productivity* [City A.M. News]. Retrieved from: http://www.cityam.com/206521/city-workers-skipping-lunch-risk-hurting-their-work-performance

► Polk, K. [Dr. Kevin Polk]. (2015, April 26). *How to do mindfulness in 5 minutes (or a lot less time)* [video file]. Retrieved from: https://www.youtube.com/watch?v=yaZNSgjdxuQ

► Wong, K. (2014, April 08). *There's no price tag on a clear mind: Intel to launch mindfulness program* (sic) [*The Guardian*]. Retrieved from: http://www.theguardian.com/sustainable-business/price-intel-mindfulness-program-employee

2

Improve focus
and productivity

'Productivity rests on focused human attention.'

Jeremy Hunter, PhD, Professor at Drucker School
(on executive management and MBA)

Among the many praises sung to the fruits of mindfulness, perhaps the loudest and most attractive to businesses has been that of the impact of mindfulness practice on increasing productivity and focus among employees. This may come as no great surprise but in this modern age the need to sharpen job-focused attention and harness specific skills designed to improve work-related efficiency has never been more pressing.

In this chapter we hope to help you understand:

▶ What it is that gets in the way of our task-focused attention and resultant level of productivity.

▶ How we can successfully navigate our way through the relentless competing demands, expectations and distractions that prevent us from getting the job done (well).

▶ How mindfulness can improve our focus and productivity at work.

▶ How to implement focused-attention and productivity-boosting mindfulness practices into your working day.

Checking-in is checking out

In a technologically advancing modern world where digital devices are taking an increasingly prominent place in our working lives, our ability to sustain focus and attention (for any significant length of time, anyway) is fast becoming problematic for so many of us. Reaching for the closest mobile device, running through the routine checks of our various online accounts, our work emails, social media, instant messages and the latest news alerts has become a habitual pattern for most of us (and that's usually before our feet have even touched the floor in the morning). These routine checks continue throughout the day and are often not planned but instead impulsive reactions to the next buzz, bleep or flashing red light being emitted from one or more of our mobile devices or just as often to a sudden thought, like, 'Ooo, I haven't checked my phone for the last five minutes!'. One cost arising from all this *checking* and *doing* is that our attention is becoming fractured into tinier and tinier pieces, and we may find that we are never actually in the one place that we intend to be or ever truly focused on the one task we had hoped to get done. In business terms this easily translates into real financial costs. The more distracted we are at work, the less productive and effective we will be. Makes sense, no? This is understandably problematic for the bottom-line profitability of any business where the prevailing model in its simplest terms is usually rather linear, and looks something like this:

Sustained focus ⟶ Increased productivity ⟶ Greater profit

Although distraction while on the job is an inevitable part of the deal in this modern day and age, more and more companies are turning towards mindfulness as a means to reduce the growing levels of inattention among their plugged-in and switched-on employees. So let's take a look at all this and see what exactly mindfulness has to offer when it comes to our work-related focus and productivity.

Keep your eye on the ball

Massive corporations and institutions have embraced this unusual technique as a means of generating higher yield, better quality services and products, and improved profit margins in the workplace, as well as having a happier, healthier workforce. Efficiency and quality are essential elements for the production of any form of work, from baking the daily loaf to the provision of financial services. So it is no wonder that businesses are increasingly using mindfulness as a cost-effective empirically supported method of increasing the productivity and focus of their workforces.

The industrial revolution and advent of the machine, as well as the more recent enormous advances in technology have all increased the expectations and pace over the past 200 years exponentially to their current global, 24-hour, 5-star gold standards. There are tighter and tighter rules, restrictions, policies and regulations, meaning that more than ever we must not slip up, and if we do, the consequences are dire – redundancy, bankruptcy, liquidation, etc. Whether it is our own face or that of our company or business, if we don't keep focused and productive (preferably to the highest level and in line with consumer demands), we are all going to end up with egg all over it and looking for another (precarious) job.

Hopefully you have not been, nor ever will go there. It isn't nice, it isn't fun and it is a huge dent to our confidence to even think about going there. On the other hand, sometimes we can feel as if it is the fear of it all going arse up that keeps us on top of the game (if that doesn't sound too dodgy a metaphor!). The thrill of the chase is the knife edge that keeps us sharp and makes us and our businesses tick, right? Wrong. Unfortunately, this simply does not hold up. When we feel stressed we react in very similar ways as all vertebrate mammals do to threat – our fight or flight response kicks in instinctively – our field of attention becomes narrowed to the perceived or actual danger, our heart rate increases, our muscles become primed for action and a whole host of other physiological reactions ensue. Despite this primal response to danger originally being intended for our caveman/woman days when we were simply trying to survive, our brain still interprets modern-day stress in the same way and our physiological responses are also identical. The necessary narrowing of our field of attention and impairment of rational thinking or complex decision-making when we need to either fend off an attacker or run like hell is a result of a decrease in oxygen to the brain and an increase in oxygen to the limbic system – really useful for running from that sabre-toothed tiger, but it makes for poor decisions in the boardroom, on the trading floor, in challenging interpersonal interactions, or any other adrenaline-inducing situation we may be faced with at work . We'll return to looking at the impact of our threat system on our focus and productivity in just a second but first off, if you commonly find that the only thing that might be preventing you being mistaken for a scatty caveman/woman is your slick business suit in place of a tatty leopard-skin loincloth, then you might like to try the following exercise.

Exercise 2.1: Mindful on the job

Take a chill pill!

If you feel that your stress levels are rising, maybe you have a zillion thoughts rushing around your mind and are finding it hard to focus or think in any clear way or maybe your body is full of tension, then you might like to try this quick exercise to cool down and regain a sense of clarity and focus once again. This is a simple exercise which involves taking some perspective on your experience by simply taking the time to curiously notice and then label it just what it is. This may sound about as useful as an inflatable dartboard especially when there's so much to get done at work, but stepping back in this way can really help you to cultivate a sense of calm and ultimately retain your sense of sharp focus when the heat is on. So why not give it a go now and then continue to practise this one regularly:

1 First, begin by noticing your breath entering and leaving your body. Pay attention to the sensations of breathing on each in-breath and each out-breath.

2 Once you feel more present and focused on your breath, continue with the following steps.

3 Next see if you can notice some of the thoughts that your mind is giving you and begin to label them with one of three categories (i.e. 'past', 'future' or 'judgement'). You may notice thoughts about what has happened (such as 'I can't believe he spoke to me like that!' or the like) so then label them as 'past'. You may notice thoughts about what is about to happen (such as 'I'm going to totally mess up this presentation, everyone is going to see I'm useless!') so then label them as 'future'. You may have thoughts about yourself, others or any particular situation, including this exercise itself (such as 'I'm not thinking any thoughts!', 'This is a stupid exercise', 'I'm/he/she/it is hopeless', or the like) so label them as 'judgement'. You might like to also imagine these thoughts as leaves on a stream as you watch them float away or as clouds passing through the sky. Notice how each one passes by when you simply label them and untangle yourself from listening to what they have to say.

4 Next notice how you feel emotionally and label it. You may feel anger, sadness, anxiety or anything else. So whichever emotion you notice, just silently say to yourself, 'I feel X right now'. If you can't feel any strong emotion, that's OK also; just notice and label that (i.e. 'I don't feel any strong emotion right now').

5 Finally, notice how your body feels. You may notice tension in your shoulders, nausea in your stomach or anything else. Or no strong sensation at all. Again, just notice and then label whatever is there, silently saying to yourself, 'I feel X in my body right now'. You do not need to fix any of these experiences or sensations, or figure them out; there is nothing to fight or flee from, just experience to notice with curiosity.

Adrenaline flunkies

As we've said, when we are fuelled by anxiety, the effect of adrenaline distorts our thinking. Our ability to make rational and balanced decisions diminishes and in fact our risk-taking increases. We are physiologically tipped into 'red alert' when we are anxious. The brain's alarm centre, or amygdala, is activated when we perceive a threat and hormones are released such as adrenaline. We also have an increase in alpha-amylase – a digestive enzyme which breaks starches into sugars – levels in saliva (if you recall the study from Chapter 1), which cause a more rapid heart rate and increase in blood flow to the muscles so that we can physically respond quickly to danger. As mentioned and as you can now hopefully appreciate, this is not as useful for our feelings about presentations as it used to be for fending off predators. The judgements we then make are suited to quick and extreme measures (flight or fight), which are simply not sensible while on the job.

Some people do love the feel of these moments, however, and justify them to themselves as how they feel the sharp edge of business and the 'killer instinct'. What this means in reality is that those types of people are more likely to make rash and risky choices and to impair their ability to consider things rationally.

> 'One need not spend much time in business settings to observe that reason does not always seem to rule.'

Donald Langevoort, Professor of Law at Georgetown University

The thrill of these moments occurs because fear is also very closely similar in physiological terms to excitement; some of us simply interpret an event (such as a presentation or meeting a predator) as exhilarating and others are scared out of their wits. So some of us love it, some of us hate it; however, anxiety/excitement impairs all of us when we need to make clear, focused and rational decisions. The 'killer instinct' is simply our caveman/woman tendencies being activated, not really the height of cool sophistication and definitely not the most effective way to run your business. Don't mistake your thrill or fear for focus and effectiveness or you may end up making a big balls up of it all. Check out our top five tips (below) to ensure that you don't let your fear get in the way (these are adapted from an article published in *Psychology Today* which you can check out from the link in the 'Useful resources' section at the end of this chapter if you wish).

Five tips for when we know fear might lead to stupid choices

1. Keep calm and get out of the way

Remember that risk and high levels of emotion are inseparable.

Why do we know this?

Because:

We are frightened of snakes, but cars are OK?! Our survival instinct is a little out of sync with modern life, clearly. For instance, we know that spiders and snakes cause us fear out of any proportion to the dangers that they pose, while fast driving, well, doesn't. A fast approaching predator would cause us to freeze instinctively, which for many predators reduces their chance of seeing you (remember that bit with T-Rex in Jurassic Park?), phew! Unfortunately this is not a good tactic when a car is speeding towards you. It is therefore important to remember the great benefits of keeping calm and appraising a situation rationally – mere instinct alone isn't always effective.

2. Keep calm and look out for the ones acting normally

Fear biases risk analysis.

Why do we do that?

Because:

Dramatic events pique our attention (that's why the news likes to report a few daily catastrophes), and as a result, we overestimate the odds of dreadful but infrequent events and underestimate how risky ordinary events are. Therefore, the more dramatic and unusual an event, the more we think this needs attention, while we are prone to ignoring the more common, frequent and familiar risks of the everyday. After 9/11, for example,

1.4 million people changed their holiday travel plans to avoid flying. The vast majority chose to drive instead. But driving is far more dangerous than flying (according to US transport statistics for 2013, motorcycling is more than 3,000 times more deadly than flying, while travelling in a car or truck is about 100 times more deadly than flying), and the decision to switch caused roughly 1,000 additional automobile fatalities, according to two separate analyses comparing traffic patterns in late 2001 to those the year before. In other words, 1,000 people who chose to drive wouldn't have died had they flown instead.

3. Keep calm, it's behind yoooou!

We underestimate threats that creep up on us.

Why do we do that?

Well, we could wait until tomorrow to answer that, but it's because:

If a risk is not imminent we tend to ignore it. So the threat of smoking or scoffing all those pies doesn't usually frighten us even though rationally we are all aware of the long-term health risks if we do these things regularly.

'Things that build up slowly are very hard for us to see', says Kimberly Thompson, a professor of risk analysis at the Harvard School of Public Health. Obesity and global warming are in that category. 'We focus on the short-term even if we know the long-term risk.'

4. Keep calm we all know health and safety is a load of old ...

We replace one risk with another.

What??

Why?

Did you know that studies have found that we speed up when we put our seatbelts on? Certain safety feature in cars (such as better brakes or four-wheel drive) have also not been found to reduce accidents, just change the type of accident. This is because people normalise their risk-taking to a certain level and then adjust their behaviour to match this, not therefore cutting the overall risk. So we'll eat the salad (hold the dressing), followed by a Triple-Chocolate-Marshmallow-Cream-Tower, please.

5. Keep calm and keep calm

Fear is bad for your health (just something else to worry about next time you feel anxious).

Not another health scare …

Go on (sigh), why?

Ebola, cancer, terrorist attack, plane crash – dramatic? Attention grabbing (did you read point 2 already?) You may even have your own special fear (hand coming out of the toilet …? No? Oh … we'll shut up now). Well, here's a lovely little factlet: the odds of dying from any of these things is teeny-weeny compared to the damage that the fear of these things does. Chronic stress harms our bodies: lowering the immune system, triggering mental health problems and causing long-term cardiovascular damage, among other things.

So what're we going to do about it?

Alright, being anxious makes you a bit silly. But we can't just STOP, can we? Go on, try … Imagine a gun to your head, and if the cat-suited assassin with their super-high-tech fear detector gets even a whiff from you (ick) on the meter, then they will shoot … feeling calm? Still alive? No. Good job this is just imaginary or we would have no readers left. We can't just push fear away because we know it is silly, ineffective and impairs our focus and decision-making. But we do know that fear is based on future, past or imagined events. For instance, fear thoughts might take the shape of:

Future fears:

I will be fired if I do/say … (something wrong).

Everyone is going to think … (something awful)

But what will happen if I … (screw up)?

Past fears:

Last time I did this … (something terrible happened)

I remember when I said … (something silly)

Yesterday it all went … (Pete Tong)

Imagined fears:

I wish I were … (anything better than this)

If only I could be … (anywhere/one better than here/me)

Actually these are *all* taking place in the imagination, created by the mind and not based on direct, in-the-moment experience. Even a memory is a construction of the imagination, as it is not real in terms of present-focused time. We can be so habituated in creating fear-based narratives and constructions of the world around us that we start to believe our own stories, and then the world does, our bodies respond 'as if' this were true and we experience stress.

'I am an old man and have known a great many troubles, but most of them never happened.'

Mark Twain

So when we focus on the present (as we invited you to try in Exercise 2.1 above), ping, our worries are gone. Our mind is massively habitual so we will inevitably go back to thinking about the stuff that induces all these anxious feelings, but attend back to the present moment again and the anxiety is just a collection of quite amazing physical sensations (rapid heartbeat, sweaty palms, nausea, etc.). Our thinking mind will scramble around to make a story out of these (Possible heart attack? Impending doom? Moment of glory?), but cut the fantasising and catastrophising, leave it alone and we can return to our observation of the continually shifting sensations of the body. Weirdly, our anxiety will naturally subside when we just take our hands off it; a few moments noticing the soles of our feet on the floor or a few breaths and we find that the mind will learn to settle, we stop struggling, we become focused. We use mindfulness to do this, to turn the mind and train it back to the present, to where there is really not so very, very much to have to figure out, nothing generally at all to fight or run from. Gradually we can then learn that to maintain this simply takes the practice of doing one thing at a time, with wholehearted attention. We lessen anxiety, we improve focus and as a result we will be more productive.

> ❝*Do one thing at a time.*❞

And yes, we did say, *do one thing at a time.* That goes to you out there stuffing your sandwich in your mouth, fiddling with your phone and jumping up and down while you read this.

Now, tell us what the hell is that all about?

The world's finest couch potato

Well, in order to make a bit more sense of our attempts to do a trillion things at once, we encourage you right now to recognise how your mind evolved to problem-solve. It was designed to scan its environment, take in any and as much data as possible, and then evaluate it and problem-solve it away. Why our brains are wired in this way we will come back to in a bit more detail soon enough, but for now, we encourage you to think of your brain as a slovenly, couch potato. Go on, as weird as it might seem, just imagine it sitting there, laid back on the sofa, feet up, gorging on junk food, snacks and sweets, without any consideration for how full it already is; with an insatiable appetite it just keeps scoffing more and more, often trying to process and digest more than one thing at the same time. Now that sounds familiar, doesn't it? Do you ever try to tackle more than one task at once? That's right, this all sounds a bit like multitasking. And that's good, as we humans are great at multitasking, right? … Well, erm … No!

Exercise 2.2: Work in progress

Multitasking experiment

Here are just a couple of tests to dispel any ideas you may have about the effectiveness of multitasking, one of the biggest myths which prevails about efficiency:

You work at BizzyBeez, an innovative, new start-up company teaching workers skills in efficiency, focus and motivation. The boss is coming and she is looking to promote the office's most focused and productive employee to the role of 'grand high Queen or King Bee'. This is the (really easy) task she has set you to find out if you can make it:

Task instructions

Do each of the following, making no errors or hesitations.

Do the whole task in under 60 seconds.

Do them all at the same time.

Task

1 Recite the alphabet.
2 Wave your left arm in a circle at least 20 times.
3 Text a message to your closest work colleague saying: 'Read *Working with Mindfulness* it is amazing'.

How did you do? Did you meet your deadline with perfection? Are you getting that promotion from the big cheese?

OK, OK, she'll give you another go (because she likes you lots) and this time she wants you to do the same exact set of tasks but this time:

DO THEM ONE AT A TIME.

How'd it go this time? How were the stress levels? Errors? Hesitations? Are you going to be 'grand high Queen or King Bee' (yes!) and if you didn't make it, then we hope you at least sent those texts!

So, joking aside (just for a moment mind, you know us by now), we're not very good at multitasking; it stresses us out, we take longer to get things done and we make more mistakes in the process. In fact, there's some ground-breaking and really interesting research[1] that came out from Stanford University that actually backs this all up. The researchers in this study found that those of us that might attempt to do more than one task at a time (erm, isn't that all of us?), like engaging in more than one email or text or social media conversation at once, while watching TV, surfing the net and trying to get some work done (we don't know, like writing a book maybe!) … are actually paying a big mental price. A hundred students were recruited into this study and put through a series of tests. Those that were 'heavy multimedia multitaskers' were easily led astray: 'everything distracts them', one of the researchers said. Despite this the researchers were still keen to find out what, if any, benefits come from multitasking and split the participants into two groups: those that tended to do a lot of multitasking and those that didn't, and ran a series of further tests. The results were astonishing. The group of students who did a lot of multimedia multitasking performed worse on all the tests; they found it harder to discriminate and filter out irrelevant information and displayed a poorer working memory. In fact, there were no positive benefits from multitasking whatsoever; those participants that tended to do a lot of multitasking were found to lose focus more easily, they felt more stressed, they took longer to do assigned tasks and they made more mistakes and experienced more physical and mental tiredness to boot.

Even though most of us can experience pretty similar, dire outcomes from multitasking our way through our working days, we still continue to multi-task. So, why do we persist? Well, what this research tells us is that the more we multitask the more we multitask; it becomes a habit and we just keep reinforcing the same old habit, doing it over and over again; it becomes our default response to the world and our work, day after day. And the habit becomes so reinforced that even when on those very rare occasions when we may find ourselves having only one thing to do (as if!), like fall asleep at night, our mind says, 'OK great, easy-peasy, let's do that but what else can I do at the same time'?! and then starts to wander off, thinking about anything and everything else it can, like WORK (getting in the way of our much needed rest). So, as we continue to multitask, we are actually increasing our distractibility more and more. And it's pretty clear (as you know too well from the exercise above) how trying to do more than one thing at once can be detrimental to our productivity and successes at work.

Increasing distractibility

So what per centage of our time awake is spent with our mind distracted away from the present moment – go on, have a guess . . . ?

Well, the research[2] tells us that on average we spend 46.9 per cent of our time awake with our mind wandering away from the here and now: that's basically half of our life (when we're not asleep, that is). The researchers of this study were also able to provide us with a breakdown of what this might actually look like during the different and specific activities that we tend to get up to most days (check out the percentage while we're at work!). Here's what one of them said:

'How does that rate depend on what people are doing? When we looked across 22 activities, we found a range – from a high of 65 per cent when people are taking a shower or brushing their teeth, to 50 per cent when they're working, to 40 per cent when they're exercising. This went all the way down to sex, when 10 per cent of the time people's minds

are wandering. In every activity other than sex, however, people were mind-wandering at least 30 per cent of the time, which I think suggests that mind-wandering isn't just frequent, it's ubiquitous. It pervades everything that we do.'

Matt Killingsworth (From an article on mindful.org; follow the link in the 'Useful resources' section for the full article)

Just think how much more productive we could be with our time at work if we could train our mind to focus on the job at hand rather than thinking about some other time or place, or all that we should or would prefer to be doing instead. In fact, this research also suggests that it is not just productivity and focus which is compromised by our wandering mind, but also our very happiness. In the Harvard University 2,250 adults with ages ranging from 18 to 88 were given an app for their mobile device and randomly interrupted throughout the day and asked three simple questions, along the lines of:

1 What are you doing right now?
2 What are you thinking about?
3 How happy to do feel?

The results were really quite interesting: those people who were focused on the present moment and task at hand were happier than those whose mind had wandered away to think about something else, irrespective of how boring, effortful or stressful the task in the present moment actually was. Yes, you read that correctly: regardless of the pleasure we get from any given activity, our happiness is decreased by mind-wandering thoughts be they unpleasant, pleasant or neutral ones – and, yes, even pleasant thoughts actually appear to decrease your happiness even when you are engaged in an unpleasant task!

Furthermore, our mind-wandering seems very likely to actually cause unhappiness rather than it being a consequence of it. For example, even if we are having a miserable journey to work and thinking about something pleasant, like having a nice hot bath later, we actually feel less happy than if we just stayed focused on the cr*ppy journey (watch the TED talk by Matt Killingsworth listed in the 'Useful resources' section at the end of this chapter if you want to hear more on this). The message is simple: when our mind is wandering away from the present moment, thinking about this and/or that other piece of work, meeting we have to get to or anything else we have to get done (exciting or not) we are unhappier than when our minds are focused on the here and now. The researchers conclude *a wandering mind is an unhappy mind'*. So, without addressing this mind-wandering, distracting, multitasking tendency, we are very much at risk of turning into one large, miserable, frazzled workforce of zombies, knocking around (and into one another) with varying degrees of attention deficit disorder, not getting much done at all (and not very contentedly).

So how well can you manage your attention? How difficult can it actually be to focus on just one thing at once? Well, if you're willing, we invite you to give this a try right now – see how you get on. We are going to give you some tips along the way. Here goes:

Exercise 2.3: Work in progress

How well can you manage your attention?

1 Close your eyes (once you have finished reading these instructions – it helps limit the billions of pieces of extra distracting data that enter our mind through our eyeballs).

2 Bring your attention to your breath (it may take a few minutes to rest your attention on your breath).

3 See if you can notice the sensations of air entering your nostrils as you breathe in – harness your attention to that sensation and try to keep that sensation at the forefront of your attention.

4 Now, just stay focused on your breath in this way ... for about the next 2 minutes (just estimate the time; it doesn't need to be exact).

Once you have had a go at the above exercise, then continue reading ...

Done? OK, so how did you do? How was that? Easy? Difficult? Were you distracted? Possibly by thoughts? Sounds? Something else?

This was a simple instruction, huh? 'Just focus your attention on your breath'. You can't get much simpler than that, but it is really difficult to be simple, isn't it? The mind is so unruly and highly conditioned. Most people tend to find that their attention is distracted by thoughts that show up in their mind. These can be really random. They can be about something that happened in the past or the future. They may be focused on the exercise itself, say with judgements, opinions or preferences about what you're doing and/or the experience you are having ('I wish that air con could just stop making that racket, it's getting in the way of me focusing on my breath!'). Whatever your thoughts happened to be about, they probably fitted into one of these categories (past, future, or evaluation/judgement). As humans, we have between 50,000 and 70,000 thoughts that show up in our mind in any given day (that's a pretty impressive amount, although we're not entirely sure how they can actually measure that!). Of course the specific content of these will vary hugely between us as we all live out our own individual, unique lives, but the themes of our thinking, whether they are concerned with the past, the future or evaluative and judgemental in some way, are the same for us all. We're all very much in the same boat and don't differ at all from one another in that way.

If your attention wandered away from your breath during this exercise, that really is absolutely fine; it's not any sign of failure (and it doesn't mean 'mindfulness doesn't work' or that you 'can't do it'!). If your mind did wander away from your breath, please do remember that is normal and just what the human mind does. Much like a puppy (or any other small being that you may have tried to train!), the mind is inquisitive and will want to rummage around curiously, sniff about a bit and pick things up. Distraction is not failure; it's HUMAN. Remember, the instruction was 'TRY' to keep the sensation of your breath at centre stage in your attention, it wasn't empty your mind or eliminate all thoughts or block out all other distractions – see the difference? Distraction and a wandering mind are also experiences that we can simply notice (with openness and acceptance) in our mindfulness practice and as soon as we have done that, BAM! we are back in the present moment, and then have the choice (should we choose to take it) to then gently return our attention back to where we intended it to be in the first place, and in the case of the above exercise, to noticing our breath.

Although we can't ultimately prevent our mind from ever wandering away from the task at hand again, we can see that just letting it run on autopilot without any effort on our part to rein it back in is not going to be helpful at all if we want to retain any level of focus and productivity at work. A wandering mind is an old habit that has been reinforced for some time and like any other entrenched habit it is a really difficult one to kick, especially in this day and age with so much demanding our attention. The other reason for this is that what happens to most of us when we attempt to multitask is that we falsely believe that the more jobs we try to cram into as little time as possible, the more we will get done, and we get a nice fat hit of reinforcing adrenaline in all the panic too. Trying to juggle a lot of things at the same time can make us feel important, showing others just how time pressured we are and creating a drama of activity to prove we are somehow 'coping'. As we've already discussed, some people find this exciting and it can be quite addictive. Unfortunately, as we've also already seen, we are usually actually being highly inefficient, genuinely getting stressed and making a bit of a boo-boo of it all. Gaining even a small foothold in all the pandemonium of our multitasking efforts seems only to reinforce the notion that it actually works, so tiny successes in all the high-stress activity feel like great gains. Basically, folks, this is not cool. Even if you get these tasks done, you are not doing them well, or definitely not as well as you could. Daniel Goleman, in his excellent book *Focus*, writes:

'Then there's what many people think of as 'splitting' attention in multitasking, which cognitive science tells us is a fiction, too. Rather than having a stretchable balloon of attention to deploy in tandem, we have a narrow, fixed pipeline to allot. Instead of splitting it, we actually switch rapidly. Continual switching saps attention from full concentrated engagement.'

(Goleman, 2013, pp. 19–20)

As addicted as we are to multitasking, it simply is not smart. So just try weaning yourself away from the urge to do it all, now, this minute and try (what your mother probably told you anyway) to do *one thing at a time* (and don't talk with your mouth full).

Setting the ground rules for multitasking

Yes we know, multitasking isn't just going to go away because we now know it's not clever and you've read about its pitfalls in this book. As we've seen, it's become a habit, right? And even though we realise it's not going to get us anywhere closer to achieving our goals in a timely, productive, calm and focused fashion, that doesn't stop the boss and everyone else at work expecting us to do it all at once anyway (until they read this book, that is), like NOW ALREADY! So how can we best navigate our way through the plethora of demands and expectations coming at us from every single angle, all at the same time throughout our working day?

Well, we thought this would be a good moment to introduce you to Tina, who works as Legal Counsel, specialising in commercial litigation, at a large corporate law firm.

Tina

Tina felt overwhelmed, exhausted and overstretched in her work when she came along for some mindfulness sessions. With a wisp of grey hair falling from her forehead onto the left-hand side of her face and concealing what appeared to be a very tired eye, circled with black rings (that's going by the look of her right eye anyway), Tina looked shattered; 'I don't know what else to do,' she exclaimed in a faint whisper of exhaustion. 'It's just that everyone wants my advice, they come to me for direction on their work all the time, and now even what they should buy their wife for a bloody birthday present! I just don't have any time to do my own work and it's all piling up on me. I keep making silly errors and my manager is coming down hard on me, accusing me of falling behind'.

It soon materialised that Tina was running on *multitasking autopilot*, welcoming anybody and everybody into her office who indicated that they might need her help, while she continued to attempt her own work. She explained that she even had a box of tissues (sounds like she might be close to doing us out of a job) and a jar of sweets on her desk as colleagues were dropping by so often and she didn't want to seem uninviting. Tina was finding it hard to say *no* for fear of displeasing her co-workers and ultimately not being liked herself. She had spent so long saying *yes* that it had become a habit, and although she feared what might happen if she didn't, she wasn't aware of any of that in the moment but just kept welcoming people in and offering her kind (yet divided) attention to their troubles. Firstly, people came with work problems for her to resolve but then this escalated to more personal dilemmas. The more knocks at her door, the more compelled she felt to answer it. Tina was continuously interrupting her work, taking longer to get it done, falling behind and making more mistakes. This left her no choice (in her mind anyway) but to work later and later in the office or from home in the evenings and on the weekend, which was exhausting, and she found that she was also then falling behind with her household chores. It was clear that Tina had lost sight of ➤

what really mattered to her. She feared letting others, down and in her struggle to eliminate feelings of being un-liked by others, she was clearly getting in the way of her own focus, productivity and well-being at work, and causing her boss to become more annoyed with her, which was her greatest fear of all.

Tina began to recognise the need to notice this people-pleasing tendency that was running on autopilot. With mindfulness practice she became better able to catch it in the moment and then discriminate between what was most important in that very moment (i.e. welcoming yet another lost colleague into her office or saying *no* assertively and getting on with her own work). Now of course, should her own manager knock on the door that might be the time to 'down tools' and pay her undivided attention to him, assuming she wanted to keep her job, of course. Another wise move that Tina acted on was to chuck the tissue box and sweetie jar in the nearest rubbish bin – duh!

Tina also found it helpful (perhaps you will too) to keep the following two rules close to hand. She wrote them on a Post-it note and stuck that to her desktop:

Two rules for multitasking

1 Choose your distractions wisely
2 Focus on one thing at a time.

To sharpen your own task-focused attention (and decrease your chances of being sidetracked by unhelpful and irrelevant distractions), try the following two exercises (and repeat them again and again, as often as you like).

Exercise 2.4: Mindful on the job

Working lunch – focus on one thing at a time

Give your undivided attention as far as possible to the following exercise. Once you have finished task X, give your undivided attention to task Y; while doing task X give your whole attention to just that (these tasks can be replaced with any other relevant activities; the idea is to give yourself a task which feels pressing and that you might normally try to do at the same time as at least one other thing).

How often do you eat while looking at messages or surfing the net, etc.? Do you bolt down a quick sandwich without even tasting it? Maybe you get hungry again later because you just forgot to notice that you even ate? Maybe you even skip lunch altogether or end up with crumbs and mayonnaise all over the keyboard (yeah, really nice)? This is a very, very common type of multitasking which is really multi-fasting: your focus is going hungry. So when you're next feeling hungry, go grab your favourite, most delicious sandwich (or whatever you fancy to eat), take a seat in front of your computer and try this exercise:

X = open and answer one pressing work email

Y = eat your delicious sandwich

1. Focus on X.
2. Feel the pull towards doing Y, or anything else; you need not act on this.
3. Notice the sensations arising in the body.
4. Return your focus to X.
5. Notice any thoughts arising about task Y; you need do nothing with these.
6. Let the thoughts alone.
7. Return your thoughts to task X.
8. Be aware of any urge to avoid this moment.
9. Continue with task X alongside any emotions/sensations (irritation, impatience, joy, hunger, etc.); you need not push these away, just let them linger as you focus on X.
10. Complete task X with the best quality of attention you can.
11. Completely finish task X, and leave it.
12. Now focus on task Y.
13. If your mind turns back to reviewing or replaying task X, bring it as fully as possible to task Y.
14. Feel the pull towards task X; you need not act on or think further on this.
15. Engage fully with the sensations of task Y.
16. Immerse yourself in this moment.
17. If you feel the pull towards the future or past, notice this.

18 Return your attention to task Y; notice what arises.

19 Allow yourself just this one moment, right here, just as it is.

20 Finish task Y and let your attention flow to the next task now.

Reflections: watch how the mind pulls towards future events, maybe trying to avoid working on a difficult or unpleasant task and leaning into a future time when it is over. Alternatively you might be avoiding the moment by constantly thinking about something that needs to be done later.

Exercise 2.5: Mindful on the job

Getting smart with your smartphone

'Meditation is the ultimate mobile device; you can use it anywhere, anytime, unobtrusively.'

Sharon Salzberg

We first included a version of the following exercise in *Mindfulness for Busy People* (Sinclair and Seydel, p. 64) and as we've been told how helpful it has been to so many readers, particularly in training their minds to be more focused while they've been at work, we thought we'd include an updated version here.

Like so many of us, you might also feel as if your mobile phone has become an extension of your body. We tend to pick them up (if we ever actually put them down) hundreds of times a day without any real awareness of doing so. One reason we continue to do this is as an attempt to quell feelings of anxiety and stress. By checking our phones regularly we feel that we can get on top of new emails and messages before they escalate and take up even more of our precious time and attention (you can read more about this in Chapter 6). We have become habituated to checking our phone and this checking behaviour and all the worries about what emails may have come through since we last checked can serve as a great distraction, a real obstacle that gets in the way of our focus and productivity with other more pressing and/or more meaningful tasks. So to really train your brain to be more focused, go grab your phone (we bet it's not far away at all) now and try this exercise and then repeat it often.

1 Start by sitting or standing with your phone either in your lap, pocket or by the side of you.

2 Take a moment to become aware of the presence of your phone, and then as you do so, take a few mindful breaths, noticing the sensations of air entering your body on the in-breath and leaving your body on the out-breath.

3 Now pick up your phone and hold it in your hand. Do nothing else with your phone.

4 Take a moment to notice the sensation of how your hand/arm is now one phone heavier.

5 Notice any urges, impulses (maybe you can notice a slight twitching in your fingers) to open and check your phone.

6 Recognise how these impulses are automatic, a response that has been reinforced by checking your phone time and time again.

7 Notice any thoughts that arise in the mind about emails on your phone, work generally or anything else.

8 Notice if impatience, anxiety or boredom (in not checking your phone), or any other feeling arises.

9 Leave all these urges, impulses, thoughts and feelings alone. There is no need to respond to these, act on them or follow them in any way. They too will pass.

10 Just notice this moment as it is – just you, just holding your phone, nothing else to do.

11 Now take your time to notice the temperature of your phone: is it warm or cool as it rests in your hand?

12 Next take a moment to gaze upon your phone: notice its colour, markings and how the light reflects off its surface.

13 Run your fingers around your phone and notice its texture, bumps, and indentations. Does it feel smooth or rough in places? Notice this.

14 Now put your phone down once again, placing it back into your pocket, on your lap or beside you.

15 Take a moment to notice how your hand/arm feels as it is now one phone lighter.

16 To end the exercise, take a few mindful breaths, noticing the sensations of air entering and leaving your body.

17 Then congratulate yourself for staying as focused and present as you could be while engaging with your phone in an entirely new way.

Reflections: training the mind to be present for the sake of our improved focus and performance takes effort and commitment. It is best done with tasks or at times when we would usually be caught up in automatic responses, just like we are most of the time when checking our phones. In doing an exercise like this, we can notice the strong pull towards habitual impulses and patterns of behaviour and thought that can lead us to distraction, away from the here and now. In choosing not to follow these impulses (time and time again), we are training the mind to be more present when we want it to be.

Training the wise mind

The exercises in this chapter (and there are more to come) are designed to help you train your mind so that you can strengthen your ability to stay focused on the task at hand when you want to. We understand that compelling distractions can come in all shapes and sizes. For example, there are demands from other people, knocking on your door, incessantly firing email after email into your inbox, sending you instant messages or calling your telephone. If it's not other people that are preventing you from getting the job done, then, as we've begun to highlight, it is often your very own wandering mind itself. But what if these irritating distractions come in other forms, you know, like the ones that we have no apparent control over. Time and time again, we are asked this question and usually by people who work in open-plan offices, whether that's sharing a large office floor with a hundred (really inconsiderate and noisy) others, hot-desking around the building or bustling about on a trading floor. *'What am I supposed to do then, well? ARGHH! I just can't stand all the noise, I can't keep focused. There's a constant hum that never shuts up!'* Well, again, we would advise that you watch out for those exact (or similar) types of thoughts themselves first, as you may find that unhooking yourself from them, simply noticing and labelling them, gives you at least a little more peace and quiet to get some more of your work done. Failing that, it might be time to think again, and maybe creatively too (see Chapter 4 for more on creativity).

The practice of mindfulness not only helps us to create space from our own productivity-defeating habits (i.e. the multitasking, the wandering mind), but within that space we might also be more open and able to think more wisely and choose a preferred practical response about what is best to be done about a particular predicament, including a noisy work environment. Like Tina in the earlier example, who realised that binning her sweets and tissues would be a good move, you too might find that making some strategic and practical changes to your immediate work environment/desk/station is just the wise move you need to take to get more work done. So, if you've got a pressing deadline and your experience tells you that the noise pollution booming out of your open-plan office is likely to get in the way, then what else could you do? Book a meeting room? Arrange to work from home maybe? Sometimes we overlook these simple (but wise) moves because we are all too often caught up in the worry and rumination, ranting about the problem in our own minds (and to anyone else that can bear to listen), expecting the world around us/others to be different or change first. Now stop that at once; it's time to get wise.

Here are our top seven wise moves (which you just may not have thought of yet!) to limit distractions:

1 Shut down all unnecessary open windows on your desktop (especially those instant messaging boxes and news alerts!).
2 Whack your phone on to aeroplane mode (better still, turn the damn thing off for a while, if you dare).
3 Book out a meeting room.
4 Let others know you're not available (do whatever it takes: stick the 'DO NOT DISTURB' sign on your door/forehead).
5 Work from home.
6 Get a sound-masking app for your phone and plug in some headphones (check out the link in the 'Useful resources' section at the end of this chapter for a fantastic, scientifically proven productivity-boosting sound app that can block out background noise – awesome)!
7 Remember: take some mindful breaths.

So why might it be so difficult to keep focused?

Our tendency to have an active mind can be traced back to the days of our cave-dwelling ancestors. They weren't a very confident bunch and needed a sharp tool to survive the threatening, survival-of-the-fittest type world in which they found themselves. They needed to be on high alert, think on their feet, evaluate and problem-solve their new environment: 'Will that roaring four-legged thingymejigy behind that bush over there, now moving closer and faster towards me (eek!), eat me or not!?' Now, whether or not that all sounds very similar to your work environment (!), the fact is that our minds haven't evolved much over this time, and today we still have this razor-sharp problem-solving tool, primed and ready to scan our landscape, designed to protect us from danger and threats to our survival. Now of course this problem-solving mind is often really useful and can help us excel in our work, BUT in this modern, information-overloaded world, that tool has a tremendous amount to take in and process (emails, instant messages, Twitter, LinkedIn, Facebook, etc., etc.), and as we have already seen, simply letting this tendency just run on autopilot (as it's been trained to do, and will continue to do unless we wise up to it) can be highly detrimental to our productivity and well-being. So, just like other tools that we may have inherited but wisely chosen to discard, substitute or upgrade for something more sophisticated, we might also do the same with this one from time to time, or we run the risk of complete psychological exhaustion and continuously dropping the ball in the process. Now, we are not saying that you need to do away with your problem-solving mind altogether. No, that wouldn't be wise (nor something that you could actually do, so don't fret about that). This entrenched mental habit is still very useful in some contexts and at certain times and places. The key is to train the mind into a state of awareness that allows you to recognise when it may or may not be helpful to be engaged in analysing and problem-solving, moment by moment while you're on the job.

For some of you out there, all this might be starting to sound rather grim and gloomy what do you reckon? As we've said, the world is speeding up with more and more information and our minds are wired a certain way: to habitually attempt to process any pieces of information that come their way! So is there any hope for us at all!? Well yes, there is. This hope comes from a branch of science called *neuroscience* and specifically with its amazing discovery of something called *neuroplasticity*.

The great brain wave

In essence, neuroplasticity is the term used to describe the remarkable ability that our brains have to adapt and modify themselves in response to the experiences we have as we go about our lives. Our brains are really quite a fascinating phenomenon – a really complex and intricate organ, full of neural networks and other super cool stuff. We have about 100 billion neurons in our brain which are effectively hubs of information connected to one another by neural pathways called synapses. There can be around 100 trillion synapses in the brain connecting neurons in this way. Now the really awesome thing (if all that doesn't sound impressive enough!) is that these connections between neurons are not static; they change over time. Every time that we think, do or experience something new, a new synapse is created and then every time that we think, do or experience that same thing again, that connection is reinforced, increasing the likelihood it'll be activated again and again and become the natural default neural connection within the brain. So effectively the brain will rewire its physical structure depending on the stuff that we choose to think, do or experience. Now how cool is that?

This phenomenon is most famously supported by a series of studies[3] involving London Taxi Drivers, who need to memorise every street and place of interest within a six-mile radius of Charing Cross in central London in order to pass the qualifying 'Knowledge' test. These taxi drivers have been shown to have larger parts of the brain called *posterior hippocampi* and smaller parts called *anterior hippocampi* (these regions of the brain are used for spatial awareness and memory) compared to control subjects. Further, significant structural changes in these taxi drivers' brains are also directly correlated to time spent driving a taxi. So in other words, more experienced taxi drivers who have been driving and practising the Knowledge for longer have larger posterior hippocampi and smaller anterior hippocampi than newly qualified drivers. The researchers of this study conclude that '*it seems that there is a capacity for local plastic change in the structure of the healthy adult human brain in response to environmental demands.*' (There's a link in the 'Useful resources' section below to a video from National Geographic about London taxi drivers' brains if you want to see more on this.) In short, this really is a groundbreaking finding which suggests that we can actually influence the structure of our brains, and that is exactly where the practice of mindfulness comes in.

The brain at work

In fact in a recent review of the research[4] there were at least eight different regions of the brain highlighted that are affected by mindfulness practice (in a good way!). Two of these regions have particular significance for our experience and performance at work and we thought you'd be interested to hear a bit more about them here.

The first of these is a structure called the *anterior cingulate cortex* which is located deep inside the forehead just behind the brain's frontal lobe. This part of the brain is associated with self-regulation which is important when we want to refrain from knee-jerk reactions at work. It also helps to retain clear focus as well as promoting flexibility around problem-solving rather than habitually continuing to use ineffective strategies. We're sure that you'd concur that this all seems crucial to ensure our very best performance in the highly demanding, ever changing and fast-paced environment within which we work these days.

Another key region of the brain is the *hippocampus* (as already mentioned in the London taxi driver studies above). This is a sea-horse shaped structure that is located behind the temple on each side of the brain. It is part of the brain's limbic system and, as previously mentioned, is associated with not only memory but also emotion. This part of the brain can be damaged by exposure to chronic stress but neuroscientific research shows us that mindfulness practice can increase the amount of grey matter in this brain region, helping to buffer against work-related stress. So this feature of the brain too seems of great importance, specifically in building resilience which is highly desirable (we're sure you'd also agree), so that we can continue to excel in the increasingly challenging and competitive world of our work.

With these findings in mind, and if you are anything like us, you might be starting to consider how mindfulness practice may not be something that you just 'might like to do' but rather something that you 'really must do' when it comes to ensuring your performance, endurance and sustainability at work. That is, if you want to maintain a healthy brain, increase self-regulation, effective focus, and improve your decision-making and productivity as well as your well-being while on the job.

It would seem that the choice is really ours to make. We can choose to keep travelling down old caveman/woman neural pathways on auto-pilot, or we can choose to behave differently (i.e. practise mindfulness) and create and reinforce new habits and ways of being. Isn't it time we develop our minds so we can begin to enjoy more and excel in this modern world of work? We'd be wise to wake up to who is actually doing all this multitasking and doing. That way we can make better choices for ourselves, improve our focus and productivity and get ahead in our work. That's exactly what mindfulness training is all about.

You might like to check out the two short videos as well as another article listed in the 'Useful resources' section at the end of this chapter to see a bit more about how the brain's physical structure changes with mindfulness practice. But please do remember that it's only through purposeful mindfulness practice (not by reading this book, an article or two, or watching a video) that you can actually positively affect your brain!

So what does the research tell us about how mindfulness can help us to stay more focused and productive while at work? Can it really help us to perform well even amidst the multiple demands of our high pressured working day? And does the physical structure of our brain actually change as we practise mindfulness – well, let's take a look.

Proven in science, smart for business

Improved performance and superior focus

Researchers in one study[5] were interested to see how a group of 25 mindfulness meditators from a range of professional backgrounds would perform on a series of attention tests compared to a group of 25 non-meditators composed of various workers from a local credit management company. The researchers found that the meditators performed significantly better on all tests: they outperformed the non-meditators in terms of efficiency and the number of errors made. This study demonstrates that mindfulness correlates with high processing speed and accurate performance. But what is most striking about this study is that mindfulness led to greater cognitive flexibility, and helps us to override automatic cognitive processes, including those that have been conditioned and reinforced over time (our old neural pathways, yep, those caveman/woman tendencies again). Those that practised mindfulness demonstrated a greater ability to bring habitual cognitive processes under control for the purpose of sustained focus. This preliminary study indicates that although many of us have reinforced a highly and easily distractible, wandering mind, with mindfulness there really is hope for us all in reining it back in when we want to.

Keeping focus in a busy office environment

In another study[6] the aim was to determine in what way mindfulness could actually help people cope with the multiple and simultaneous demands flying at them within a busy office environment and what effect mindfulness has on our attempts to multitask. Thirty-eight human resources professionals participated in this study and were separated into three groups: one group received eight weeks of mindfulness training, another group eight weeks of relaxation training and the third acted as a control group (no relaxation or mindfulness intervention). To test the workers in these three groups against one another, they were asked to perform a series of standard office tasks within a certain time frame while being disrupted with unrelated demands and other interruptions. Although the mindfulness group didn't perform the tasks any faster than the relaxation or control group, they were able to sustain attention on individual tasks for a longer time and were 20 per cent less likely to jump around from one task to another. The researchers conclude

➤

---

that mindfulness meditation increased focus and 'reduced task-switching' – an admirable ability to enhance productivity when we think about trying to get stuff done at work while having to contend with so many other irrelevant competing demands and irritating interruptions.

Improved memory and performance on tests

In a further study[7] researchers were keen to understand the effect that mindfulness might have on the relationship between a wandering mind and academic performance among a group of university students. Forty-eight undergraduate students were recruited into the study. A two-week mindfulness training was provided to 26 of the participants, while the remaining 22 received just nutrition training. The results showed that mindfulness training predicted better performance on the Graduate Record Examination (GRE) reading and comprehension tests and a greater working memory capacity. Furthermore, it was shown that the better performance from students who had trained in mindfulness was due specifically to decreased levels of their mind wandering compared to their peers in the control group. In short, mindfulness can improve our memory and performance on tests and lead to greater academic success, and this study confirms that it can do that even more than other lifestyle changes like diet and exercise.

Improved focus from gazing at the greenery

In a very recent study[8] from the University of Melbourne, researchers gave 150 participants a simple, menial, computer-based concentration task. After five minutes the participants were given a 40-second break while instructed to remain sitting at their desk. During this break an image of a rooftop surrounded by tall buildings appeared on their computer screens. Half the participants saw a plain concrete roof while the others saw a roof covered with a green, flowering meadow. After the break both groups then resumed the task. The results showed that following this mini break, concentration levels fell by 8 per cent among the people who saw the concrete roof and their performance grew less consistent. However, among those who saw the green roof, concentration levels rose by 6 per cent and their performance held steady. The researchers concluded *'engaging in these green microbreaks – taking time to look at nature through the window, on a walk outside, or even on a screen saver – can be really helpful for improving attention and performance in the workplace'* (you can read more about the benefits of taking a 'mindful green break' in Chapter 4).

➤

Dealing with complaints and difficult customers

Researchers in a further study[9] gathered together a sample of service industry workers. They found that the workers who were measured to have higher psychological flexibility following ACTraining were also better able to display more positive emotional responses towards customers who complained, despite an understandable level of stress on the job. The researchers propose that higher psychological flexibility *redirects energy and attention away from the intensive regulation of emotions ... and toward other more professionally relevant and less psychologically consuming tasks*.

Better focus and performance on new tasks

Researchers in a replication study[10] were keen to investigate the impact of ACTtraining on the behaviour of call-centre operators working in a financial institution. The findings showed that higher levels of psychological flexibility predicted better mental health and job performance (fewer work-related computer errors) on a newly trained task. The researchers propose that staff with greater psychological flexibility, who are not distracted by or trying to avoid the frustrations with the learning curve have better training outcomes when learning a new work-related task.

Changing the physical structure of the brain

Just in case you're putting all these positive outcomes down to silly ideas like, 'yeah, but surely mindfulness just relaxes people and that's why they perform better on tasks', etc., take a look at this other well-documented and fascinating study[11] in which researchers were keen to see what, if any, actual structural changes might be occurring in our brains when we practise mindfulness. Thirty-five participants were recruited for the study. Eighteen of these participants were allocated to the mindfulness condition which involved participation in eight weekly 2.5-hour sessions, and one 6.5-hour session during the sixth week of the course. The remaining 17 people received no mindfulness training whatsoever. Both groups received two MRI scans approximately two months apart (pre- and post-training). Astonishingly, the results showed that grey matter concentration increased within certain brain regions of the participants from the mindfulness group, including the left hippocampus, the posterior cingulate cortex, the left temporo-parietal junction and the cerebellum. This shows how mindfulness practice can influence grey matter concentration in brain regions involved in learning and memory processes, as well as emotion regulation, self-referential processing, and perspective taking – awesome, huh?

So with all that said (and again, if you're anything like us), we bet you're eager and just itching to practise some more mindfulness straight away, and start positively influencing those little grey cells – oh, go on then, it'd be rude not to … let's do it …

Exercise 2.6: Mindful on the job

Body-focused attention training

You can do this practice while sitting at your desk or just about at any other time that you choose to (you might choose to do it standing or sitting on your train journey in to or back from work). Throughout the exercise we're going to invite you to focus your attention on your body (but remember: this is not a body exercise but an exercise of the mind – an exercise of resting in awareness – and we just happen to be using the body as something to focus on). Some pointers:

▶ It's helpful to close your eyes, to limit further distractions as best you can. But if you don't feel comfortable to do that, just droop your eyelids and focus your gaze on a still spot or object in front of you.

▶ As you focus attention on your body, thoughts or other distractions such as sounds, emotions, sensations, etc. will likely try to pull your attention away – try to just notice any distractions; let them come and go, rise and fall as they naturally will, as you then return your focus of attention on to your body at that moment, as best you can. Every time your attention is distracted (which is completely normal and not a sign of failure!) just notice the distraction, congratulate yourself for noticing it, and then return your attention to your body, again, and again and again.

▶ The purpose of this exercise is to cultivate a non-judging awareness of your experience of focusing attention on your body, accepting any distractions that may arise, returning your attention to your body, moment by moment, nothing more or less, simply that.

Ready? OK, let's begin:

1 First, bring your attention to your feet. You may notice a sensation at the soles of your feet where your feet touch the floor and/ or the sensation of your feet against the inside of your shoes. If you

can't notice any sensation, that is absolutely fine too; just notice the absence of sensation. Remember, this is not about sensation but about open and non-judgemental awareness of what is, just as it is.

2 So, there they are, your feet (with the presence or absence of any sensation) and then there is you noticing your feet, allowing your feet to take centre stage in your awareness right now.

3 Notice where your attention is now – if it is not focused on your feet, then gently guide it back to doing just that.

4 Now as you allow your feet to dissolve from your awareness, guide your attention to your legs.

5 Take a mental snapshot (much like a camera would) of how your legs are right now in this moment – notice and acknowledge their position as you sit in the chair or stand. Hold just your legs alone at centre stage in your awareness right now. Nothing more, just your legs.

6 Notice the presence or absence of sensation at your legs.

7 Next, as you allow your legs to dissolve from your awareness, gently bring your focus of attention to your arms. Hold just your arms at centre stage now; notice their position, take a mental picture of just your arms. There are your arms, the left and right one and then there is you noticing them, just them, nothing else for now.

8 Now, bring your attention to the sensation of air where it meets the surface of your skin. Maybe you can feel the sensation of air against your skin on your face, your neck, hands or any other exposed body part. Just be curious and open to noticing the sensation of air against your skin. If you can't notice this sensation, just acknowledge the absence of it; that is absolutely fine too.

9 Next, begin to scan your body, from your head down to your toes and toes back up to your head with your full undivided attention. As you do this, acknowledge any warmer sensation that you may come across versus cooler sensations. It may feel warmer where your body meets the chair that you are sitting on or different body parts rest against each other. Acknowledging these warmer sensations is much like tipping your hat to a passerby as you might acknowledge them walking along the street, 'ah, warmer sensation, I see you'. Keep scanning up and down, for the next.

10 Notice where your attention is now; if it is not scanning your body for warmer sensations, then just guide it back to doing just that.

11 Now, expand your awareness to include your entire body. Allow your whole body as it is right now to take centre stage in your

awareness. Take a mental snapshot of your body, notice its position and posture as you sit in the chair/stand. There is your body and then there is you holding it at the forefront of your awareness.

12 Take a moment to recognise how your body changes; it is not the same body that you had as a young child. You may have had things cut out or put into your body. The skin at the surface of your body may have suffered scars or blemishes. Your skin may have grown hair in certain places or lost some in others. The temperature of your body can change from day to day, moment to moment. Your body can feel tired, energised, painful or relaxed or anything else. The experiences of your body change, but THE YOU that is aware of these experiences never changes; it remains the same and unaffected by these changes.

13 To end this exercise, narrow the focus of your awareness once again to zoom back on to holding just your feet alone at centre stage, as you did at the start. Maybe take a moment to marvel at the amazing ability of your awareness to expand and narrow at your will.

14 So there they are again, your feet, the left and right foot, with the presence or absence of sensation and then there is you, noticing your feet and holding just your feet alone at the forefront of your awareness – just your feet, just this one moment.

15 Now, begin to expand your awareness once again, bring to mind some of the objects that are around you, as you gently open your eyes and ground yourself back into the environment that you are in.

So how was that?

In doing this practice you may have come to experience a sense of calm, peace, tranquillity or relaxation. Remember that this was not the purpose, as this was not a relaxation exercise but an exercise of the mind, an exercise of resting in awareness, while focusing your attention on the here and now, being present and, in this case, aware of the sensations of your body. The fortunate by-product of being present in this way is improved well-being (aka relaxation) and also, from the cultivation of a clearer mind, we often will experience improved performance and functioning too.

You may have also noticed how, although your experiences (such as your experience of bodily sensations and your attention of these) are forever changing and shifting, the part of you that notices and is aware of these experiences never changes. Your awareness is much like the sky, in that whatever passes through the sky – the birds, clouds, aeroplanes, weather, rain, scorching sun, night, day, etc., the sky seems to be able to make room for it all and it remains unaffected by these events. Your awareness is the same: whatever passes through your awareness, thoughts, feelings, sensations, etc.; your awareness has room to hold it all and remains unchanged by these events.

This part of your mind is 'pure awareness', the ability to notice what is going on in the 'here and now', with openness and acceptance. There are no thoughts occurring in your 'awareness', as they only show up in your thinking mind, often demanding your attention. The part of your mind that can simply observe, acknowledge, notice and watch all your other experience (including where your attention is) is non-evaluative, non-judgemental and therefore by nature implicitly accepting, curious and kind. That is why we often come to experience relaxation and an absence of any stress in a practice such as this, as stress is only a consequence of thoughts (evaluative, judgemental, past or future oriented) that we are choosing not to follow with our attention.

More than this is that we tend to spend most of our time struggling with and/or defining ourselves by our ever-changing experiences, and as these are constantly shifting – whether that be one thought followed by another, one success replaced by a failure or one bodily sensation or behaviour being substituted by the next – we find ourselves in a perpetual state of fluctuating stress and instability. By stepping into the part of our mind that simply is aware of all these changes, we can again make contact with the stability and clarity of mind that resides within the present moment and enjoy the natural sense of ease, focus and productivity that comes with it. We begin to see thoughts as thoughts and feelings as feelings, rather than events that have to drive our behaviour. By widening this gap between stimulus (i.e. a thought, a feeling, etc.) and response (i.e. engaging with that thought, trying to eradicate that feeling), we have more choice about how and/or whether or not we do react. We can relate to our inner world experiences as an object of our attention rather than as a subject that we must identify with or immediately act upon without any awareness or reflection. This gives us a greater sense of calm, composition and assuredness and we are then free to choose to take wiser and more effective actions while on the job.

Balancing messy people

Generating optimum productivity, efficacy and focused attention among a workforce is a clear aim for any business in a competitive environment.

However, to balance productivity and focus alongside well-being and sustainability is a fine art (more on this in Chapter 7) and raises complex questions regarding the whole ethic of any business, let alone each individual. Encouragement and incentive can swiftly swing towards bullying and job insecurity, or lack of encouragement or incentive to sloppy, ineffective work and job dissatisfaction. As a business owner, manager or grass-roots employee, we have to make constant decisions about how our values, energy and motivation fit with the desire to grow our company or compete with others to be bigger, better, faster or greater.

Therefore there are certain questions raised beyond the obvious 'how do we improve focus and productivity?' to 'should we/I? Is it timely? Is there energy? Does this fit with the long-term goals and ethics of the business/myself?'

Psychologists have long struggled with how to compete with 'harder science' (such as Newtonian physics) because human beings simply have so many, often unpredictable variables. For example, push a billiard ball on a smooth surface with a stick and it will roll away, but push a human with a stick and it will probably push you back, cry, fall over, take the stick and ram it up your ... well, you get the point. With humans, there are always unpredictable forms of behaviour; we are basically messy when it comes to science and doing what we're told, or what is logical, rational or expected. Sorry, folks. Trying to tidy this up has itself led to even more problems. The results of statistical analysis are often criticised within psychology for removing the 'outliers', (or test scores which are outside of the norm) because they distort test results and make them really tricky and not the neat, sensible results which would make us feel reassured and safe, in the knowledge that humans are predictable. In other words, every time we pushed a human on a smooth surface with a stick they would always roll away. Try this experiment at home; we do not expect you to have great success.

In order to accept the exceptions to the 'rule', we are required to let go of predictability. A new paradigm emerges which is not based on (Newtonian or positivist) science being king. Eeek.

The metaphor of 'man as machine' is outmoded. People are not predictable in their actions all of the time, continually relentless in their energy or immune from ever making errors.

But before we all jump off cliffs or ram-raid the off-licence, we can also recognise that we need not descend into chaos either. In fact, the urge to categorise, make sense of and understand our world and fellow beings is natural and *hardwired*. The need to look towards trends, predictions, forecasts and probabilities helps most of us who work in business to form some kind of model, to manage budgets, to develop goals and strategies and to plan. This is stereotyping at worst and categorising at best: generally efficient and systematic but potentially dogmatic and narrow-minded.

So stop trying to work out the perfect formula or psychometric test to pigeon-hole yourself or your employees into their perfect role and to increase company output. That is not to say that many of us will act within the norm much of the time, but even this is not easy to predict. How many of us? How much of the time? For how long? And what will those who aren't toeing the line be up to? This means we can open our eyes to fluctuations, changes, minorities, minutiae and exceptions. Working life becomes fluid, dynamic and creative (more on this in Chapter 4). We can potentially hold the value of the efficient and verifiable alongside that which is rich in potentiality and fluent. In ethical terms this means constantly evaluating the balance of productivity and meaningful work output with the energies and capabilities available at any given time. It translates business into both science and art; if we sacrifice one for the other we compromise the long-term functionality of our work, either as individuals or as the collective workforce. Place too much emphasis on dogmatic, structured and target-driven work paradigms and burnout, discord and stress will be high, decreasing productivity, morale and focus; too little emphasis and laziness, indifference, poor quality work and lack of commitment ensue. Like fine-tuning an instrument to achieve the most beautiful quality of sound, we too can attune ourselves to the amount of applied effort required of us and our employees to encourage optimum efficiency and focus. We can understand when working overtime, for example, is a manageable and valuable strategy for ourselves and our workplace and when it becomes untenable and demotivating (more on this in Chapter 7). Yes, there may be times when we may struggle (to stay awake in that meeting about auditing, for example) or have to restrain ourselves from doing something that we think is grossly unhelpful (for example, when we repress the urge to tell the presenter to shut their cake hole), but these become less frequent and more manageable as we retrain the mind. We learn to take our foot off the gas, and learn to help and allow our co-workers and colleagues to do so too, knowing that the anxiety we hold about our work is not beneficial to us or them, and in its place we allow our enthusiasm and engagement to renew, so that focus and clarity become abundant again and productivity is increased. The natural ease which exists in the absence of our work-fuelled anxiety becomes gradually more accessible with persistent mindfulness practice and our effort at work is alive, fresh and engaged.

How to learn this with mindfulness

1 Watch the commonly held notion that mindfulness requires 'no effort', or should not involve effort.

2 Watch your view that 'effort' means wilfulness or a punitive form of discipline.

3 See if you can allow effort to be both attentive and at ease.

Exercise 2.7: Mindful on the job

Pencilled in

Practise on the effort required to balance a pencil on your finger:

1 Extend and hold one finger (or two if you're just getting started) out.

2 Gently place a pencil onto your finger/s and balance it there.

3 Watch the mind as you do this: any habitual self-criticisms, judgements.

4 Notice how similar-themed thoughts might manifest in your working day.

5 Do these motivate you? Increase your focus? Improve the outcome?

6 Try to let these thoughts be; refocus on your moment-by-moment experience of balancing the pencil.

7 How would it be to just leave these thoughts alone?

8 As you end the exercise, notice what your mind tells you when you 'get it right' or 'get it wrong'.

In this chapter we have seen how mindfulness can help us to retain and also sharpen our focus, efficiency and productivity. We find ourselves working in a day and age where we are bombarded with incessant digital information which in turn increases distractibility, and ineffectiveness ensues. Mindfulness is just the tool to help us cope with this. We can now understand that to improve our focus and productivity we need not necessarily reduce the amount of work that we do or at second best chuck all our mobile devices onto the nearest scrap heap, but instead we can choose to simply do one task at one time to enhance our efficiency and effectiveness. With practice we can unveil the sharp-edged focus and productivity that naturally lies just beneath our anxious, excited and often all too busy-doing-nothing exterior; we retrain our minds and as a result become more effective workers. Practising mindfulness is a mental workout. By returning our wandering attention to our present-moment experience – to the breath, the body or anything else that we choose – time and time again we are strengthening the neural pathways that increase our ability to stay focused and more effective. While at our desk, our mind wanders to another inbound email, that other piece of work, the latest news flash maybe, the sounds from the office floor or what's for dinner that evening, and then we purposefully guide our attention back to the task at hand, or our breath, etc. This simple yet highly effective practice (if continuously repeated) is not to be underestimated; it has the power to rewire our brains, reduce our tendency to drift off and become lost in unproductive patterns of thought; it has the power to keep us present, stable, attentive and productive on the job.

❝Practising mindfulness is a mental workout.❞

Mindfulness top tips to go

From this chapter you might like to remember that:

▶ Stress, whether from excitement or anxiety, can seriously impair rational judgements, reasoned decision-making, focus and productivity. Start being effective at work by using mindfulness to do just one thing at a time.

▶ 'Just focus your attention on your breath or body'; practise this very simple instruction for two minutes, watching the unruly nature of the mind; maintain this daily and you will train your mind to be more focused and productive, even changing the very structure of the brain in the process.

▶ Distractions will occur; recognise the cost of judging these as 'failures'. Instead refine your awareness of the habitual tendencies of the mind and choose to mindfully 'take your hands off' them.

▶ A few moments noticing the soles of your feet on the floor or a few breaths and you will find that the mind will learn to settle. You will learn to stop struggling and become more focused.

▶ Learning to be sensitive to the balance of effort and ease required in mindfulness will increase your awareness of this in daily working life, helping you to remain steady, focused and stress-free.

▶ Practising mindful, focused attention will not only help you with the tasks you face at work, but will also improve your well-being, your enjoyment of your working day and the long-term success of your business.

So how are you doing? Still with us? We hope by now that your interest and appetite is growing. Mindfulness really does have so much to offer us in our work and business and we have only just started to scratch the surface of all this. We are really keen to turn your attention to the application of mindfulness for work-related stress and well-being, our relationships with colleagues at work, a healthy business culture, our creativity and, specifically, workplace confidence next, if you're up for it? Oh go on … there's loads more insights and practices to come.

Useful resources

▶ Board, F. (2015, March 31). *Free 'Study' app for more productive working* [article on the soundagency.com]. Retrieved from: http://www.thesoundagency.com/2015/sound-news/free-study-app-for-more-productive-working/

▶ Killingsworth, M. (2011, November). *Want to be happier? Stay in the moment* [video file]. Retrieved from: http://www.ted.com/talks/matt_killingsworth_want_to_be_happier_stay_in_the_moment

▶ Killingsworth, M. (2013, August 1). *Does mind-wandering make you unhappy* [article on mindful.org]. Retrieved from: http://www.mindful.org/does-mind-wandering-make-you-unhappy/

▶ National Geographic. (n.d.). *London taxi drivers' brains* [video file]. Retrieved from: http://video.nationalgeographic.com/video/london-taxi-sci

▶ Scientific American. (2013, October 31). *How does meditation change the brain? Instant egghead #54* [video file]. Retrieved from: https://www.youtube.com/watch?v=q0DMYs4b2Yw

▶ Smiling Mind. (2015, February 2). *Mind the bump – mindfulness and how the brain works* [video file]. Retrieved from: https://www.youtube.com/watch?v=aNCB1MZDgQA

▶ Stromberg, J. (2015, August 27). *What science says about meditation: it improves your focus and emotional control* [Vox.com; science and health article]. Retrieved from: http://www.vox.com/2015/8/27/9214697/meditation-brain-neuroscience

▶ Szalavitz, M. (2008, January 1). *10 ways we get the odds wrong* [*Psychology Today* article]. Retrieved from: https://www.psychologytoday.com/articles/200712/10-ways-we-get-the-odds-wrong

Boost confidence

These days we find that business owners and managers are increasingly recognising the potent power of self-confidence that exists in the members of their teams. Employees with higher self-belief and greater confidence can have a significant effect on business interactions and successful outcomes. In our work with clients who may be suffering with feeling anxious, stressed, burnt out and/or lacking satisfaction and meaning in their work, the issue of confidence (and usually the lack of it) arises time and time again. More and more individuals, as well as organisations, are recognising how the practice of mindfulness can play a fundamental role in helping to rebuild broken confidence at work and also to boost it in ways that can bring about greater business successes.

In this chapter we aim to provide you with a practical overview of the relationship between workplace confidence and mindfulness.

Specifically, we will take a look at:

▶ What confidence is and what it's made up of.
▶ Why confidence is so fundamental to getting ahead in business.
▶ What psychological processes erode our confidence.
▶ What mindfulness has to offer in building up our confidence.

If you are hoping for the usual gamut of 'confidence-boosting' practical tips and tricks, we're sorry to disappoint but you won't find them listed here; instead we are offering you something different and far more effective. Repeating positive self-affirmations, ensuring that you are well versed and well prepared with a soothing, cool bottle of water (say, before you give that presentation to your manager) may all sound (and can be) helpful to some degree, but we find that ultimately on their own they are pretty overrated when it comes to cultivating a more stable and reliable sense of confidence at work. You have probably heard them all before anyway. So if you are willing to take a look at something completely different, then you're in the right place; read on.

So what exactly is confidence?

Confidence often seems like some elusive part of the make-up of 'other' people: you know, the ones who keep their cool, are fazed by nothing, with the magazine looks and exuding a magnetic charm. Even if we temporarily feel like this, our self-assuredness can desert us in the most inopportune and inconvenient moments and leave us feeling exposed, ashamed and vulnerable. In essence, confidence is a quality that does not appear to be consistent and reliable (and HOLD THE FRONT PAGE! as, contrary to what you might believe, that actually goes for all of us), but it is still much prized and necessary for our own sense of self-worth, feelings of competence and the trust that this instils in others about our skills, products and/or services. Yes, even those who look like they are brimming over with self-assurance may well be feeling pretty uncertain about themselves and simply winging it – in fact, others might regard *you* as poised, cool and sure of yourself when the reality is that on the inside you are quite as much of a faint-hearted jelly as everyone else. In short, confidence is the fundamental sense of being acceptable, safe, assured and capable – a sense that so many of us seem to lack at work these days.

The Lion's Roar

We have lost count of the number of CEOs and senior business leaders that have walked into our office looking lost and directionless, full of self-doubt, explaining that they often feel like a 'square peg in a round hole', suffering from some kind of *impostor syndrome* and anxiously anticipating the day when they are no longer able to 'wing it', exposed as an incompetent fake and lose their job. So, why do so many of us and even those that may be at the very top of their game seem to lack so much self-worth and self-confidence?

Well, most of us spend our time anticipating what's about to happen, what's about to go wrong. We have a sense that something terrible will occur; the good won't last, and when that happens we won't be able to cope, so we'd best be prepared: forewarned is forearmed, right? All this leaves us tense, our body full of adrenaline and we are primed ready for fight or flight. All well and good, and this sounds pretty sensible on the face of it, but ask yourself:

▶ What does your experience tell you about the usefulness of this protective tendency?

▶ How does it work out for you?

▶ Is it effective?

▶ Does it keep you feeling safe and assured as you navigate your way through your working day?

▶ And how about your efficiency and productivity: does it help you get the job done?

▶ Do you walk into work each day with a profound sense of capability?

Well, unless your office has just been moved into the deep Amazon jungle, leaving you to rough it with a host of wild tropical animals, we'd expect that most of this just gets in the way of any sense of self-assuredness, your performance, your ability to get ahead at work and also the enjoyment of what is actually right here and right now.

So what would it be like if we dropped this anxiety-fuelled protective suit of armour? What would be revealed and what sits behind it? Well, that would be your confidence, free to naturally flow as it always would. Within each of us there is the sense that everything will be OK; sometimes we can sneak a peek of it deep down inside of us, usually, however, only when we offer some advice to our colleagues, clients, friends or family members in response to their own predicaments. At other times, if we are lucky enough, we actually tell ourselves the same when we are faced with some of the daily stressors and even bigger sh*t that work throws at us from time to time. But all too often this sense of self-assuredness is far out of reach, often trampled over by another fearful part of us that we tend to reinforce unknowingly (we'll return to this in a moment). This buried sense of confidence is within us all; it has sometimes been described as the 'Lion's Roar':

> 'It's the confidence that allows us to say, 'No matter what life presents me, I can work with it.' When that confidence is there, we take incredible joy in the moments of our lives.'

> **(Brach, 2012, taken from: http://blog.tarabrach.com/2012/03/lions-roar.html)**

This is the deepest sense of confidence that mindfulness can help us to uncover, reconnect with and cultivate more of. Mindfulness can help us to cease running from the next threat around the corner and to allow our inherent sense of confidence to naturally flow once again. There is a natural sense of stability and assuredness that arises when we make contact with the present moment in an open and accepting way. Much like a tree, rooted into the ground, we can stand firm and secure when we refocus our attention towards now.

Exercise 3.1: Mindful on the job

Holding your nerve

Try the following exercise as a quick method for holding your nerve and finding a little stability when you feel your confidence waning (you can repeat this exercise often and as regularly as you like to ensure that you continue to cultivate a deep sense of inner strength and confidence):

1 Whether sitting or standing, find your centre of gravity – through the feet, the hips or spine. Feel the centre of the body upright, dignified and open; adjust your posture if necessary to support this intention.

2 Repeat gently 'I can work with this', meaning that even if you are a bundle of nerves, you can both acknowledge your present state and cultivate further confidence.

3 Repeat gently 'all will be OK, I've got this', meaning that you can acknowledge your anxiety and put it in perspective.

4 Find your centre again physically. Breathe in, breathe out mindfully.

5 Continue to hold your nerve with kind attention, repeating 'I can work with this', 'all will be okay' and 'I've got this'.

As many of us begin to practise mindfulness even in the absence of any particular panics, wobbliness or fear, we very quickly realise just how uncomfortable it is to simply *be still*, as if there is something weird and abnormal about just *being* rather than *doing*. In experiencing this common and natural discomfort, we soon notice that actually we aren't very comfortable in our own skin after all. With more regular practice, however, we begin to recognise how we can in fact be more at ease with ourselves. By continuing to explore this discomfort, we begin to strengthen the natural confidence in being who we are, just as we are. This allows us to cultivate and transfer a greater sense of confidence to everything else that we do.

While there are definitely ways of helping our chances of tapping into and maintaining confidence using mindfulness, as with the exercise above, mindfulness can also help us to recover well when we inevitably do f*** up from time to time. Throughout the rest of this chapter we are going to turn your attention to how we can cultivate more confidence while at work and on the job. For now, here's an interesting fact for you to consider . . .

If you sometimes feel a little useless, offended or depressed... *

*Remember ....

... you were once the fastest and most victorious sperm out of millions.

The real confidence zapper

How often have you noticed that your confidence has suddenly plummeted to a non-existent level? Maybe just before you give a presentation, show up for a job interview or appraisal meeting with your manager? If not in these situations, then maybe you can think of your very own unique times at work when you've turned into a quivering, weeping wreck. The truth is that our confidence waxes and wanes (and more often the latter) when we do challenging stuff and more so when that stuff really matters to us; how about that daunting appraisal meeting that could lead to a fantastic promotion and a really exciting new role? Feeling confident? Nope. We thought not.

If you are anything like us, at such times your mind is probably full of all sorts of self-doubts, worries about what's likely to go wrong and what ifs. *'I'm not really skilled to do this job!' 'What if I don't know the answer?' 'I'm going to totally mess this up!' 'What if I go blank?' 'What if they think' 'I'm incompetent, uninteresting and not good enough?'* Buying into all these thoughts is quite understandable as they're designed to help us prepare and problem-solve any obstacles so that we can ensure we deliver the best performance possible and succeed, but in actuality they are circular and potentially never ending, and trying to answer them can be a proper pain in the arse. But also consider now, that while trying to problem-solve the worst-case scenarios, we are also simultaneously telling ourselves the worst about ourselves (continuously commenting on our failings and rejection). A few hours pondering over these sorts of worries and questions in our mind can often leave us feeling like we have been totally flattened by a high-speed juggernaut – splat!

Michael: To say I was elated when I received that email is an understatement. Let's just say I was more akin to a cat on heat, shrieking with unabated excitement. Could this really be true? It was a request for me to deliver a talk alongside some VIPs that could also make a really big difference to some less fortunate people's lives. I read and re-read that email at least one hundred times. But by the end of the day my excitement didn't seem so strong. I could hear a faint whisper of self-doubt at the back of my mind. I listened to that doubting whisper all the way home and it got louder and louder; my feelings of low self-worth came creeping in. 'You can't do it!' 'No way!' 'What if you f*** it up?!' 'What if word gets around?' 'You'll ruin your career if you even try!' The following morning I was totally wiped out.

I felt as if I had spent the whole night going ten rounds with Mike Tyson. Having to return to work was my only saving grace; the referee called time – ding, ding . . . and we have a winner (Mike T. obviously!). I arrived at work looking haggard, feeling vulnerable and a bit shaky to say the least – such is the power of that worrying, self-critical and self-doubting mind. My mind had got the better of me. In my mindlessness I had exhausted myself and chased any sense of confidence I may have had far away. It was now time to recognise all this confidence-zapping worry and self-criticism, and instead bring a little more mindful attention and compassion towards myself.

It's got to be perfect

Anxiety-fuelled perfectionism often erodes our sense of self-confidence – an underlying fear of not being perfect, as if failure is an absolutely, unacceptable no-no. Our attempts to avoid feelings of failure, rejection and shame often hold us back in progressing in our work and career. Our fear of saying the wrong thing and others not liking us for it prevents us from speaking our mind and leaves us hesitant to share new ideas and answer questions. Unless we are 100 per cent certain that what we've got to say is right, interesting or inspiring, we may keep shtum in that very important business development meeting chaired by the CEO who has just flown in especially from the New York office to hear some new ideas, and then just beat ourselves up when Brian from the IT department says exactly the very same thing that was on our mind (smart-arse!). Unless we feel fully competent and qualified, we may shy away from going for that promotion, new role/job and generally taking risks at work/in our career/business. All this perfectionism just feeds back into undermining our confidence further, ironically, preventing us from getting much done at all. It also tends to drain all the satisfaction and fulfilment we could gain from our work and career at the same time.

When engaging with these perfectionist thoughts and worries, we can notice the anxiety rising in our body, and when this happens these stressful situations have just got a whole lot more stressful. We become a prisoner of our anxiety, fearing that others may see our weakness. We become anxious about being anxious and get locked into a battle with our anxiety. Now, along with delivering our top class performance, we also find ourselves preoccupied with trying desperately to push the anxiety aside, hide it away or even, better still, eliminate it completely, all at the same time; and by now we know all too well what the effects of multitasking are (if not, take another look at Chapter 2). All this struggling leads to a disconnection from ourselves and the actual moment we are in: we begin to talk louder, faster (wishing we had been born a chameleon, praying that the surroundings would just swallow us up), and we can make more mistakes and find ourselves bringing on our worst fears (i.e. failure, rejection and shame). What's that saying again, oh yeah – what we try to resist persists! Fighting anxiety in this way is like fighting a losing battle; we are bound to fail, and that's the greatest confidence zapper of all time – yep, that's the real deal, folks. So how can we manage all this? Well, mindfulness training is the way to successful regulation of our emotions and a calmer, clearer and more confident mind. With mindfulness we can unveil, retain and boost our confidence even in the most stressful work situations.

The art of public speaking

'There are two types of speakers: those that are nervous and those that are liars.'

Mark Twain

For most of us the idea of public speaking can leave us feeling pretty jittery, unsettled with a kaleidoscope of butterflies flittering around in the stomach. Whether that sounds a bit like you or even if you're one of trillions of others who quite frankly would rather run naked across the office floor than get up to do any form of actual public speaking – whether to your closest teammates or to hundreds of delegates at a professional conference – either way there's no need to panic anymore as there is hope for us all. Mindfulness has been shown to help sufferers of social anxiety disorder who typically fear the negative appraisal of others and who consequently find any form of social interaction (let alone addressing a crowd) absolutely debilitating.

In a study at Stanford University[1], researchers explored the impact that nine sessions of mindfulness training would have on the experience of people suffering with social anxiety disorder. Following the mindfulness intervention, participants were less anxious and also changed their beliefs about themselves, thinking of themselves in a more positive light. The mindfulness intervention helped people to reduce the amount of times that they thought of themselves as a 'coward', 'weak', insecure' and 'afraid' and instead chose to describe themselves by terms such as 'strong', 'able', 'admired' and 'loved'. The mindfulness training helped people to break old habits of thinking about themselves in a certain way. The researchers conclude that mindfulness *'might make it easier for people to shift between ways of viewing themselves'.* In summary, these findings demonstrate how mindfulness reduces emotional reactivity and enhances emotion regulation as well as reducing behaviours that function to avoid social anxiety (like running away to hide – the actual behaviours that really maintain and undermine our poor sense of self-confidence). So this is excellent news for those of us that would like to get a handle on our lack of confidence and associated anxiety about public speaking, especially if our attempts to avoid getting up there and presenting (like running to the toilet or taking a sickie!) are getting in the way of our progress at work. Well, you know the drill: in order to benefit from this stuff, you need to practise it. So next time you have the opportunity to speak up in a meeting or present to an audience, take it and try the following exercise.

Exercise 3.2: Mindful on the job 🎧

Finding confident ground

This goes out to anyone who is even a teeny bit anxious about speaking in public to an audience (or anyone that you want to impress). This could equally be speaking up in an interview, a meeting, pitching a new product or giving a lecture or presentation. We are going to assume you are well prepared and have a good knowledge of whatever it is you intend to present, whether that is a profit forecast or your feelings about the interpersonal dynamics in your team. Make sure you are well informed and well prepared with any facts and figures you need (i.e. do your homework first! But don't go into perfectionist-overkill and feel like you need to remember everything you want to say word for word – trying to remember these words will just get in the way). Also prepare yourself physically: make time for a wee, a drink of water, avoid the coffee, try to get a good night's sleep, eat something, take any necessary (legal!) medications and acknowledge that if any of these things aren't or haven't been possible, even though you might benefit more if you have done them, you will still be OK (you are not going out to fight a gladiator after all). You can practise this exercise anytime, but try it before your presentation, giving yourself time with each stage if you can (one to two minutes maybe). Then, during your presentation/meeting, you can use all or parts of the practice, even fleetingly, to help anchor yourself in the present and enhance your confidence.

1 First, find your feet. Feel the ground solid beneath you.

2 Feel the sense of solidity in your body, especially with the contact of your feet against the floor, in your calves, thighs, hips and pelvis.

3 Notice your body breathing. Ragged and short breaths are as fine as long slow ones.

4 Notice if your mind turns towards catastrophic thoughts, notions of failure, negative appraisals, or doom. Leave the thoughts alone, let them be, see them gently float away as you focus back on your feet/body/breath.

5 If you feel afraid, anxious, apprehensive or unsettled, let yourself know that it is OK; it's just this one moment; this shall pass; even if this is hard, you are choosing to face the challenge. You are showing up in your life. This is courage, this is where confidence flows from. Here you are in this moment, confident, nervous, brave, confused … showing up.

6 Feel the sense of solidity in your body, especially with the contact of your feet against the floor, your calves, thighs, hips and pelvis.

7 Find your feet. Feel the ground solid beneath you.

'Anchoring' exercises like this are great to help us move out of our thinking (worrying) mode of mind and into more of a sensing mode of mind (as we direct our attention to the lower half of our body). The effect of this will usually automatically alter your physical, cognitive and emotional response (remember however that this is a fortunate by-product and not our intention or expected result) allowing you to feel more grounded and stable so you can act in a more reasoned and therefore productive way. You can do this kind of exercise with your eyes open or closed, while sitting or walking around, anywhere at all.

Remember, even if you do make a tit of yourself, (even with the great practice of mindfulness beside you), at least you showed up in your life and the ground is still right there beneath you. Well done fellow human. You might also like to remind yourself of these wise words:

'Opportunities are like buses – there's always another one coming.'

Richard Branson

Act confidently and do what matters anyway

'May your choices reflect your hopes, not your fears.'

Nelson Mandela

We have yapped on now about how our anxiety and fear of failure keeps us behaving in unhelpful, protective ways. Recall, just for now how these habitual tendencies are likely to be outdated, reactive and confining, cramping to your confidence and well-being. You don't initially need to *do* anything dramatic, or make any grand commitments or gestures; simply take a moment to reflect on Brené Brown's questions:

▶ What would you attempt to do if you knew you could not fail?

▶ What's worth doing even if you do fail?

(Brown, 2013, loc 501)

As we spend so much of our time thinking about what we are not, what we cannot do/achieve etc., we can lose sight of what is actually possible today or in this very moment. With mindfulness, we can free our minds up to notice the numerous possibilities open to us in each and every moment, possibilities that we might grab if only we had the confidence to do so. These may be tasks we put off working on or even larger goals that we have brushed aside or ignored. It may be that we would choose to relate to others or even ourselves differently if we had more confidence to do so. Try the following exercise to set your mind free and focus on building your confident self.

Exercise 3.3: Work in progress

Wake up to confidence!

Imagine that when you wake up tomorrow, as if by magic you find that you are as confident in your work/business as you possibly can be. With this confidence in mind, now reflect on your answers to the following questions:

If you had all the confidence you ever wanted (and imagining you would still choose to work) …

▶ What would your day ahead look like?

▶ How would you act differently at work (i.e. walk, talk)?

▶ How would you treat others?

▶ Who would notice this?

▶ What would they notice that was different about you that told them you were now totally confident? (i.e: in your demeanour, character, speech, behaviour, etc.)

▶ What other personal qualities would your confidence demonstrate (calm, assertive, generous, kind, etc.)?

▶ What would your confidence enable you to do that is meaningful to the larger picture of your work/career?

▶ How would you talk to yourself differently?

▶ What would you feel proud of at the end of the day?

Now, reflect on these further questions:

▶ What aspects, if any, of the answers to these questions above are already present in your life right now?

▶ What aspects, if any, might be (partially or potentially) possible for you to take action on now?

▶ Can you act in these ways that demonstrate your confidence tomorrow, today? How about right now?

Building your confidence with mindfulness is most certainly possible, but, make no mistake about it, it can be a challenging process and it can take some time. You can speed this process up by putting yourself into situations that might scare the pants off you (initially anyway), but be assured that the more you step into the feared unknown (time and time again) armed with the powerful practice of mindfulness, the more confident you will begin to feel. So, if you are someone who tends to say:

'I'll do that (presentation, talk with the boss, etc.) when I feel more confident/ready.'

It might be time to switch that around to:

'I'll do that (presentation, talk with the boss) now anyway, despite not yet feeling 100 per cent confident/ready.'

The truth is that we will never feel 100 per cent confident/ready and if we wait until then, well, we'll never get anything that may present as challenging done, ever. If we act as if we are confident now (despite not yet feeling so), we are more likely to begin to experience confidence growing within us. It's time to take a leap of faith, step into the unknown, breathe mindfully, use the practices in this chapter and watch your confidence grow (to learn more about how our willingness to feel vulnerability can lead to very great things for us, please watch the excellent TED Talk by Brené Brown, listed in the 'Useful resources' section at the end of this chapter).

'You must do the thing you think you cannot do.'

Eleanor Roosevelt

Take note: stepping into feared situations mindfully is not about ignoring or pushing your vulnerability aside. On the contrary, it is about making room for it, allowing it to be there and being willing to feel that way as you strive forward with what is most important to you. Move into your feared situations with respectful attention and acceptance towards your vulnerability. You may find that repeating these few words can help:

'I can do this (scary stuff) AND feel vulnerable/under-confident at the same time'

Also you might like to remember that when you fail (and know that there is no 'if'; to err is to be human after all), you're in good company. These products, by market giants, all bombed:

▶ The Ford Edsel (epic fail): overpromoted, too expensive – especially at the time of the late 50s recession. It did not meet expectations and was criticised to be just the same as any other Ford, apart from the bodywork of course which looked a lot like female genitalia! Ford finally ended the car's production after losing $350 million on it!

▶ Sony Betamax (ouch!): killed off when Sony chose to take the moral high ground and refused to license its technology to the pornography industry. With such a demand for porn, competitor JVC saw an opportunity and moved in with its own product (VHS). Also, Sony apparently misread the market and stuck to their guns, assuming that viewers wanted just an hour of tape to record stuff; again, competitor JVC saw the opportunity and created the four-hour tape so people could enjoy watching football games and films (including porn!), despite the lesser quality of the VHS product.

▶ Apple Newton (apparently not everything turns to gold): overpriced at $700 – $1,000 and it was too big and clunky. Despite its handwriting-recognition software being promoted as 'unprecedented', it was highly inaccurate and just plain annoying!

▶ McDonald's Arch Deluxe (flop): $100 million was spent on advertising this product in an attempt to attract a more adult and classy customer with a refined palate. But nope, not even a processed piece of round bacon could 'whet the appetite' of this demographic; they were just not interested in this kind of fast food – duh!

▶ Microsoft Zune (please, really?): revenues declined by 54 per cent in one quarter while at the same time the iPod's increased by 3 per cent. With poor quality design, it lacked the style and simplicity of its competitor products. Most importantly though, it was not compatible with the most dominant product in the market – Apple's iTunes programme.

▶ Pepsi A.M (just wrong!): this new drink was rolled out in response to an apparent decrease in the amount of coffee drunk by consumers in the mornings while they were still keen for a caffeine kick. But Pepsi was unable to convince people that a cup of cola first thing was a better idea! The branding was prescriptive and therefore it restricted the market size.

► Frito-Lay Wow! Crisps (so very wrong!): sales exploded to $347 million but then dropped in just two years to $200 million. Olestra was the fat-free alternative, secret ingredient in these crisps that first really did wow the market but then consumers soon realised that it made them want to go to the loo (a lot!) much like a laxative – stomach cramps and diarrhoea prevailed!

Confidence leads to success

When it comes to business success, confidence may be just as important, if not more so, than competence. It would seem that studying and working hard, gaining knowledge and skills in the hope of moving onwards and upwards to excel in your career, is not the only talent needed: confidence really matters too.

In a series of studies at the University of California-Berkeley[2], researchers were keen to test how the social status of people was enhanced by their confidence. They found that overconfidence led to a higher social status and also certain behaviours that make people appear confident to others. They also found that the hunger and motivation from people to gain higher status promoted their overconfidence. Specifically, and most interestingly, these studies showed that people who are overconfident in incorrect information are actually more effective in building peers' trust and respect than people showing less confidence in the correct information (so it would seem that acting confidently not only helps to boost confidence but it will also help you get ahead in your work – if getting ahead in your own work means gaining the support of others, that is). Although this does not necessarily mean that always assertively communicating false information will make you more confident and liked by others, it does demonstrate how having self-belief and confidence is a powerful tool in being noticed and influencing others. The researchers conclude that *people might so often believe they are better than others because it helps them achieve higher social status*.

From our experience, it would seem that organisations are recognising the integral role that confidence has in bringing about business successes. Psychometrics measuring confidence form part of the selection and recruitment process as well as regular performance reviews for staff in a growing number of organisations, who now, more so than ever, value the confidence as much as the competence of their key players.

Mindfulness is gaining significant traction as a viable way to train confidence in managers and business leaders, and, taking a look at the research, it is easy to understand why.

In a recent study[3], researchers at the University of Westminster in England were interested in the effects that a 12-week mindfulness training programme could have on the confidence and self-perception of skills among a group of CEOs and senior managers in the London area. The results of this study demonstrated how this mindfulness training significantly enhanced the overall confidence of this group of managers as well as some of their specific individual skills, such as inspiring a shared vision and demonstrating moral intelligence.

So it would seem that mindfulness really does help to promote self-confidence. Let us now look further into just what 'being confident' involves, so that you can deepen your understanding, making this whole topic all the more relevant and meaningful for you and your working life.

❝ *Mindfulness really does help to promote self-confidence.* ❞

Do I believe in myself?

Confidence is not just the mysterious air we have about us, like a bottle of trendy aftershave or perfume. Confidence is, at least in part, something we believe about ourselves. Our self-beliefs are sometimes referred to as our personal narratives or stories and we are continually creating, re-telling, reinforcing and reinventing these. There are many ways in which we do this, such as how we describe our personality ('I'm really driven/kind/supportive'), attribute certain habits to our history ('I don't do public speaking', 'I've never been good at presenting'), look for a persona we can 'fix' upon and wear 'those' clothes ('I'm just like him/her/them'), talk 'that' way or listen to 'that' music, etc. The problem with all this arises when these stories have firmly fixed beliefs about ourselves which are at odds with the situation that we find ourselves in and/or what actually matters most to us, often culminating in a big dollop of dissatisfaction and more likely leaving us quivering in our boots. Most of us will recognise a certain personal journey through childhood hobbies and obsessions, teenage fashion disasters, early adulthood ambitions, and so on. Simply by seeing this history, and the stories we have tightly clung to and told about ourselves, we see that actually our sense of ourselves, and the confidence we feel as a result of this, has gone through many shifts and changes. The good news, therefore, is that even if you struggle with confidence, it is a mutable and malleable thing open to a certain degree of reconstruction if we dare. Are you ready to let go of your 'Self Story'?

'I am not what has happened to me. I am what I choose to become.'

Carl Jung

Try the following exercise to begin to reflect on the stories that you have told about yourself and the impact that these have had on your confidence and choices at work.

Exercise 3.4: Work in progress

How old is that story?

1 When you were at school/university/previous jobs, what was your role? Were you the clever one? The funny one? The popular one? The shy and quiet one? What tasks did you do well and not so well in? What tasks/personal qualities did you get praised/criticised for?

2 How have you reinforced this early image/assumption/belief of yourself over the years? What types of jobs have you put yourself up for? What roles have you taken? What types of tasks do you avoid doing? Do you wait for things to happen for you or do you make them happen?

3 Have you held beliefs and assumptions about yourself based on where you were born/grew up? Who your family is/what your family do? How your family related to you? Have your work-related choices, actions and reality been affected by these assumptions/early relationships in your life? Are you happy with these actions?

4 Do you ever change the image of yourself to please others around you? How has that worked out for you in your career?

Faking it to prove it

The temptation may be to build or rebuild our 'self-belief' to rhino-skin thickness (like, try the 'in every day in every way I'm getting better and better' mantra in the bathroom mirror ten times a day) and charge forth into the world of work trampling anything and anyone in our path (I'm NOT a failure! I AM a success and I WILL be recognised!). We ignore caution, advice, physical tension, headaches, teammates' viewpoints, reviews or predictions and stick faithfully to our set path shielded by thick, impenetrable armour. This can work, to an extent, for some of us; however, it is rarely sustainable in any deeply satisfying way as we tend to disconnect from others and our authentic selves. The need to be connected with others, socially accepted and part of a community is a hardwired human condition (more on this in Chapters 5 and 7). There's no way of getting out of it, we are social apes who love a good grooming from one another (remember to tell this to your next date). Therefore if we cut off from others as an attempt to protect our vulnerable, underconfident self, we actually end up feeling even more isolated and dejected. Take note: rhino suits are not the answer!

'It may easily come to pass that a vain man may become proud and imagine himself pleasing to all when he is in reality a universal nuisance.'

Baruch Spinoza

The other component of this is because a 'hard shell' of simulated confidence is actually a way of masking our genuine inner feelings, which can feel too painful to bear, so we cut off from these too and instead turn to defining ourselves on tenuous and unpredictable external events (such as successes and positive feedback at work) and comparisons working in our favour (ignoring the rest). This is a bit like the gambler believing that he or she is on a lucky streak and piling more cash into a game of pure chance. We may, further, engage in behaviours which are bullying or perfectionist in an attempt to control others or our environment in order to sustain this precarious position and eliminate our vulnerability. But of course, when the wheel of fortune eventually turns, we may find that instead of our ego being puffed up like Toad of Toad Hall we feel more like something the cat dragged in (and maybe everybody sees it too, especially if you have a spectacular f***-up).

Hubris blinds us to an inner fear of being seen for 'what we truly believe we are' (read in this case: vulnerable, unlovable, not good enough) and sadly often makes most of us look and act like total prats. If you lack confidence, on the other hand (which, remember, is every one of us at some time or another), this can sometimes be expressed in ways which are judged by ourselves or others as a 'weakness', leaving us feeling very exposed and uncomfortable. We can feel as if, contrary to our rhino-friends, we 'have no skin'. If this shows up for you, then the reaction is generally one of withdrawal of some kind, perhaps defensiveness, self-deprecation or just wanting to hide. We surely all have stories of our own crushing embarrassments, the inner hurts which we carry about and hope no one else will discover unless we are either very drunk or very trusting.

Underconfidence, either shown through pleasing others, arrogance or belittling yourself/others, does not inspire trust from others, certainly in the long term, and can be a cause of great stress. Let's give some examples:

Alicia works at Coffee-Bean-Tastic in the accounts team and is about to have her annual appraisal. She has been working in the job for the past year, after completing her accountancy exams. She has worked hard, but still feels very junior when comparing herself with her more experienced co-workers. At her meeting she is actually up for a promotion, which she is not aware of. These are her possible answers to 'how do you feel you are getting on at Coffee-Bean-Tastic?' and the associated body language/ behaviours:

1　She speaks quietly, making poor eye contact. She says that she is well aware that she is not as good as the rest of her team and she is working really hard, but still feels she doesn't know that much and she's very sorry because she doesn't want to be letting everyone down and taking up too much of your time. She stops talking and looks towards the door.

2　She is fidgeting and speaks very fast. She tells you that she has really liked working with her team and is learning loads of new things on the job and is getting very interested in the company. She then goes on to tell you that she has Googled the senior staff members and noticed that they have travelled frequently to Costa Rica and that the carbon footprint must be pretty large, and the coffee isn't actually fair trade and she buys her coffee from Green Beans and actually she already had 17 cups of it before the appraisal and isn't that funny?

3　She begins to talk, loudly, before you have finished asking the question. She tells you how passionate she is, that she will put in 110 per cent to any task given her. She is glad you are having this appraisal as she thinks she must be up for promotion after a year of, frankly, doing all the hard work. It is probably time they took on someone else to do the menial jobs and let her get on with something more important, because frankly, with results like hers she is simply wasted in her current role and everyone knows it. She is happy to step on anyone who gets in her way to achieving success.

Having read the above examples, consider your answers to the following questions:

▶ Which 'Alicia' would you give the promotion to?

▶ Maybe you can recognise some of your own qualities and expressions of underconfidence from these examples?

▶ Which of these do you think seems more or less like you?

▶ What messages are you transmitting at work by your own behaviours, body language, etc.?

▶ Perhaps you are drawn to traits similar or different from yours?

▶ Can you recognise your aversion to or desire for a particular way of being, or combination of contradictions?

It can be helpful to know how we are drawn into our own 'self-stories' and our narratives about ourselves (with no claim on what is right/wrong/true/untrue/real/fantasy) and how this can shape our decisions and behaviours. We are then able to begin to see the influence of these limited views upon our working environment and how they continue to play out a particular 'script' we might have purposefully or accidentally set for ourselves of 'how I must be'. This is usually with some intent of controlling life's outcomes, protecting ourselves from feeling anxious, overwhelmed, ashamed or vulnerable. As we work with mindfulness further, we can begin to see that our way of being and our choices at work are not inevitable eventualities; we are actually free, at any time, to try something different and look at things afresh. The first step to this process is to make some careful observations.

The underconfidence trap

Our lack of faith, fear of disgrace and underconfidence in ourselves is transmitted and communicated to others via an array of behaviours such as:

▶ going blank or forgetting what we are saying;

▶ stuttering or stumbling over words ('um, your err, umm');

▶ failing to speak up for ourselves;

▶ blushing, sweating, shaking, etc.;

▶ saying 'silly', 'inappropriate' or 'unkind' things;

▶ talking too fast, too quietly or mumbling;

▶ openly denigrating or degrading ourselves/others, or letting others do this;

▶ participating in activities which go against our values or ethics;

▶ compensating for our lack of confidence by drinking, taking drugs, talking too loudly or talking over others;

▶ not listening properly;

▶ rigidly holding on to our views and having to prove that we are right;

▶ fiddling with things (pens, papers, hair, your...err...um);

▶ rushing through a task carelessly;

▶ checking (and re-checking) work for reassurance;

▶ taking on more and more work;

▶ showing off about ourselves;

▶ being overly apologetic;

▶ our own unique ways.

These behaviours and self-judgements tend to compound themselves into vicious cycles and may look a bit like this when they show up:

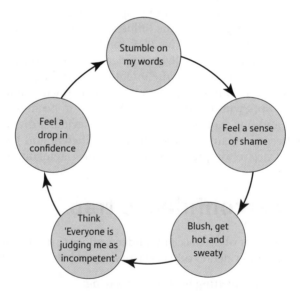

Of course, many of us also add to the joy induced by this delightful list of mishaps by imagining them all for hours/days/weeks or maybe even months beforehand, rehearsing all our potential disasters or our defining career moments (and as we know from Chapter 2 we do love a bit of drama) and totally upping the emotional ante. We have already discussed the adrenaline addiction and its poor partnership with rational decision-making, and here we see it in action again. Then we make a ballsup somehow and spend the next hours/days/weeks or maybe even months replaying the carnage in our minds and giving ourselves a bollocking for everything we should have done differently. Which then might look something like this:

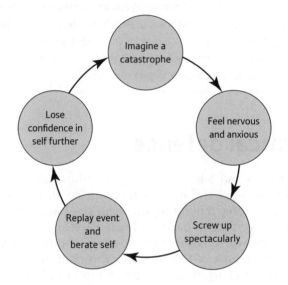

Even if this is not our own particular brand of 'messing up', we can surely recognise plenty of times in our work where we have felt overwhelmed by a situation and unable to function well under the pressure. If we have enough resilience, we might be able to turn the lemons into lemonade; however, sometimes we just get mindlessly reactive to a situation and end up in fight (be arrogant, complain, bully or attack) or flight (withdraw, resign or self-sabotage) mode. Take the case of Peter, for example:

Peter

With a strong but hidden sense of vulnerability, Peter worked as a Partner in a large private equity firm. He was driven by deep fears of failure and rejection and his perfectionist ways were evident for all to see. He tended not to delegate work to his team as they were 'just incompetent wastes of space'. His fellow partners were annoying time wasters too, who didn't have the first clue about how to run a successful business and couldn't tell the difference between their arses and their elbows. Peter would ruminate on the mistakes, flaws and incompetency of everyone around him. ➤

In time he found it hard to hold his frustration in and would display his upset with sarcastic comments: 'really, did you really think that was going to work?!', 'Oh right, OK then, I'll just make this work even though I have no resources and a team of absolute dimwits to do the job, wish me luck then!' Peter's sarcasm wasn't going unnoticed: a few of his team had made a complaint to senior management and Peter was increasingly being pulled up on his attitude and approach to others. Although he held firmly on to his belief that everyone around him was useless, he had begun to fear that his comments might cost him his job. He turned his critic on himself and began to berate himself for his sarcastic and angry outbursts. This didn't seem to help and he became more and more frustrated. He decided to seek some help.

The critical defence

Berating ourselves and others for our/their failures and mishaps seems sensible on some level and may sound a bit like this: 'I need to know what I/they did wrong, remind myself/them (over and over again) what a total pillock I've/they've been, to learn a lesson/know the worst so I can prevent the worst happening, especially if I don't feel too confident to face the trauma of failing again'. Criticism in this sense can be viewed as a super-charged, problem-solving machine, activated and ready to protect our underconfident, vulnerable, gooey soft centre from any future pain (remember those cavemen/women in the previous chapter and how they needed a tool to protect themselves?). But chastising ourselves/others in this way is not always the answer, as it just continues to undermine our own self-confidence, further increasing our sense of vulnerability and helplessness, giving rise to more attempts to protect ourselves. Although some of these slights and the attacks on others might not at first appear like personal attacks on the self, they will also penetrate our own self-confidence in the most detrimental way.

Attacks towards others are in fact ultimately highly self-critical also and therefore as confidence-zapping as the most obvious and explicit self-criticisms (such as 'I'm a total loser'). Pointing the finger in blame (i.e. 'you are a total loser'), criticising everyone else (and their mothers) only actually damns yourself as lacking any useful substance and as helpless and incompetent to independently change your own reality – so: he/she/they is/are useless effectively translates into I'M USELESS! All types of criticism can therefore be seen as both the cause and effect of underconfidence. This creates a perpetual cycle; it's really not clever and leaves us stuck in an underconfidence trap (having to endure all the associated performance-hindering anxiety and frustration to boot) which looks a bit like this:

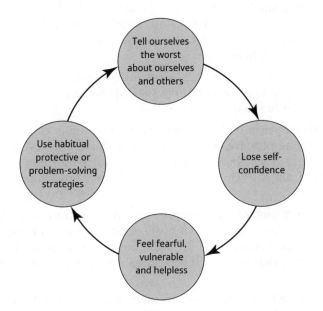

So if you are with us on this (which really we hope you are) you'll probably agree that it's time to start letting this critic know who actually is boss around here. Enough with this *old blame game;* it's time to get wise to your critic before he/she/it batters your confidence down even further. You might like to try this next exercise to really begin to start noticing your inner critic, while lessening the negative impact that he/she/it is having on your confidence.

Exercise 3.5: Mindful on the job

Paper pusher – origami

This practice can actually be done with any task at all, not just one that involves folding paper. Anyway, for now go get a piece of paper and follow these instructions:

1 Take a square piece of paper.

2 Fold each corner into the centre.

3 Turn the paper over so that all the folded-in edges face down – you will have a smaller square now. (Did you fold that right? Are you doing this properly? What would your boss think? Or notice any other ways your inner critic is questioning you, hounding you or berating you right now.)

4 Fold the corners of this square into the centre (Is it good enough? Are you making a mess of things (again)? See if your critic is visiting and what it has to tell you.)

5 Fold the paper in half, both ways (Does your inner critic have a particular tone of voice, a gender or other characteristics? Maybe you can notice if you have internalised the voice of a parent, carer or teacher from your childhood? Maybe it's your boss/competitive rival at work?)

6 Now pinch each of the corners by putting your fingers into the little squares underneath. (Very clumsily done? Or are you achieving perfection? Ridiculous exercise! What are they on about? This is stupid! Watch that critic as it attacks us now – that wasn't very nice, was it?)

7 Squeeze the four outside corners together into and up to the middle. (See your critic for what he/she/it is: an outmoded, outdated, misguided mechanism for self-protection (armouring). You may wish to tell it to 'shut up', 'no thanks', 'bye bye'. You really don't need it anymore and look …)

8 You have made a fortune-teller. (If you are judging your fortune teller, criticising yourself, this exercise, the world, then OK.)

9 Now see what else you (with the help of your critic) have made along with this folded piece of paper …

Fortune-teller + frustrated critic (waste of time) = bad world

Fortune-teller + unhappy critic (misaligned corners) = cr*ppy exercise

Fortune-teller + scared critic (strange looks from others) = unworthy person

Fortune-teller + self-aggrandising critic (perfect construction) = smugness

Fortune-teller + undermining critic (perfect construction) = doubt

Fortune-teller + your own brand of critic (any paper creation) = anything essentially lacking in care, empathy, wholesomeness or connection to yourself/the world around you.

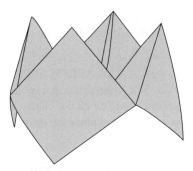

If you want to use this (no judgements from us!), you can also look on YouTube for further instructions. You can find a link to a tutorial video on how to make an origami fortune-teller listed in the 'Useful resources' section at the end of this chapter.

It's likely that you will be familiar with your own internal critic; for many of us it has become an entrenched mental habit. The fact that it is a habit, common and familiar (in one form or another) among all us human beings speaks to the fact that at some point in time it has been useful (remember the tools needed by our cave-dwelling ancestors?) – as intelligent human beings we wouldn't do something unless it made some sense to do it, now, would we? The truth is that our critic might be useful (as a motivator, say) at some points in time and in certain contexts. However, we do need to remain mindful of it (as in the exercise above), as otherwise it can go into overdrive and cause havoc with our sense of confidence, as described earlier. We need to do little more than to notice and become aware of our critic (more on this to come) to stop it in its tracks. In simply stopping to notice and observe it, we also remind ourselves of the fact that it is just a habit of the mind, and in that moment of observation we reconnect with our deeper sense of solidity, stability and assuredness, even in the most stressful moments on the job.

Confidence in the now

When we comprehend the intimate relationship we have struck up with our perfectionism, the way it is fuelled by anxiety to rid ourselves of the least desirable parts of, well, ourselves (which is actually impossible) and therefore the way it perpetuates dissatisfaction and even more failure, we can see how our confidence suffers. The key to developing confidence, in the face of our fear (real or imagined) is to understand that our anxieties are not present focused, they tend to have a flair for the dramatic and they are habitual. Using mindfulness, then, we first become aware of our own special brand of screwing up.

> '... *without self-awareness, you would have little ability to moderate and direct your behaviour ... You need this capacity to free yourself from the automatic flow of experience, and to choose where to direct your attention. Without a director you are a mere automaton, driven by greed, fear or habit.'*
>
> (Rock, 2009)

So let us see the inner critic as that which is driving us habitually by fear or greed. We first need to develop mindfulness to catch him or her 'in the act', just like we did in the origami exercise just now. Once we notice and recognise the voice inside ourselves so ready to undermine our confidence, we can use mindfulness to re-focus on our present experience, to see life as it is just in the moment instead. There is no need to make any attempt to engage with the voice which attacks and undermines us; we don't need to struggle with it by attempting to think positively instead, or by trying harder or by berating ourselves further for even having an inner critic (that would be simply beating yourself up for beating yourself up!). When we get out from under the Monty Python-like foot of our critic, we can then start to see that we are actually OK.

Disengage and disarm

No, not a pitch for CND, but certainly a way of putting aside the biggest weapon of mass destruction – namely your inner critic. Beating ourselves and others up is familiar to so many of us. As we have seen, it is our attempt to eradicate and hide from our vulnerability and associated emotional pain. In this light we can see how our critical mind does actually really care and has our best interests at heart; it is motivated to help us feel better, safer and more assured; however, it is just making a total balls up of it all, so maybe we can let it off the hook, and, as we've said, not beat ourselves up for beating ourselves up. It is wise to notice how engaging with our critical mind is usually essentially an act of self-loathing; it is rejecting of ourselves, therefore exacerbating our sense of low self-worth and poor confidence. So instead of trying to fix our and others' imperfections (including our self-criticism itself!), mindfulness offers us another, more productive way to manage our innate insecurities and to cultivate more confidence in the ever changing, highly competitive, and sometimes scary world in which we work.

Mindfulness has been shown to not only enhance our self-esteem and confidence but also cultivate more confidence irrespective of our successes, and even in comparison to those around us, no matter how rampant our self-critical thoughts about our failures might be. Researchers in a series of two studies[4] carried out at Griffiths University in Australia firstly found that, among a group of student participants, mindfulness skills strongly correlated to high self-esteem. Specifically, the four components of mindfulness practice that predicted higher self-esteem in this study were:

▶ labelling internal experiences with words, which prevented people from getting consumed by self-critical thoughts and emotions;

▶ bringing a non-judgemental attitude toward thoughts and emotions, which helped individuals have a neutral, accepting attitude toward themselves;

▶ sustaining attention on the present moment, which helped people avoid becoming caught up in self-critical thoughts that relate to events from the past or future;

▶ letting thoughts and emotions enter and leave awareness without reacting to them.

In order to be certain whether mindfulness practice was actually the cause of higher self-esteem or down to some other factor/s, the researchers divided participants into two groups where one engaged in a 15-minute mindfulness practice while the other read a story about the Venus Fly Trap for 15 minutes. Both groups were given questionnaires to complete that measured their level of mindfulness and self-esteem before and after the 15-minute tasks. Those that participated in the mindfulness intervention group showed significantly higher levels of mindfulness and self-esteem after their practice while there was no change in the scores of these measures for the group that only read the Venus Fly Trap story. Although further research is necessary to ensure that mindfulness training can have longer-term effects on self-esteem, the researchers conclude that *'mindfulness may be a useful way to address the underlying processes associated with low self-esteem, without temporarily bolstering positive views of oneself by focusing on achievement or other transient factors. In brief, mindfulness may assist individuals to experience a more secure form of high self-esteem.'* This study confirms that we don't need to do any more than to notice our self-critical thoughts with mindful attention (read here: attending to them in the moment with openness and acceptance, while not trying to change them, thinking positively or beating ourselves up for having them), allowing them to come and go naturally. This is how we can lessen the impact that our self-criticism has on our self-confidence.

Unworkable persistent positive optimism

Many therapies, tools and techniques encourage us to try relaxing, thinking positively (i.e. challenge and reappraise that critical voice) and setting ourselves goals to attain. This can work fantastically for a time, but then, if it all goes tits up (which it inevitably will again), our inner critic is reactivated. The shame of failing at what everyone else has been touting as the next great thing (and yes, mindfulness, if not taught clearly, can fall into this trap too) either causes us to give up, or if you have strong perfectionist tendencies, to try again. This can lead to a tyrannical pattern of endless rejection of ourselves, our community, our world: 'I'm not good enough', 'you're not good enough', 'work's not good enough', 'life's not good enough'. Brené Brown calls this the culture of 'scarcity', and in her research she asks her participants to fill in the blank in the phrase: *'never … enough.'* Examples include: interesting, smart, nice, safe, perfect, thin, powerful, good. How many can you come up with?

Exercise 3.6: Work in progress

Nothing is ever enough!

Have a think about what your critic might happily insert into the following blanks (if your critic is anything like ours, you might find that you have more than one for each sentence, which is fine!). This is a useful exercise to continue your work on noticing your critic's voice and disarming its power:

▶ I'm never … enough

▶ He is never … enough

▶ She is never … enough

▶ It is never … enough

▶ They are never … enough

▶ This book is not … enough

Sometimes, in fact perhaps often, we can clearly see the merit in loosening our habitual, narrow and restricted views of ourselves and the world as we think we/it should be, and how we/it fall/s short of that. Like 'yeah, it would be great if I stopped buying into the belief that "I am never confident enough"', because we know that this feels bad and actually undermines our confidence further. Nevertheless, it can be very challenging to relinquish our grip on these views, even if we know they are not beneficial, as we also do not trust in or even know any alternatives. So we ask ourselves 'what does it look like in this moment not to buy into the belief that "I am never confident enough"'? and come up with: 'I don't know', 'scary', 'too difficult to imagine', etc. So, if you are able and this type of response shows up for you, then just let this insight be enough for now. Rob Burbea, a Buddhist teacher, writes about 'the confidence to let go'. He states:

> '... There may be times, for example, when we know it would be best to let go of an unhelpful attachment but somehow we just can't. Perhaps at a certain level we feel desperate, and unable to imagine that we could be okay without this thing that we are clinging to. Perhaps even unconsciously we worry that letting it go would render us bereft of what we believe we need for our survival. If, however, we can have access to, and develop, a reservoir of profound inner well-being, it makes letting go of what is not helpful much easier. We feel that we have enough, so letting go is not so scary.
>
> Over the long term, repeated and regular immersion in such well-being supports the emergence of a genuine confidence.'

(Burbea, 2014, loc 922)

Exercise 3.7: Mindful on the job

Developing a reservoir of profound inner well-being

Well, you heard the man (see above; no, not the sky, above in the text!), we need to repeat this one regularly. This practice will help you find space in times when the inner critic is on a rampage, and enhance and deepen groundedness and trust in yourself at work. Take time to allow this skill to develop, to broaden the reservoir so that any work struggles have somewhere soft and spacious to land. With time, you will see that this practice is another significant key to unlocking your genuine, authentic confidence in yourself (without relying on a shortage of positive self-affirmations or looking to transient work-related successes/achievements) and unhooking from the tyrannical struggle of your critic.

1 Find a spot to sit; somewhere restful helps, but is not essential. If you have a few minutes alone at your desk, in the park at lunchtime, or even in the loo cubicle (don't forget to flush!), use it for this. If you don't have time for that, then that sounds like a challenging place to be in, so don't sweat trying to do this 'perfectly' and just do what you can when you can.

2 Feel the contact of your feet with the floor or surface they are resting on, or notice the absence of contact (for those high fliers out there).

3 Feel the sit bones on the chair or loo seat. Notice your body.

4 Take a breath and notice the journey of that in and out of your body. This is you, and this is you noticing your breath.

5 Check in with your mental state; it may be busy, still, engaged, distracted or something else. Whatever is there, just let it linger for a while. Just notice and perhaps say to yourself 'I am noticing the busyness (or other quality) of my mind right now'.

6 Check in with your emotional state; it may be open, angry, indifferent, anxious or something else. Whatever is there, just let it linger for a while. Just notice and perhaps say to yourself 'I am noticing the openness (or other quality) of my emotions right now'.

7 This is you, as you are right now, no more, no less.

8 Now say to yourself, 'Hello (your name), I wish you well' (no one can hear you!). You might feel silly at first; just notice this too. You might also want to say, 'Hello silliness, welcome'. You may feel stuck, unsure, like you don't get the point of this, calm, or anything else; just welcome them each in.

9 If you lose focus, that's OK; welcome that too. You can return to step 2 at any point.

10 Whatever arises, continue to wish yourself well, just in this moment, just for now.

The relentless critic

Despite all the detrimental effects of engaging in criticism (whether directed towards ourselves or others), many of our clients continue to question how they could possibly manage without it. Many of us are so utterly used to having an inner bully, and attributing that to anything we achieve at work that the thought of quitting this self-deprecating habit leaves us feeling at a loss, scared and vulnerable. What would we do/be without our critic? How on earth are we supposed to motivate ourselves to improve? How would we get ahead without telling ourselves that we should do better?

You might like to take a moment for your own reflection.

Exercise 3.8: Work in progress

Critical reflection

▶ What does my inner critic say about how I have to be right now?

Example: Josie: You need to be smarter, clearer and cleverer. You need to work harder and impress everyone. If you fail, you will feel crushing, burning shame and everyone will know what a stupid, bumbling fool you really are.

▶ What do I notice when I don't look to my inner critic to define myself right now?

Example: Josie: I feel calm, spacious and still in my body. I am not sure what will happen, but that feels OK right now. Actually without all the stress of beating myself up, I feel free and more energised to get stuff done.

Because we are so used to turning to what we believe is a voice of authority (which we have internalised as our inner critic and made super-tyrannical) to keep us on the straight and narrow and keep us 'safe' from failure, most of us feel a little uncertain about trusting our deeper, more centred sense of self and can feel quite vulnerable, certainly at first. In our often cut-throat, demanding, highly critical and competitive work environments, it is perfectly understandable to hide our sense of not-knowing and being unsure from others – for fear we may be eaten alive! So, hanging on to these beliefs for as long as you may have or continue to do so, is also OK too, as after all, you are only (an imperfect) human. And it is really difficult to be an imperfect human where the culture demands 100 per cent perfection. We are forever told that our best just isn't good enough, so, with a little help from our inner tyrant, we end up working in a perpetual state of anxiety, fearing our mistakes and failures and constantly striving to do better. Oh, if only we could be good enough, wouldn't it then all be OK? But, the truth is that no matter how much we try, we will mess up, fail and fall out of line, at least some of the time. Because we fear this failure so much, because it feels painful, our critic tries to help us to avoid it – but, dear friends, this is such hard, hard and futile work, simply eroding confidence faster than we can defend against it; we are caught in trying harder and harder still. Since our inner critic is so pervasive and convincing, let's help you reflect further. Here are our top two facts to keep in mind.

Why criticism leads to failure (not success) ...

1 If you really think about it, the main reason that we procrastinate or avoid new challenges at work is due to our fear of messing up. When there is even a distant whiff of failure, the self-critic is let loose ('I'm so useless at this!'). We know this about ourselves all too well. Also, when we beat ourselves up in this way, well, that feels really very sh*t! So to prevent that occurring, we continue to beat ourselves up ('I'm useless at that,' 'I can't do that!') to protect ourselves from ever going there – we know, ironic, right? This can also look something like:

'Cr*p, I did a really poor job of that, but I mustn't think negatively, I must stop berating myself, it is only making me worse, I must try harder to be more positive, I'm really bad at that, why am I no good at being positive? What's wrong with me?'

But that's the truth here: the driving force behind our self-criticism is an attempt to avoid further failure. All sounds like a vicious cycle, doesn't it? Well, that's because it is. And it kind of makes sense: what better way to avoid any sudden feeling of failure than to have your critic keep that feeling alive for you all the while; you'll certainly never be shocked by that feeling of failure again, now, will you (just the ticket if you tend to lack confidence)?

2 Getting caught up in a critical mind is a messy affair, which clouds our vision, and amongst all the feelings of stress and low self-worth that it induces, we can find it hard to take a really good look at ourselves and where we might actually be able to make a change for the better, even if we wanted to. So our critic really isn't the best aid in our attempts to motivate or improve ourselves so that we can reach our desired targets and goals; it just keeps us in a constant state of intense negative emotions, feeling as if we are not good enough and failing, undermining our confidence and motivation.

In essence, engaging in this critical mind, although on the surface may look like the smart thing to do, isn't actually the most useful strategy for bettering our performance and helping us get the results we want in our work. Self-criticism is actually performance-hindering as it triggers our stress response (fight or flight). Our self-critic alerts us to a threat (read here: our own imperfections) and we then begin to attack that threat (which in this case is actually ourselves!) with more self-criticism and eventually we then shut down in a defensive position, and become depressed – which we're sure you'd agree is not the most motivational mental state to find yourself in. You may think that arguing with your critic is the answer but you needn't do that either (that sounds like being critical of your critic again) – the truth is that your critic is basically a total smart-arse and will always try and convince you of its righteousness. You will totally recognise this if you've ever tried to engage in a debate with someone who is convinced they are right (no matter what logic, facts or convincing counter-arguments you may provide).

So what are we supposed to do without criticism? How will we better ourselves, improve, excel and strive towards achieving more of what we want and what matters to us in our work? The fact that we don't really know how to operate without a bully whipping our backs and making constant demands, is NOT evidence that we couldn't actualise all our desires without it. No. We can do all these things, but we must recognise the obstacle that criticism actually is to achieving them and instead cultivate a new, more viable and productive way of operating.

So what is this alternative way? Well, just for a second, let's suppose that it is wiser to accept the fallibility of being human. What do you think that might be like? However scary this may sound, just for a moment, let's consider it as, let's face it folks, despite our very best efforts we are not, nor will we ever be, 100 per cent perfect. Owning up to our limitations and flaws and responding to our, and others', mess ups and mistakes with genuine kindness and compassion rather than punitive criticism is the way that we can continue to retain the confidence to move on the things that are most important to us in our work and which lead us to greater work success.

Is self-compassion really the new self-criticism?

'Don't be embarrassed by your failures, learn from them and start again.'

Richard Branson

Reminding ourselves of our gains, successes, and wins as a way to promote our confidence and self-esteem, as we strive through our working day and our career, means that we are going to need a constant stream of external validation to feel good about ourselves. Yes, this false sense of self-esteem comes with a proviso and creates a boom or bust cycle. Of course it all works extremely well when we succeed as our self-esteem rockets sky high but when we inevitably fail again, our critic is set loose, damning us as a failure, or not good enough, and our self-worth, confidence and motivation then plummets. However, by adopting a more self-compassionate approach on the other hand, our self-worth, confidence and motivation remain more stable and secure.

With self-compassion we are warm, caring and kind to ourselves, particularly in times of failure, stress or hardship, in the same way that we might be toward a close colleague, friend or loved one. For example, when you'd usually berate yourself endlessly for mistakes you might make at work or damn yourself as a failure for setbacks or any flaws or inadequacy you notice in yourself, with self-compassion you might instead warmly acknowledge the upset you feel, talk kindly to yourself, remind yourself that you are only human and then coach yourself in a more supportive way and wish yourself well. Self-compassion is not about judging ourselves negatively or positively but more about taking a realistic and more helpful perspective on the situation we find ourselves in and choosing to relate to ourselves with kindness and acceptance; it's about being truly accepting of ourselves, warts, flaws and all.

Kristin Neff, PhD is a leading researcher in the field of self-compassion and has outlined three components of self-compassion:

1 **Self-kindness:** Instead of self-criticism, we choose to talk to ourselves with kindness, patience and empathy, much like we would speak to a close colleague or friend.

2 **Common humanity:** Recognising the natural common 'imperfection' in being human. Rather than comparing ourselves to others we notice the similarities (i.e. weaknesses, flaws, inadequacies) between us and others.

3 **Mindfulness:** Simply noticing and practising acceptance of our unwanted and unpleasant experiences (i.e. failure) rather than trying to eliminate or suppress them. We need to accept our suffering before we can be compassionate to ourselves.

When we bring compassion (read here: mindful attention of acceptance and kindness) to ourselves (the bad as well as the good parts) at work, there is nothing to fear, as deep down we know that we are only human, and as a human we will make mistakes, and that there are some factors that we simply cannot control. So, although in hindsight I know that *my behaviour wasn't all that it was cracked up to be*, I can still be assured that *I am still all that I am meant to be!* So self-compassion gives us the tools, strength, motivation and confidence to take risks at work and tackle new challenges as we feel better prepared to face difficult feelings, like failure, as and when they may arise. In being self-compassionate, we recognise that suffering and inadequacy are part of our shared human experience; we are all in the same boat in that way. So when we are confronted with personal failings, we respond with more understanding, acceptance and self-care. Mindfulness practice helps us to practise and cultivate self-compassion, as we repeatedly meet our busy mind, and any difficult thoughts and feelings, without judgement, in an accepting way.

In not beating ourselves up when we fail, but instead offering ourselves expressions of kindness and acceptance, we retain visibility on where and how we can make a change and also, as importantly, we remain confident to take wiser actions even if they feel difficult to do. We will return to this topic later (in Chapter 5) where we will see the transformational power that mindful compassion can have, not only upon ourselves and our own confidence in the workplace, but also upon our wider working community. We'd really encourage you to take a look at the excellent TED Talk by Kristin Neff, listed in the 'Useful resources' section at the end of this chapter to find out more about self-compassion and how it compares to self-esteem and especially how self-compassion is a much more effective motivator than self-criticism to help us get ahead at work.

> **"Self-compassion is a much more effective motivator than self-criticism."**

If you are anything like us, you're probably thinking that this all sounds great but is any of this actually backed up by science? Does a more compassionate approach really help with our confidence and consequentially our motivation to face challenges and therefore excel? Will self-compassion really help you to succeed in your work? Well, yes. Take a look at this:

Proven in science, smart for business

Self-compassion leads to personal improvement

Research supports the use of self-compassion as a means of motivation for self-improvement and specifically the fact that when we are more self-compassionate ➤

---

we tend to take more responsibility for our actions rather than none at all (as many of us might fear). Researchers at the University of California conducted a series of four studies[5] looking at self-compassion in relation to personal weaknesses, moral transgressions and test performances. When compared to a self-esteem group, a positive distraction group and a no-intervention control group, the self-compassion participants showed significantly greater motivation to: make amends and avoid repeating a recent moral transgression; spend more time studying for a difficult test following an initial failure; make an upward social comparison after reflecting on a personal weakness; change the weakness they identified. These findings suggest that, somewhat paradoxically, taking an accepting and compassionate approach to personal failure may make people more motivated to improve themselves. Researchers in another study[6] found that when participants were instructed to be self-compassionate when thinking about a past mistake, humiliation or failure, they were more likely to accept personal responsibility for what happened rather than blaming things on other people or events.

Self-compassion reduces negative emotions

In very recent study[7] (hot off the press! – at the time of writing this, anyway), researchers found that mindful compassion was more effective than other cognitive approaches in reducing the impact of harmful thinking (such as criticism) on our emotional state. A total of 207 undergraduate students were randomly assigned to either the compassionate thinking condition or one of three other conditions (cognitive reappraisal, responsibility attribution or self-deflection) or a control group. Participants who engaged in compassionate thinking and cognitive reappraisal reported significantly lower levels of negative emotions compared to those in the other groups. However, even more interesting is the finding that the habitual use of self-compassion reduced negative emotions across all the conditions.

So we can see that self-compassionate, mindful people still set high standards for themselves, they retain confidence and are motivated to take action towards their desired goals. The difference between them and those that rely on a critical mind for motivation is that they are not as thwarted, despairing or clouded by a fog of stress, negative feelings and anguish or feeling quite as underconfident when they don't meet their goals, leaving them more motivated to try again. Self-compassionate people have a more stable sense of confidence and motivation in their work as their drive to work hard is based on their desire to learn and flourish and not because they need to prove anything to themselves or avoid the negative appraisal from others (i.e. eliminate feelings of failure). In short, self-compassion is not about taking the easy way out, increasing the chances that we never step up to responsibility or take productive action towards making any improvements. In fact it's a tried and tested way of ensuring that we excel and reach our fullest potential in our work.

So if you are with us on this, and to ensure that you cultivate a more self-compassionate mindset (rather than habitually relying on self-crit-icism) to enhance your confidence and motivate yourself at work, you might like to begin increasing your awareness of your self-compassionate attitude. You can start to do this with the following exercise (which has been adapted from the 'ACT with Compassion' work [www.actwithcom-passion.com] of Jason Luoma et al. at the Portland Therapy Center in Oregon USA and based on the 'Self-Compassion Scale' by Kristin Neff, which you may also choose to complete online to see how self-compas-sionate you actually are; see 'Useful resources').

Exercise 3.9: Work in progress

Noticing self-compassion in your work

▶ To really start to build a more self-compassionate attitude we would suggest that you work through this exercise regularly (at least 3–5 days per week).

▶ Before you finish up your work for the day, or maybe on your way home, take a few minutes to work through this exercise to increase awareness of how you treated yourself throughout the working day. Reflect on any moment(s) when you were struggling, upset, under-performing or feeling highly self-critical.

▶ Over time, you can monitor your progress and see how your scores may change (the higher your scores the more self-compassionate you are).

▶ Carefully read each statement before answering.

▶ Rate how often you behaved in the following ways over the working day:
1 = not at all, 2 = a bit, 3 = sometimes, 4 = mostly, 5 = all the time

1 When things went badly for me today, I saw the difficulties as part of normal working life that everyone experiences.

2 I tried to be kind towards myself when I was feeling upset at work.

3 When I was feeling down or upset today, I reminded myself that there are lots of other people at work feeling just like I am.

4 When things were difficult at work today, I tried not to be self-critical and tough on myself.

5 I was caring towards myself at work today.

6 I saw my failings as part of the human condition.

7 When I felt painful feelings today, I tried to be mindful and approach my feelings with curiosity, acceptance and openness.

8 When I struggled at work today, I was not disapproving and judgemental about my flaws and inadequacies.

9 I was tolerant and patient towards those aspects of my personality I don't like.

10 I was able to acknowledge the importance of self-compassion.

We are now going to look at another mindful way of building confidence through self-compassion. This is not, as you might imagine, by trying to think positively instead and conjure up a sure-fire solution to the shortcomings and failures of ourselves and the people we work with. Rather than yet again unleashing your ferocious, snarling critic in the hope of chasing all your vulnerabilities away, why not try holding your discomfort and soft spots with mindful attention and some unconditional kindness and compassion; after all, you do seem to really care. Why not try this radically different approach now and practise it regularly to boost your self-confidence:

Exercise 3.10: Mindful on the job 🎧🎧

Enough is enough

For the following exercise recall the phrase of scarcity – 'never . . . enough' – a favourite of our inner tyrant, which you considered earlier in this chapter.

▶ Close your eyes or allow them to rest softly on a still object in front of you.

▶ Repeat the phrase, 'I'm never . . . (insert your own word) ... enough' (or whatever expression resonates as your self-critical voice more); be gentle in your tone to yourself.

► Scan your body to see where you can locate any feelings and sensations (i.e. of anxiety, frustration, sadness, etc.) arising as you say this. Notice what is alive in your body right now.

► Allow these feelings to linger for a while.

► Allow yourself to feel this and breathe: no stories, no dramas, just stay with the physical sensations in your body. See this with your attention and allow yourself to comprehend the experience at hand.

► Let go of the phrasing now, leave any compulsion to embellish a story, resist sensations, distract away from your experience alone as much as possible. If this feels impossible, just see if you can observe the habitual hanging on and simply notice this.

► Use the breath and the bodily sensations as your point of reference to the here and now.

► Can you allow yourself to experience just this?

► Now, hold your hand up, palm facing towards the discomfort in your body (is it at your chest, stomach, some other place?).

► As your hand gently rests against your body where this discomfort resides, hold this pain gently (as you might support the head of a baby) and breathe consciously.

► Repeat the words (silently if you wish), 'I care about this pain/suffering/imperfection/vulnerability. This is part of my experience, this makes me human'.

► Can you allow yourself to have this?

► Continue to breathe mindfully while you support this vulnerable part of you: no need to avoid, escape or eliminate it – just allow it to be.

► Continue to breathe mindfully and repeat the words to yourself, 'I am sorry that you are experiencing this pain, I am here for you'.

► Take a few more mindful breaths.

► When you are ready, begin to open your eyes again and continue your day with a rejuvenated sense of confidence in being who you are, the full you, supported by YOU.

Through this exercise we learn to simply allow ourselves to feel (through emotions and physical sensations) the experience that we usually attempt to divert from when we are questioning our belief in ourselves and engaged in self-criticism. If we cease to engage with reactiveness (criticising yourself and everyone else) around the vulnerabilities we experience, in the hope of eliminating them once and for all, we can instead start to gently examine and allow ourselves to know our 'soft spots'. We don't need to talk about them or share them, although this can really help sometimes, but instead we allow them to be seen by our own careful, gentle gaze of mindful/compassionate attention. If it is hard to find a 'gentle gaze', kindness towards your struggles, a sense of allowing or 'anything much' in relation to this exercise, don't worry. Merely paying this quality of attention (mindfulness) to ourselves is enough. The rest (including our natural sense of confidence) will unfold anyway, if we just give it the space. Essentially, in an exercise of self-compassion such as this, we can recognise but not challenge, embellish or celebrate our inner bully as we might usually do, and in doing so our self-criticism tends to quieten down; we begin to doubt ourselves less, allowing us to create a more stable source of self-confidence and self-worth in our work.

Here are our top summary tips for you to take away from this chapter:

Mindfulness top tips to go

▶ Watch your self-belief and the stories you tell about yourself. Notice the behaviours that transmit your underconfidence at work. Use mindfulness to keep centred and grounded and aware of when you can let some of your unhelpful habits go.

▶ Practise mindfulness of worry, performance-hindering and perfectionist critical thoughts, both self-criticism and criticism towards others.

▶ Identify what's most important to you at work and what you would do if you knew you would not fail – who and what do you want to be about?

▶ Take opportunities to practise success and confidence, and do things that matter even if it scares the pants off you – do presentations, public speaking, etc., and remember to practise mindfulness as you do so.

▶ Act confidently even when you lack confidence; keep showing up to challenges in your work.

▶ Watch your critical mind and develop a more mindful, accepting and compassionate mind to boost confidence and motivation in yourself.

▶ Practise self-compassion exercises as an alternative to confidence-zapping attempts (self-criticism) at ridding yourself of your human imperfections.

As we end this chapter, we do encourage you to remember the amazing discovery of neuroplasticity (if you need a recap, go back a few pages to the previous chapter and take another look). In short, the more we choose to think, do and experience stuff a certain way, the more we can think, do and experience that stuff again. This is just as relevant to building up confidence at work (by using the exercises in this chapter) as anything else. Confidence can be learned, enhanced and rejuvenated (even after a mighty crash!) – don't forget that. We hope that this chapter has helped to provide valuable insight as well as practical tips about how you might continue to build your confidence at work with mindfulness. Next, we are keen to turn your attention to creativity and how mindfulness can help us to ensure that we remain as fresh, open and innovative as we can while on the job.

Useful resources

▶ Brown, B. (2010, June). *The power of vulnerability* [video file]. Retrieved from: http:///www.ted.com/talks/brene_brown_on_vulnerability

▶ Neff, K. [Tedx Talks]. (2013, February 6). *The space between self-esteem and self compassion: Kristin Neff at TEDxCentennialPark-Women* [video file]. Retrieved from: https://www.youtube.com/watch?v=IvtZBUSplr4

▶ Neff, K. (2015). *Test how self-compassionate you are* [www.self-compassion.org]. Retrieved from: http://self-compassion.org/test-how-self-compassionate-you-are/

▶ Strubickmubie. (2008, May 14). *How to make a paper/origami fortune teller* [video file]. Retrieved from: https://www.youtube.com/watch?v=BYarlKnetRs

Get creative

> *'Companies have to nurture [creativity and motivation] – and have to do it by building a compassionate yet performance-driven corporate culture. In the knowledge economy the traditional soft people side of our business has become the new hard side.'*

Gay Mitchell, Executive VP, HR, Royal Bank Financial Group

Organisations with high levels of creativity demonstrate a clear edge in both developing new services and products, and outwitting rivals by doing the job faster, better and/or cheaper. Research confirms increased market growth, profit and capitalisation from creative business. And even if these are not your own or your company's goals, creativity in the workplace has consistently been found to enhance job satisfaction, reduce stress, inattention and burnout. The link between mindfulness and workplace creativity is fast becoming widely recognised. More and more organisations are realising that a present-moment-focused mind is more likely to have better ideas and novel solutions to the pivotal as well as the common challenges that we all face while on the job day to day.

The Walt Disney Company was an early advocate of mindfulness-enhanced creativity at work. Just over 30 years ago, the company felt lacking in any creative direction. To help them along, the 'Imagineers' (the company's team of design creatives in charge of design, development and innovation) called in a mindfulness trainer, and after a series of mindfulness-based creativity workshops they went on to develop Tokyo Disney, Disneyland Hong Kong and Disneyland Paris. It might be of interest to know that Disney's Imagineers are still considered some of the best in the business and continue to lead the way, pioneering developments in innovative 3D virtual-reality displays and animatronics today. General Mills and Intel have also both spoken openly about the link between mindfulness practice and workplace innovation.

So, could you, your team or your company do with more creativity on the job? Well, in this chapter we are going to take a look at the role of mindfulness in helping us to get more creative and innovative at work.

In this chapter we are going to look at:

▶ What creativity actually is.
▶ How creativity is relevant to the workplace.
▶ What is involved in the creative process.
▶ What stops us from being creative at work.
▶ How we can boost and tap into more creativity with mindfulness.

As you know by now, we are really keen for you to experience what we're talking about in this book rather than for you to just read about it on these pages. So, get ready to get your creative juices flowing. Here goes...

What is creativity at work?

For some of us the word creative may conjure up unsettling images of a floppy-hatted, kooky artist staring deeply into a blank canvas with a paint brush pressed tightly against his lips or a mad scientist feverishly mixing colourful potions in a littered and smoky basement lab somewhere. Yes, we might fear that any sudden dramatic flurry of imaginative and abstract ideas could leave us looking a bit like *Back to the Future*'s Doc Brown driving off in his DeLorean Time Machine (not the greatest look if you want to impress the boss, your colleagues or clients!).

This association (between the wacky and the creative) has often led to confusion around the appropriateness and relevance of creativity within a business context. If this sounds like you, then please take note: creativity is crucial for business, as among its many benefits it helps to promote improved problem-solving and also stimulates innovation. Please also remember that it's just as relevant for folks working in the accounts department as it is for others engaged in more obviously creative endeavours at work, like design, developing or marketing. Yes, we can all do with a bit of creativity while on the job.

We encourage you to recognise that whatever your own daily work involves, even if you don't consider yourself to have a particularly creative part to play (say, like the folks at Disney we mentioned earlier), a certain amount of free-flowing creativity can help us all out of tricky situations, assist in getting the job done and help us to progress further in our career/business. Creativity helps us to find solutions to everyday work-related problems; these could be anything from how we might get into work when our usual route is blocked (by yet another public transport strike), where to go for lunch when we're bored with the same old café down the road, how we might continue to work when our computer crashes, to redesigning products and services, or opening up to new possibilities when we feel like it's time for a change of job/career.

We can all relate to those moments at work when we just can't see the wood for the trees – maybe when we've been handed that important brief and instructed to design that new project or maybe when sat in that team business development meeting and the boss is expecting some insightful contributions (after all that is what she pays you for!). At these times you may find yourself praying to the gods for some (even the tiniest piece of) inspiration so that you can get stuck into some exciting and meaningful work again and impress the bigwigs too. In these absences of any creativity, we can become knotted in a cognitive loop of uninspiring thoughts. We become increasingly frustrated with ourselves, and also with the divine Muse herself (who has clearly taken it upon herself to go for an early lunch!). At these moments work can feel like really hard labour, a real drag and often an excruciatingly painful experience. So how do we escape from the binds of normality and get our creative juices flowing once again? Well, we'll be taking a look at just that in no time at all, but before we do, let's just consider the ins and outs of creativity a little more.

Essentially, creativity can be described as: *the ability to perceive the world in new ways; to generate new ideas that may be useful in solving problems.* But in business terms, coming up with lots of original ideas is not where the creative process ends. In business an idea must be appropriate, effective, actionable and profitable – not just original. It must have a positive impact on how business gets done, for example by either improving a product or advancing the process of getting that product made. The actual creative process does involve more than this (which we'll come to in a just a moment) but for now, why don't you put your own creativity to the test and have a go at the exercises on the next page. This way you'll also get a better understanding of what's involved in being creative.

Exercise 4.1: Work in progress

Shifting perspective

How many different ideas for the use of this object can you come up with right now? Take your time and try to think of as many as you can, giving yourself a few minutes to really allow the mind to go to town on this one, before you read on.

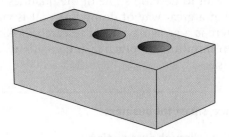

So, how did you do? Feeling stuck? Has your Muse gone AWOL, leaving you with nothing more than 'build a house', maybe? Or maybe you were able to come up with lots of ideas. Either way, have a go at the next task.

Connecting the dots

Can you think of a common association between these three words?

There's no right and wrong with this, just see what comes to mind. Go on, it's an easy one.

glass building person

What do you think?

'Tall', maybe?

If you did well on these tests, then it is likely that you are a creative person and possess some particular qualities. Creative people tend to be:

▶ curious and inquisitive;

▶ good listeners;

▶ observant;

▶ explorative.

'I have no special talents, I am only passionately curious.'

Albert Einstein

'Curiosity about life in all of its aspects, I think, is still the secret of great creative people.'

Leo Burnett

Does this sound like you? Whether it does or it doesn't, the good news is that creativity is something that we can all continue to cultivate and release from within ourselves. If you want to enhance your creativity, then you might want to develop some of the qualities listed above, and it would seem that a great way of doing just that is via the practice of mindfulness. There is a growing arm of research looking into the relationship between mindfulness practice and creativity, and here's what some of it has to say.

Proven in science, smart for business

Boosting creativity through observation

In one study[1] carried out at the University of Amsterdam in the Netherlands, researchers aimed to discover which specific mindfulness skills predicated creative performance. The study found that people with robust observation skills, whether inherent or learned through extensive mindfulness training, showed superior creativity levels compared to other participants. The researchers conclude that *'the ability to observe and attend to various stimuli consistently and positively predicted creativity'*. This is an interesting finding that helps to develop our understanding of the link between mindfulness and creativity. As you know all too well by now, mindfulness practice is all about observing your present-moment experience, in a particular way, without judgement or evaluation and so it would seem that turning the mind to this simple practice, again and again is a sure-fire way to also boost your creative skills. Excellent!

Generating new ideas

In another study[2], researchers at Leiden University in the Netherlands were keen to explore the effect that two different types of meditation might have on creativity, and specifically two separate types of creative thinking, namely, divergent thinking (the ability to generate lots of ideas – like the 'brick' exercise you did earlier) and ➤

---

convergent thinking (the ability to connect those ideas into one amazing concept or, in other words, conjure up a solution to a particular problem – like the other exercise involving a 'common association' between three words). Following participation in each of the different types of meditation sessions, the 16 participants were asked to complete a series of creative tasks (just like the two you did above) to measure the effects of mindfulness practice on both divergent and convergent thinking. This study found that mindfulness meditation significantly improved both divergent and convergent thinking. Interestingly, the type of meditation performed had an impact on which type of creative thinking was improved. For example, open-monitoring meditation (i.e. open the mind to any occurring thought or sensation, with a non-judgemental attitude) improved divergent thinking more than focused-attention meditation (i.e. focus attention to particular parts of the body). Now don't panic, as both these types of meditation are implicated in common forms of mindfulness training, so you're good to go with mindfulness.

Being creative is not about all feeling positive

If you believe that you need to be in a good mood to broaden your mind and get your creative juices flowing, then you may be missing out on other opportunities to get creative. Apparently our creativity is affected more by the motivational intensity of our emotions rather than simply by negative or positive moods. In one study[3], participants were shown funny video clips of cats (triggering emotions of low motivational intensity, i.e. pleasant, amusing) and clips of delicious-looking desserts (triggering emotions of high motivational intensity, i.e. desire). Even though both evoked positive emotions, the cat videos, which were simply amusing, broadened the mind (measured by participants making more holistic matches to a target stimulus), whereas the dessert clips that evoked emotions with higher motivational intensity *narrowed* participants' scope of attention (they made more detail-oriented matches to a target stimulus). Interestingly, this was the same when participants watched video clips that triggered negative emotions. For example, sadness (an emotion of low motivational intensity) broadened attentional focus, whereas disgust (an emotion of high motivational intensity) *narrowed* focus. These findings suggest that if you want to keep an open mind and see the bigger picture at work, it's probably best if you're just in a pleasant or even sad mood. If, however, you really need to focus on making a new idea practical, emotions (negative or positive) with high motivational intensity could help. So it would seem that staying mindful of the motivational intensity of your emotions (rather than whether you are simply in a good or bad mood) is key to understanding the quality that you are likely to bring to your creative endeavours. ➤

Being mindful of mixed emotions leads to more creativity

If you ever feel like there are a whole range of emotions running through you, then that might actually be the best time for you to get creative. A study[4] carried out at the University of Washington found that participants who experienced 'emotional ambivalence' (an unusual mixture of emotions like excitement and frustration at the same time) were better at recognising unusual relationships between concepts which, as the researcher of this study concludes, is '*an ability believed to be important to organisational creativity*'. Our work environment can often bring up a mixture of emotions for us, say, when we first start out on a new job, or feel a mixture of excitement and anxiety when presenting our work to others, and these findings suggest that it might be at these times that we are at our most creative. The researcher adds that perhaps managers '*would benefit from scheduling creative-thinking tasks for these time periods or could assign creativity tasks to new organizational members* (who are likely undergoing socialization processes)'. So remember to remain mindful of your emotional state, as it may be that when you experience a mixture of unusual emotions you are in fact at your most creative.

This is all certainly excellent to know. It would seem that mindfulness can really stimulate our creative side and also help us to get creative by increasing our chances of noticing when we are in the optimal mood state for creative endeavours. This is all great news for our performance at work, as well as our stress levels, sense of satisfaction, inattention and burnout while on the job. But before we rush on to practise more mindfulness and get our creative funk on, let's first take a closer look at the creative process in a bit more detail.

The creative process

In order to be creative at work, to think in new ways or in an unusual combination of ways, finding new patterns, connections or solutions, we need to fire our imaginations. But as we said, that alone is not sufficient. Imaginative ideas, then, need to be able to be produced in some way either in a service, artefact or result. To be creative, you need to not only have ideas, but you need to also then act on them. Furthermore, how you act on them, to whom and when are also absolutely critical if you want your ideas to have wings. Therefore we have outlined several steps necessary in the creative process within the exercise which follows. Have a go at working through this creative process for yourself right now by reflecting on your answers to each step in the exercise (we have provided some example answers to help you along).

Exercise 4.2: Work in progress

Seven steps to the creative process

1 **Outline your purpose:** What is my goal or purpose? (To make a spaceship for Mum)

2 **What is my motivation?** (To free up my creativity and see Mum smile)

3 **Imagine the possibilities:** What are my ideas? (To use washing-up bottle and tin foil, scrap metal, visit Mars, steal ride-on toy from outside Asda, etc.)

4 **Filter your ideas to what is practicable:** What is workable? (I only have 50p, better use the washing-up bottle)

5 **Develop your clarity: How do I communicate these?** (I draw diagrams and make a model)

6 **Enhance your confidence: Am I ready for this?** (I read Chapter 3 and I am breathing mindfully)

7 **Target your audience:** Who do I communicate these to and when? (My Mum after she's had a sherry)

Take note: If you skip a step in this creative process, you may end up in trouble. Here's a classic cautionary tale from the world of psychology:

'In 1619, Italian philosopher Lucilio Vanini was burned alive for suggesting that humans evolved from apes. Over two centuries later, popular society still reserved its sharpest contempt for evolutionists, as illustrated in this caricature of Charles Darwin, published in The Hornet in 1871. Yet a literal interpretation of Genesis started to unravel long before Darwin published On the Origin of Species and The Descent of Man. Europeans were deeply disturbed by the anatomical similarities they saw between themselves and apes, and they struggled to find logical explanations.'

(Retrieved from: www.strangescience.net/stfor2.htm)

125

Also, we do advise you to take a good look at your confidence (see Chapter 3), because if you put yourself out there and dare to be creative there will be many times that not only your ideas get rejected or scorned, but also you might make mistakes along the way – but don't worry, you'll be in very good company.

> 'In William Golding's (1911–1993) novel Lord of the Flies (1954) one character, Piggy, is teased by the other boys because he is fat and wears glasses to correct nearsightedness. Later (Ch. 2) they use Piggy's glasses as a burning glass to start a signal fire. What is wrong here? Nearsightedness is corrected with negative (diverging) lenses. A positive (converging) lens is necessary to focus sunlight. Therefore a burning-glass must be positive. Piggy's negative eyeglass lenses would not work.'

> **(Retrieved from: www.lhup.edu/~dsimanek/whoops.htm)**

All those English literature students across the world will agree: we're glad he wrote the book anyway and we forgive him, don't we?!

You may like to revisit the questions listed in the exercise above whenever you need to engage with the creative process, to help you map out your steps in a useful way. But, let us now look specifically at the sticky parts of this process and how mindfulness can help us with those.

Creativity and vulnerability go hand in hand

First off, we'd like to remind you of what we just said, as, if you are going to be creative, you really must be prepared to fail. It is often our unwillingness to experience vulnerability that dries up any trickle of creative juice that may be there, just bubbling below the surface. The fear of our ideas going down like a lead balloon can lead to a billion and one excuses for why we are 'just not the creative type', or why we won't pitch any creative ideas even if we have them (there's that perfectionism again). Brené Brown speaks of 'vulnerability as the birthplace of innovation' … 'without vulnerability how can we innovate?' (check out a short video with Brené Brown on this topic listed in the 'Useful resources' section at the end of this chapter). If failure is not an option for you, then it is highly unlikely that you will ever find yourself being creative at work. The truth is that being creative, putting yourself and your new ideas out there is a scary place to be, and you WILL feel vulnerable. So if you value creativity, it seems that you will need to be courageous also, as vulnerability and innovation are inseparable and most certainly poured from the same vessel. As we have said, if you lack the confidence to face feelings of failure and rejection, please revisit Chapter 3, as your willingness and confidence to experience discomfort and vulnerability will be crucial to help get your creative juices flowing once again.

What else is possible?

'Creativity is a gift. It doesn't come through if the air is cluttered.'

Often attributed to John Lennon

Mindfulness, with its simple instruction of seeing into the nature of reality as it stands, right in this moment, is already a great challenge to habitual, fixed and narrow ways of thinking. Rigid thinking is a contraction of viewpoint which really hinders creative thinking. The problem here is that our minds tend to run on autopilot, repeating and reinforcing the same patterns of thinking, experiencing and associating time and time again. This can make it extremely difficult to break free from habitual ways of seeing the world and generate new and novel viewpoints to a range of work-related dilemmas that can arise day to day.

Have a go at trying to solve the puzzles in the following exercise. Notice how hard it can be to think outside the box and to release your creative mind (try not to jump to reading the answers until you have given each question some good consideration). Notice how the mind tries to make sense of our world in its usual habitual way, holding on to the logical, obvious, tried and tested ways of seeing the world and how challenging it can be to free up our thinking from these rehearsed viewpoints.

Exercise 4.3: Work in progress

Thinking outside the box

Q: A man rides into town on Friday, stays one night and leaves on Friday that same day.

How is that possible?

(A: Friday is a horse.)

Q: An ordinary American citizen with no passport visits over 30 foreign countries in one day. He is welcome in each country and leaves each one of his own accord.

How so?

(A: He is a mail courier who delivers packages to the different foreign embassies in the USA. The land of the embassy belongs to the country of the embassy, not the USA.)

Q: A father and son have a car accident and are both badly hurt. They are both taken to separate hospitals. When the boy is taken in for an operation, the surgeon (doctor) says 'I cannot do the surgery because this is my son'.

How is this possible?

(A: The surgeon (doctor) is a woman. She is the boy's mother.)

Q: A man is alone on an island with no food and no water, yet he does not fear for his life.

How come?

(A: He is a policeman on a traffic island.)

Q: A man marries 20 women in his town but isn't charged with polygamy.

How can this happen?

(A: He's a priest; he is marrying them to other people, not to himself.)

Q: A riverboat filled with passengers suddenly capsized, drowning most of those on board. There were no other boats close by. The riverboat was in good condition, the weather and river were calm and there was no carelessness on the part of the crew members.

Explain.

(A: The boat was travelling along a river in India and a large snake fell on to the deck. The passengers all rushed to one side of the boat, so overturning it. This is apparently based on a real-life incident reported in the *World Almanac*).

> *'I think 99 times and find nothing. I stop thinking, swim in silence, and the truth comes to me.'*

Albert Einstein

Problems only remain a problem if we continue to feed them with our repetitive, habitual thinking. When you step back from a busy mind, creativity is there and able to naturally flow again. Mindfulness practice helps us to disengage from repetitive and relentless thinking patterns and instead be more curious, to notice new things and give up preconceived and rehearsed mindsets, thus unleashing our natural creativity. This is supported by scientific evidence. Take a look at these two studies:

Proven in science, smart for business

Mindfulness helps us to recognise and solve problems in a novel way

Researchers at the University of Groningen and North Dakota State University were interested to explore their hypothesis that mindfulness practice could help to improve awareness and the filtering out of other unhelpful mental processes during creative tasks. In this large two-part study[5] (157 participants in total) the researchers found that mindfulness training predicted and improved '*insight problem solving*', which is the ability to recognise and solve problems in a new way. Mindfulness training improved participants' ability to solve problems that required creative and non-habitual responses. This study was the first of its kind to document a direct relationship between mindfulness and creativity and is rather ground-breaking. It is often thought that our history and past experience limits our creative flow, and the authors of this study conclude that mindfulness practice may in fact be one way that we are able to '*overcome the inertia of our past*' when it comes to the creation of novel ideas and solutions. Impressive stuff!

With mindfulness we can overcome cognitive rigidity

In another study[6] researchers at Ben-Gurion University, Israel, were eager to discover what impact mindfulness training would have on cognitive rigidity and whether it could in fact improve cognitive flexibility. A total of 76 participants were randomly assigned to two groups, either an eight-week mindfulness training group or a wait-list group (control). All the participants were given a set of logic problems to solve. The first set of these problems required complicated solutions, involving several steps, while the second set of problems could be solved with the same complicated solution or with a much simpler solution, using just two steps. The next and last batch of problems could only be solved with the same ➤

simple, two-step solution. The researchers found that the participants from the mindfulness training group were able to notice and use the simple solution more often and more quickly than the participants from the control group. The control group continued to use the more complex method, seemingly out of habit and appeared to be blinded by their past experience. The researchers conclude that mindfulness practice *'reduces cognitive rigidity via the tendency to overlook simple novel solutions to a situation due to rigid and repetitive thought patterns formed through experience'*. This study demonstrates that mindfulness can enhance problem-solving skills and help us to notice novel ways of overcoming problems so that we are not limited by our past experiences.

So, along with keeping stuck in old habitual patterns of thought and ways of seeing the world, what else can get in the way of our creativity? Well let's take a look.

Creating balance

As we have already covered, anxiety, rife in the workplace, tends to severely hinder open-mindedness and the mind instead fixates and obsesses as a way of compelling but ineffectual problem-solving. There can of course be many anxiety-triggering factors within the work environment which can all be detrimental to work performance and creativity, and included among these is the way in which we can relate to one another. We will come back to team dynamics a little later (in the next chapter) but for now we thought it would be of interest to hear a little more about how creativity specifically can suffer when there is an imbalance towards a less civil and, dare we say, more hostile working culture.

Falling victim to acts of incivility at work has been shown to negatively affect creativity. In a series of studies[7,8] participants who were treated rudely by others were 30 per cent less creative than others who were not. When the victims of rudeness did come up with responses to what they might do with a brick, their ideas were less original and imaginative and more logical than others who were not treated rudely, for example they said 'build a house', 'build a wall', 'build a school' while others who were not subjected to rudeness from others responded with ideas such as 'sell it on eBay', 'use it for a goalpost for a street soccer game', or 'decorate it like a pet and give it to a kid for a present' (brilliant!). So it would seem that if we want to ensure the optimal conditions for creative flow, we'd do well to keep an eye on how we are speaking to one another at work. Balancing out any stress-induced rudeness with more civil, courteous and kind actions seems the way to go.

Creativity and innovation are also likely to flourish in a work environment where a sense of fairness and respect for individuality flows throughout the company culture. In an article published in the *Harvard Business Review* (which you can find a link to in the 'Useful resources' section at the end of this chapter), Teresa Amabile describes *'how to kill creativity'* as a manager at work and suggests that the stress that arises from a lack of autonomy can be a real creativity flattener for employees. She advises:

> *'People will be more creative, in other words, if you give them freedom to decide how to climb a particular mountain. You needn't let them choose which mountain to climb. In fact, clearly specified strategic goals often enhance people's creativity.'*

> **(Teresa Amabile, 1998; for full article see 'Useful resources' section)**

So it would seem that a certain amount of autonomy, but balanced with leadership, can take a team quite far along the creative road.

In short, high-stress environments can restrict creativity. This can occur to such an extent that some companies have attempted to redress this in other (novel and creative) ways: by instilling playful and quirky features in their offices, for instance:

> *'Employees of product development company Davison work in a life-sized toy racetrack, tree house and big boot in the eccentric office space named Inventionland. Other quirky features of the 75,000 square foot work space include a waterfall, pool, rocky cove and castle complete with turrets and a drawbridge.'*

> **[from www.weneedofficespace.com, see 'Useful resources' for full details]**

"*High-stress environments can restrict creativity.*"

Playfulness can promote plasticity of the brain, helping to strengthen a particular brain state which gives rise to creativity. When we are playful our brains release dopamine which is rewarding and reinforces our playful and exploratory nature, further increasing our chances of seeing things in a new light. Although we often try to separate work from play, from a neurological perspective bringing some fun and games or novel approaches to tasks into the work arena would actually seem to make good sense for business. When it comes to the generation of creative thoughts and innovation, having a good time with colleagues, joking around together and even allowing time for a bit of 'idle' daydreaming may not be such a waste of time after all. A bit of playfulness or simply attempting routine tasks in a fresh and unusual way can stimulate our explorative and creative minds while on the job. By injecting a bit of fun into our work we bring the part of our brain alive that is conducive to creativity: we are more likely to see things from a different perspective; we are more likely to innovate.

Now, letting our hair down or stepping outside of our usual frame of reference may work for some of us, but for others this can just increase the sense of pressure, inadequacy and discomfort. So there is no need to unleash the artistic temperament within by bouncing around the office on a space-hopper, while drinking wheat grass juice, and proselytising about Nietzsche, especially if no one else gets it (just taking some time to relax, cracking a joke or two with some colleagues or inventing new ways to approach a routine task may at times be just enough to get the creative juices flowing once again). Remember also that being overly 'loose' or 'out there' and presenting ideas in an unstructured and uncontained way may not be the most effective way to get the job done, even if it might seem quite freeing (or just plain mad). The process of creating of a working system, theory or design is extraordinarily valuable in allowing those systems, theories and designs to be constructed, reproduced and ultimately improved upon (if possible). In essence, clear communication and formulation as an aspect of the creative process becomes a way of allowing social groups, ideas or products time to assimilate, to be found of value or not and to be accepted or ultimately rejected. However, if we just allow things to remain completely stable, then we are also at risk of stagnation and inertia. Again it's all about balance.

Your creative endeavour needs tempering with the purpose of that endeavour and is therefore, in business, inextricably linked to the unique goals of that particular company and what it is they are producing (services, ideas, products, etc.). Clear goals and intent, which are easily transmitted to others, make the creative object replicable, which is absolutely necessary for spreading ideas, concepts and products. As such, creativity, with movement, becomes innovation:

'Innovation is creativity that ships.'

Often attributed to Steve Jobs

Motivation for the inspiration of your innovation without complication

Remember that the particular focus of a creative process may not be your great passion, but it is nevertheless important to know what is motivating you to engage with this process. Lack of motivation will find you procrastinating and drained of inspiration. If you can find a wee spark of joy, interest or energy, you can then harness that with mindfulness and this can carry you through the inevitable dull or challenging parts ahead. For example, updating the company policies and procedures may not set your world on fire, but you might find an improved level of clarity and standardisation around equality and fairness in the workplace very motivating. To identify a form of motivation, even if it is the pay-cheque waiting at the end of the month, will really help you through.

Exercise 4.4: Mindful on the job

Sparking the inner fire

The following exercise is a further development on the 'Deciding how we choose' exercise from Chapter 1. With some idea of mindfulness under your belt, you can begin enhancing your skills of referring to the present-focused sensations which arise in the body and using these to deepen your inquiry and self-awareness.

For this practice you need only identify a task ahead which requires motivation. Frankly this is anything, otherwise we would simply atrophy. Examples might include: updating company policies and procedures, reviewing the minutes from your last meeting, phoning a client, designing a new web page, going to the water cooler for a drink, getting the train home, etc. Let yourself know that whatever arises is exactly what you are seeking right now; everything is welcome; you do not need to be, think, feel or sense anything else than this, just as it is.

1 Feel your feet on the floor and the contact you have with any supporting surface (floor, chair, wall, etc.).

2 Scan your body for areas of tension or unpleasant sensation; do this quite quickly, just sensing in a broad brushstroke from your toes up to your head.

3 Scan your body now for any areas of softness or pleasure, again, in a generalised way, not getting too hung up on any particular area.

4 Scan your body a third time now for any areas that feel neutral, numb or lacking in any particular sensation; again doing this from your toes to your head quite swiftly.

5 Now bring the specific task to mind. Allow yourself free rein to observe any thoughts or images or emotions that should arise. Allow these experiences to linger for a moment or so.

6 Ask yourself 'As I sit here observing my body, what motivates me to do this task?'

7 See if your body, mind or emotions reply! You don't need a right answer, just look for what arises: any thoughts, emotions or bodily sensations. The clue has just arisen.

8 Repeat steps 1–7 as many times as you like.

This is obviously not a guaranteed formula for getting an answer, but if you find nothing much there, then clearly you can see that your motivation is low and you are very unlikely to find inspiration without it. If you feel stuck or frustrated with the exercise, then that is also a clue as to your feelings about the task. Don't panic! You can always do the exercise again; with practice, your attunement will become more subtle and you can then identify more easily what comes and use that to discover motivation. On the other hand, if you continue to find nothing or only obstructive thoughts, sensations or emotions, and this is a task that for some reason you really must complete, then you really might need to acknowledge that and gain support with this task from colleagues, delegate it to someone else (see Chapter 5 for more on delegation), change the task, or even invent a motivation (e.g. give yourself a treat when you complete it).

Along with these tips for keeping motivation alive, we'd also advise that you make efforts to recognise even small gains and wins along the way as you continue to work on your project or task. Keeping a record of your progress and what you have achieved day to day, even if these seem the smallest of accomplishments, can help keep your positive emotions alive (about yourself and what you are doing) which will help you remain motivated and creative. So if you notice you have done something that has moved you along (even if it's not what you had planned to do), something that matters to you or the people you care about and/ or work with, then keep track of it. When you feel stuck and demotivated with the task at hand, revisit this log which may help keep your motivation alive for the sake of further inspiration and creation. Remember that creative ideas are more likely to arise when you are motivated to work on something. You are unlikely to feel motivated if you don't find your work interesting, involving, exciting, satisfying or challenging in some way. So try your best to look for that source of motivation and keep it alive in your mind.

Michael

Task: writing this book

1 Contact with floor and stool

2 Discomfort: tension in head, aching hips and buttocks

3 Pleasure: softness in the chest, comfort in the soles of the feet

4 Neutral: Lack of sensation in middle back area

5 Scanning bodily sensations and feeling tension in the stomach, emotions of dread

6 Feeling a lift and a desire to honour my colleague and our commitment to this work

7 Noticing a greater clarity about my motivation and still feeling dread.

Even if you find that you have more motivation than a scooter ride down Mount Everest, it still won't completely address underlying difficulties in generating creative thinking. We might plan endlessly, clarifying goals, finding meaning and purpose for our endeavours and be raring to go, but with no good ideas we may still be left a bit clueless, lacklustre and confused. So what next?

Unleashing the creative (without the space-hopper)

Sitting about moping, berating yourself for your lack of genius and comparing yourself unfavourably with the talents of others is doing nothing for you (remind yourself of the detrimental effects of self-criticism in Chapter 3 if you need refreshing). If this is all sounding a bit familiar, then our following four tips might also help to reignite your creative flare and keep it burning brightly:

1 **Refresh your skills.**

   You might find that keeping abreast of developments in your area of expertise or even reading up on some new skills that lie outside your strengths may help to spark new associations and generate some novel ideas for the task/s at hand.

2 **Seek out differing perspectives.**

   Speak to other people working in different areas to get their perspectives. Don't just seek information from your own field. There's really no need to hold back with this one; you may find that looking outside of your own industry for inspiration, or maybe talking to someone with very little (if any at all) experience or knowledge of your work may be the very thing that helps you to shift perspective and free yourself from a mental block.

3 **Immerse yourself in unfamiliar experiences.**

   Sticking to what you know, and what is tried and tested is unlikely to inspire you. Take up new hobbies, do things you are not familiar with, and even try out new foods – maybe something that you didn't like when you were younger. You may find that having new experiences will help to generate new perspectives and connections between ideas.

4 **Take your time and don't rush creative decisions.**

   New ideas may pop up at unlikely times when you least expect them to. You may find that it's when you are thinking of something completely unrelated that your mind suddenly gives you that fresh new perspective on the task that you've been struggling with for so long. So don't pressure your mind into solving problems right away. Instead give your mind some time to find its way while it collects new information and joins the dots. Have faith in your mind's creative ability while you watch it do its job. So, try your best to hold off making a final creative decision until you really have to make it.

If you find that you are still stuck, even after trying to free your mind in these ways, we'd say that it's definitely now time to give your brain cells a break before they blow, and try going for a walk.

'All truly great thoughts are conceived while walking.'

Friedrich Nietzsche

It's OK, that's where the Nietzsche quotes end. Nevertheless, walking has a fabulous evidence-base as a great method for freeing up creative thinking. On a physiological level, walking increases the rate of oxygen to the brain, like any physical exercise, which in turn helps to improve memory and attention and decreases the rate of decline in neurotransmitters. Unlike more strenuous forms of exercise, however, the relatively slow cadence of walking means that the central nervous system is enlivened but not overstimulated. Our inner speech has been found to align to the pace of our thoughts – so if you are feeling mentally racy, angry or fired up, then try gradually slowing your pace. Mentally sluggish, low in mood or uninspired? Then walk a little faster. Add to these findings the power of mindfulness, and mindful walking can become an easily accessible tool in the cultivation of deeper insights, intuitive thinking and creativity.

'People usually consider walking on water or in thin air a miracle. But I think the real miracle is not to walk either on water or in thin air, but to walk on earth.'

Thich Nhat Hahn

Exercise 4.5: Mindful on the job

A refreshing stroll

Take a walk; it might be in the park (see below) for a double stress-buster, along the corridor to the water cooler or the photocopier, to the canteen/your favourite café for lunch, or through the streets on the way to work or home. In this way, the practice might be a one-minute stroll each way to getting a glass of water, or a twenty-minute lunchtime amble: any length of time is fine. Start with Part 1 of the exercise below to bring the mind into the task and focus yourself on the present. Then try Part 2 to allow the mind to expand and develop breadth; this will help free up your creative thinking. Alternating naturally between Parts 1 and 2 will allow you to play with the balance of being focused and clear and then opening awareness out to include broader sensory experiences.

Part 1: Walk in

1 To help you focus, if your mind is wandering somewhere other than where your feet are, you might like to silently count your steps from one to ten.

2 One … I am lifting and placing my right foot.

3 Two … I notice my left foot lifting and moving.

4 Three … I feel the ground beneath my right foot.

5 Four … I feel the ground beneath my left foot.

6 Five … I am breathing in as I step forward.

7 Six … I am breathing out as I step forward.

8 Seven … Just this one step.

9 Eight … Just this one moment.

10 Nine … Just walking.

11 Ten … Just walking.

Part 2: Walk out

1 Noticing your feet contacting the ground in the rhythm of your walk.

2 Feeling the sensations of clothing and/or air against your skin as you propel forward.

3 As you walk, being aware now of the temperature of your body generally.

4 Noticing the movement of the feet, then the legs, the torso, the arms and the head as you move.

5 Becoming aware of sounds passing and arriving as you walk; just let your mind open to these.

6 Taking in the sights, the colours, movements and textures of the visual world around you.

7 And now, noticing the smells, scents or taste sensations. Allow these to come into your awareness and to pass on.

8 Free your attention and notice where it chooses to alight on the experiences of this present moment.

Walking spaces

Walking around outdoors really is a great way to tickle the fancies of your muse and it also has so many other benefits besides (recall the study on increased performance after 'gazing at greenery' in Chapter 2). So it might be a wise move to peel yourself away from your desk as often as you can (at least once a day – even for 5–10 minutes) as well as trying to incorporate more walking into your journey to and from work. Here are a few interesting facts about walking:

▶ Walking, like other physical activities, releases endorphins which improve mood and reduce stress and anxiety and improve your sleep.

▶ Walking, as a form of physical exercise, not only reduces the risk of depression but is also at least as effective as antidepressant drugs in treating mild and moderate depression – and has positive rather than negative side effects.

▶ Although only a preliminary study, Cook and Croft, two researchers at the University of Oklahoma, recently installed a temporary walking meditation labyrinth, using a theatrical spotlight, in the university library. They wanted to assess the effects of walking mindfulness on students' stress and mental and bodily fatigue within a limited space. Comments from respondents stated that they found it was *'Surprisingly peaceful. Very quick stress relief'*, and also that for some *'Concentrating on my walking was very freeing'* (you can read an interesting article about this work listed in the 'Useful resources' section at the end of this chapter).

▶ A small but growing collection of studies suggests that spending time in green spaces – gardens, parks, forests – can rejuvenate the mental resources that man-made environments deplete. Attention is a limited resource that continually drains throughout the day. A crowded intersection – rife with pedestrians, cars and billboards – bats our attention around. In contrast, walking past a pond in a park allows our mind to drift casually from one sensory experience to another, from the trickling of water to the rustling of reeds.

▶ These great thinkers were also renowned for their love of walking: Aristotle, Wordsworth, Dickens, Henry David Thoreau, Søren Kierkegaard and Beethoven.

If freeing your backside from being welded to the office chair has still done nothing to free your mind, then there are plenty more ways to lift yourself from the mental rut you may be in. Conversely, the first of these, after having a good walk, that is, is to work on your *acceptance*. Having writer's block, falling out of love with your muse, finding life dull and work uninspiring, may well all be perfectly natural parts of your experiences, utterly logical and just as things 'should' be, given the circumstances. Facing up to things being a bit drab (including yourself) might be the very ticket to beginning to unweave the knots around your creative thinking, and we do know by now (don't we?), that beating yourself up about wanting things to be different (including yourself) ain't gonna work. The key to this one is accepting that you're in the doldrums.

'You weren't thinking and you weren't paying attention either. People who don't pay attention often get stuck in the Doldrums.'

(Juster, 2008)

Leaving the fog alone

Sometimes, looking more clearly into the present moment might just allow us to face up to the bleak, cloudy, grim weather front we are sitting in (mentally or physically), wishing we were anywhere but here or anyone but this. In fact we work so hard to deny, resist and defend against reality that instead of accepting things being 'grey', we tend to get stuck and actually hinder our journey through this weather front.

Tom

Take the case of Tom, for example: a promising graduate, Tom had been asked to come up with some fresh new ideas for the marketing team he had recently joined. He had always excelled in creative thinking and, in fact, this was probably the one area of his CV he was most proud of and felt gave him the edge which secured his role. However, suddenly filled with nerves and feeling like he was being 'put on the line', Tom now found his creative thinking was paralysed by fear. In an attempt to ease the tension, Tom had started to drink heavily, and as a result was finding it even harder to cope. He felt increasingly out of his depth and initially insisted that he simply had to keep working and trying harder in order to get his nerve, and his mojo, back. After some discussion, Tom started to appreciate the reality of his situation; he recognised that he felt pressurised, on the spot and inexperienced compared to his colleagues. With the help of mindfulness he was able to begin to notice the tension in his body, to allow himself simply to feel this and not to react in habitual ways, but rather to simply breathe and notice. He was amazed to see that the feelings, and the bodily sensations did not last more than about five minutes before they began to change. He saw that he had uncertainty, but also excitement and a sense of spaciousness that could be open to seeing things differently, once he stopped habitually resisting the reality of the daunting task ahead. Tom was able to then ask a senior member of his team for some ➤

---

help, and as such he understood that the expectations were not for him to 'be perfect' but instead to share his ideas and integrate with the team. When Tom started to consider that his team were also excited about him and wanted him to build relationships with them, the sense of paralysis lifted and he soon found his creativity flowing again.

Stories like Tom's illustrate the natural ebb and flow of emotions and their accompanying reactive behaviours that often occur in our lives. If we step back from trying to stop ourselves feeling (especially 'negative emotions' but it could equally be true for 'positive' ones) and un-attach ourselves from the accompanying stories, we also liberate the mind from fixed points of view, leading to enhanced creative thinking. Without allowing ourselves to progress through a spectrum of emotions, like Tom, we can get stuck. Once we feel and allow space for what is difficult, painful or dull and let ourselves embrace that experience fully (by mindfully paying attention to bodily sensations, for instance), we can let the cr*p drop to the floor and become the fertile ground for something new to actualise and grow.

The creative cycle

According to a branch of psychological theory known as personal construct psychology (PCP), proposed by George Kelly (1905-1966), our definition of reality is based on our subjective, phenomenological perception ('construction') of the world around us ('events'), and this is what has meaning to us in our lives rather than any objective reality that may exist independently of ourselves.

Either we must *loosen* our constructs in order to accommodate a new event, i.e. increase their range of convenience, or *tighten* the construct to preserve predictability, i.e. decrease their range of convenience. This process is called the *'creativity cycle'*; it is a continual cycle of change and reformulation of events (see Fransella and Dalton, 2000).

Mindfulness invites a flow and a creative loosening of having to see things (events, ideas or objects) in a limited way. Through the exercises already presented in this book, all asking you to recognise this tendency of the mind to grasp hold of certain ways of operating in the world – to recognise this and to stop meddling in the endless construction of fixed views – we are already awakening to a new form of creativity. By not insisting that the world should, must or ought to be 'like this', we instead allow ourselves to experience the world (ourselves included) as it actually is, in this very moment. When we start to look deeply into that, we uncover the constant constructing and deconstructing that the mind does in order to try to make sense of the world. Let's consider this with this next exercise. You can do this at your desk, in an open-plan office, on your commute to or from work: anywhere will do.

Exercise 4.6: Mindful on the job 🎧

Here-ing sounds

1　Listen in to the noises around you right now.

2　Identify one sound and name and label it.

3　Notice what you have chosen to name it.

4　Is there another possible way to also label and name this sound?

5　Can you let go of this sound and of labelling it now and hear afresh?

6　You may notice the mind looking for definitions of the collection of oscillations, vibrations and variations in sound around you. Hear this experience too as a sound within the mind. You can choose to tune in or tune out like a radio.

7　Notice how you can tune in to a particular noise, or broaden out to include all or many of them. Practise this for a moment.

8　In relationship to this or these sounds right now, see if you can sense between the sound being external to the ear/mind and internal to the ear/mind.

9　What happens to the sound, the label of sound and the absence of sound when you no longer focus on them?

10　Listen to the sounds around you, knowing there are sounds, that somehow you know this, that there is a construction of meaning around sounds and then there is an end or change to the sounds and a corresponding deconstruction of meaning. This is the mind grasping for meaning. Notice how you can free yourself from fixating, how you can play with the mind's habitual urges.

The mind looking for meaning or making sense is not 'wrong'. But in doing an exercise like this, we can see that we are not bound by any particular way of hearing, seeing or sensing the world around us; at any moment there are multiple variations of possibility. This recognition can not only free our creativity, but also liberate us from confined or automatic thinking, and as such we can then be open to seeing the world and our work afresh; even the seemingly mundane can become magical. We can then begin to see mindfulness as a tool to enhance our awareness of the full spectrum of experience. At one end we develop focused concentration, stabilising the mind to see the present moment more clearly. Repeated practice of retuning the mind to a focal point (such as the breath) gradually trains our attention, taming the inherent 'busyness' of our minds to find rest, singularity and depth of attention. At the other end of the spectrum, mindfulness can allow us to cultivate a spacious quality, freely flowing as our attention opens to the unfolding of our daily experiences. With practice, we then become increasingly skilled at regulating our attention, assessing the appropriate skill we require in a given situation and recognising when the mind feels too tight or, conversely, too loose. We gradually develop what can be termed as a '*discriminating awareness*', very different from the tendencies to judge or criticise as right/wrong, good/bad, etc., and instead find a deeper wisdom within ourselves.

> '*By stilling your mind through concentration, opening your awareness to whatever is present, and letting wisdom emerge, you can learn to live a joyful and skilful life – one that keeps stress to a minimum and promotes internal and external peace.*'
>
> (Smalley and Winston, 2010, p. 166)

That's where this chapter ends, folks. We hope that in reading through the chapter and trying the exercises listed above, you have come to realise that your creativity is always there. Even if you don't tend to feel so creative at work, you can tap into more creativity whenever you want – it is something that resides in us all. Remember that creative ideas aren't reserved for a special group of people; they can in fact come to anyone of us if we increase our awareness with mindfulness and choose to change our mindset. In opening up our minds and really noticing the abundance of possibilities in this world, we soon discover that creative ideas are not necessarily something that we need to conjure up, but are in fact out there already, just waiting for any one of us to recognise and bring into reality and fruition. Yes, you can access your creativity and realise its full potential within each and every moment through mindfulness practice. Ellen Langer, a Professor of Psychology at Harvard University, writes:

'Creativity is not a blessing some special few are born with or receive from above. Our creative nature is an integral part of our daily lives, expressed through our culture, our language, and even our most mundane activities.'

(Langer, 2005, p. 4)

Just before you go on to read the list of the top take-away tips from this chapter, you might like to read the following poem, attributed to Chanie Gorkin, a 14-year-old secondary school pupil from Brooklyn, New York. We think that this poem is not only an excellent example of creative work but it also reminds us that when we dare to break free from habitual ways of responding to our world and instead take new perspectives, our experiences can be dramatically different. Hopefully this poem may inspire you (as it does us) to get creative. Also, if you like this kind of thing you may also like to take a look at another similar piece of creative writing, this time by two renowned ACT therapists, Jason Luoma, PhD, and Jenna LeJeune, PhD, from the Portland Psychotherapy Clinic in Oregon, USA (you can find a link to a video of their poem in the 'Useful resources' section at the end of this chapter – we think it's awesome!).

Worst Day Ever? *Chanie Gorkin*

Today was the absolute worst day ever
And don't try to convince me that
There's something good in every day
Because, when you take a closer look,
This world is a pretty evil place.
Even if
Some goodness does shine through once in a while
Satisfaction and happiness don't last.
And it's not true that
It's all in the mind and heart
Because
True happiness can be attained
Only if one's surroundings are good
It's not true that good exists
I'm sure you can agree that
The reality
Creates
My attitude
It's all beyond my control

And you'll never in a million years hear me say
Today was a very good day

**Now read it from bottom to top, the other way,
And see what I really feel about my day.**

Chanie Gorkin, www.poetrynation.com

As always, here are your summary top tips to go from this chapter:

Mindfulness top tips to go

▶ To enhance your creativity and successful innovation at work, follow the 'creative process' step by step. This includes generating original ideas, ensuring that these ideas are relevant and useful to your business and then communicating them and putting them into action.

▶ Be prepared to experience vulnerability and failure if you want to be creative; practise mindfulness to retain and strengthen self-confidence.

▶ Practise mindfulness regularly to enhance fundamental qualities of creativity, such as curiosity, openness, observation and exploration. Through your practice, you will also naturally increase your creative ability to generate ideas (divergent thinking) and problem-solve (convergent thinking).

▶ Practise mindfulness of your emotions to ensure that you are in the best emotional state to get creative.

▶ Try to help your working culture remain civil, fair and respectful with a degree of autonomy; this way you and your colleagues are more likely to get creative.

▶ Bring more acceptance to your experience of 'stuck-ness'; remember 'this may be just as it is for now'. From a more accepting mentality like this, your creativity is more likely to start flowing again.

▶ Practise mindfulness to connect with your motivation, and therefore inspiration, to carry out work-related tasks. This motivation is crucial for harnessing, implementing and disseminating your creative endeavours.

▶ Practise mindfulness of your walking (try to spend at least 5–10 minutes walking mindfully in the outdoors each day; if you think you don't have 5–10 minutes, then do it for 20 minutes!).

▶ As well as mindful walking, practise mindfulness of sounds to unhook yourself from habitual patterns of thought and narrowed perspectives on the world. These practices will release your creative mind.

We hope you are enjoying the book so far and that this chapter has enhanced your enthusiasm to continue your exploration into the many interesting facets of *working with mindfulness*. Next we are keen to take a look at our relationships with our colleagues at work and what mindfulness can offer us in how best to succeed in teams. So whenever you are ready, let's take a look ...

Useful resources

► Admin (2011, July 9). *Quirky space with a pirate ship and lollipops* [from needofficespace.com]. Retrieved from: http://www.needofficespace. com/servicedoffice-blog/quirky-office-space-with-a-pirate-ship-and-lollipops-9850.html

► Amabile, T. (1998, September). *How to kill creativity* [*Harvard Business Review* article]. Retrieved from: https://hbr.org/1998/09/ how-to-kill-creativity/ar/1

► Brown, B. (n. d.). *Vulnerability is the birthplace of creativity* [video file]. Retrieved from: http://www.inc.com/kimberly-weisul-andrew-maclean/vulnerability-and-innovation.html

► Cook, M. and Brennan Croft, J. (2015, June). *Interactive mindfulness technology: A walking labyrinth in an academic library* [College & Research Libraries News]. Retrieved from: http://crln.acrl.org/content/76/6/318.full

► Luoma, J. and LeJeune, J. [portlandpsych]. (2013, March 20). *The ACT therapist (Acceptance and Commitment Therapy)* [video file]. Retrieved from: https://www.youtube.com/watch?v=n1HlSezYyzs

5

Succeed in teams

'Coming together is a beginning; keeping together is progress; working together is success.'

Henry Ford

Successful outcomes in business are dependent on our effective interactions with one another. This is as true for someone who may have delegated the entirety of the daily operations within their successful business to someone else, or someone working in their own small business alone, as it is to a manager leading a team of 30 employees, or a grass-roots employee working in a team of 50+, hoping to work his/her way up through the ranks of the organisation. Forging a close-knit team and/or building strong working alliances is crucial for our work and business successes. We simply cannot achieve success without input from others, whether that be from colleagues, mentors, managers, educators, suppliers, customers, clients or the guy who cleans the office every day.

Technological advances, screen uses and social media might be engaging and necessary at times, but they are also shown to detract significantly from our social development and skills, which are imperative to our chances of success in work and business. In this modern age, businesses have an ever increasing and pressing need to help teams work better. Bill Ford (in conversation with Jack Kornfield at Wisdom 2.0, discussing mindfulness and business) says that although technology is awesome:

'Business is always about the people ... any business is about human interactions.'

**Bill Ford (See the 'Useful resources'
section for a link to a video of this interview)**

Mindfulness can help improve effective teamwork, interpersonal processes and working cultures, which all leads to greater team success. A successful team easily translates into increased bottom-line profitability for any business. So, in this chapter we will be taking a closer look at:

► Why social connection and interaction are crucial for team success.

► What qualities of interaction can be strengthened to foster greater team effectiveness.

► How to manage feedback, criticism, performance appraisals and delegation amongst a team.

► How to manage conflict well and interact successfully with distressed colleagues.

The costs of social disconnection

The most common challenge we hear about from our clients when it comes to effective teamwork is how to overcome problematic interpersonal dynamics within the team. Of particular concern is the apparent difficulty that members of a team have in actually listening to one another and communicating productively. This can be especially problematic when it comes to managers and those leading a team, who understandably set the tone for group interaction and teamwork. When members of a team are engrossed and distracted by their smartphones rather than paying good attention to one another, or caught up in other distractions in their minds, then communication suffers. It is then easy to understand how the team as a whole is unlikely to be able to establish cohesion and a sense of a group identity and shared purpose.

When team members are present in communication, however, and able to effectively manage the difficult thoughts and feelings that can get in the way of productive interactions, the team is better able to communicate effectively and it can then establish a set of shared values and a stronger sense of group identity, efficacy and purpose. With the tools for productive communication in place, the team is able to make collective group decisions on what specific and effective actions each team member needs to take for the team to reach its desired goals and targets. Furthermore, without skills to effectively manage the thoughts and feelings that get in the way of good communication, team members are more likely to feel unheard, disrespected and undervalued by one another – not the best recipe for ensuring the success of collective, group endeavours.

There are, of course, many established and effective models and strategies within the business literature that can be implemented to enhance successful teamwork, including a range of performance-management systems that we could write about here, but space is limited and we wanted to offer you something different, so we'll leave that to the business gurus (which may even be you). In Chapter 7 of this book ('Build a healthier business') you will read about a set of design principles and other characteristics that may help a working group to better cooperate, succeed and thrive, but for now in this chapter we are keen to share how mindfulness can improve communication in a team to increase the likelihood of that team's success. In our humble opinion, fundamental to the success of any team are the tools to ensure *productive interaction and communication* between team members; without those in place, any other strategy designed to help a team to succeed is bound to not work.

Not only are our social skills necessary for business interactions and success, but they are also fundamental to our health and well-being. We, as evolved apes, are intrinsically social beings who rely upon one another for survival from infancy to old age, physically and mentally. Social isolation was a form of death in times past and still is for our most vulnerable citizens. In fact, the absence and poor quality of social relationships has been shown to be a stronger predictor of mortality than cigarette smoking, obesity, alcoholism, physical activity and hypertension[1] and is a large factor in most mental illnesses. Multiple research findings have also shown that social isolation can be a predictor of morbidity and mortality in both cancer and cardiovascular disease as well a host of other immunological and inflammatory illnesses[2]. We are simply not meant to go this life alone. No infant could survive without another human being, and those with low and poor human contact have been repeatedly shown to 'fail to thrive', falling far short of reaching normal developmental milestones or physical growth expectancies.

In terms of our mental well-being, loneliness and social isolation have been linked to:

- ► depression and suicide;
- ► increased stress levels;
- ► decreased memory and learning;
- ► antisocial behaviour;
- ► poor decision-making;
- ► alcoholism and drug abuse;
- ► altered brain function.

Furthermore, the (no longer ethical) psychological studies of the past, performed on rhesus monkeys who were denied social contact, were shown to produce aggressive and violent animals incapable of forming the healthy relational bonds necessary for survival and procreation.

We are not saying that you need to go and have a group hug, although don't let us stop you (!), but more, to recognise the very centrality and meaningfulness of our social interactions, particularly when considering the potential for a thriving and successful working team and business. Spending time alone is highly valuable for us too, but this is entirely different from social withdrawal, isolation and loneliness. The clue, as always, is in the internal state that you find yourself. Recognising, yet again, the influence of your own personal *perception* of events, whether you are physically alone or in a group, is absolutely critical. A recent study[3] from Carnegie Mellon University showed the wonderful effects that Mindfulness-Based Stress Reduction (MBSR) could have on the lessening of perceived loneliness in healthy older adults aged 55–85. Mindfulness is an invaluable way of recognising and beginning to perceive our sense of aloneness, relinquishing that which keeps us (perceiving that we are) in isolation, and ultimately tuning into our very real and important need to connect and belong.

'Too much self-centred attitude, you see, brings, you see, isolation. Result: loneliness, fear, anger. The extreme self-centred attitude is the source of suffering.'

Dalai Lama

Before embarking on any exercise of connecting with others, it is fundamental to first contact and develop the sense of connection you have with yourself. Most of us do spend our days disembodied, dissociated and out of touch with reality (i.e. the present moment) to a greater or lesser extent. Just think about how often you may have:

▶ Travelled to or from work, or maybe on a business trip of some kind, with no recollection of what has happened for all or part of the journey?

▶ Listened to a colleague talking and then realised you have heard nothing that has been said?

▶ Walked into a room, maybe to see a colleague and forgotten why?

▶ Found yourself lost in a daydream, feeling a sense of isolation/aloneness even though you are sat in a room/office/train carriage full of other people?

▶ Been introduced to someone at a work do and then two seconds later completely forgotten their name?

▶ Forgotten dates/times? (Oops! Weren't you supposed to sign in to that conference call right now?)

▶ Had trouble recalling an article you have just read? (Go on, back to the start of this chapter, please!)

Don't worry, you're not alone. We all do this. So begin by recognising that your doolalliness is a shared human experience – and you belong here with us. Now you might like to try the following exercise to reconnect with yourself:

Exercise 5.1: Mindful on the job

Here I am, connected

This is a very simple practice to help you remember yourself in your rush about your working day. You can do this walking about, sitting at your desk or in a meeting. It need only take a couple of minutes (or fewer!), but of course, you are welcome to take longer if you wish. Try this as often as you like, especially at times when you feel disconnected from your team or colleagues.

1 Notice your Self. Do this by becoming aware of your body. Here you are, here is your body. Just this.

2 This very body is here because of your connection to others, through genetics, nurturing, loving touch and more. This body would not be possible without that connection. Sense that with your body.

3 This awareness may bring sadness, animosity, wonder or nothing much. Simply notice, be present with whatever arises. Bring yourself into close contact with your experience, just as it is right now.

4 Here you are. Welcome.

5 Notice your Self. Do this by becoming aware of a breath. Here you are, here is your breath. Just this.

6 This very breath is here because of your connection to others, through the cycle of oxygen, planting and care of trees and plants, medical advances in health care and more. This breath would not be possible without that connection. Breathe that in.

7 This awareness may bring joy, dismissal, ease or nothing much. Bring yourself into close contact with your experience, just as it is right now.

8 Here you are. Welcome.

9 Notice your Self. Do this by noticing what you see. Look around you; take in the sights, objects, people, and surroundings. Just this one panorama as it is right now.

10 These sights are there for you to view due to your connection to others. None of this would be there if it weren't for this interconnectedness; gaze upon what you see, notice your sense of sight.

11 This awareness may bring relief, closeness, anxiety, anger or nothing much. Be present with whatever arises. Bring yourself into close contact with your experience; see it, just as it is right now.

12 Here you are, connected. Welcome.

Communication breakthrough

If we want to create a healthy, sustainable business, we need to pay great attention to our business community, our shared goals and shared humanity. Beginning with ourselves, using practices in mindfulness, such as the one above, we not only can begin to find room for our own human nature, but we also become increasingly aware of our communication with others and how this connects or separates us from them. Deeply fragmented teams with poor communication demonstrate unhealthy working dynamics and function ineffectually. So the skilfulness of our communication within a team is critical for the ongoing well-being and success of our business.

This may sound obvious but it's worth recognising how any modern place of work, whether a large or small business, will rely on effective teamwork, collaboration and client/customer interaction in order to succeed. But even if you aren't too fussed about the overall success of your organisation, it would seem that brushing up on your own communication skills is still of vital importance to help you get ahead in your own work and career. The good news is that in doing so, your team and company will benefit anyway.

'Not only will better recognition and promotion of soft skills benefit the UK economy, it will also make a significant difference to the businesses, careers and lives of young people.'

James Caan, entrepreneur and venture capitalist (Please see the 'Useful resources' section for full article)

Yes, in order to get ahead at work it seems that being intelligent, ambitious and technically competent is not all that counts; you also need to be pretty savvy when it comes to social skills. In a study carried out by the global management consultancy firm, Hay Group, involving 450 HR Directors and 450 graduates based in India, the USA and China, it was found that, of business leaders and HR Directors surveyed:

► 85 per cent believed that emotional and social skills, over and above technical skills, are what sets new hires apart and are the real differentiator to future business success;

► 90 per cent consider that employees with strong people skills are better able to deliver significant commercial impact;

► 91 per cent believed that employees with enhanced people skills tend to advance faster in their careers.

(For more on this study, please visit: http://web.haygroup.com/worth-their-weight-in-gold)

Although a strong intellect and relevant technical skills and experience may help someone to secure a job, they are not enough to help someone keep their job or even excel in their career thereafter. Maybe you can think of someone who has lost their job (that may even be you), and consider for a moment the main reason/s why they were fired – you may find that more often than not it is for a lack of good teamwork and/or a solid set of adaptable social skills rather than for any technical incompetency. Yes, 'soft skills' really do matter. They are necessary to form and maintain healthy and productive relationships at work and they are essential to help you get ahead in your career. More so, however, these skills soon translate into bottom-line profitability for the team and the organisation as a whole and the fact is that they make good sense for business. A recent research campaign in the UK led by McDonald's and backed by other organisations including the CBI, Barclays and learndirect, as well as the UK-based entrepreneur James Caan, found that these sorts of soft skills, including communication and teamwork (amongst others), contribute a staggering £88 billion to the UK economy, and this figure is predicted to increase to £109 billion over the next five years as organisational structures continue to evolve and globalisation speeds up.

The good news is that mindfulness can help any one of us to develop and strengthen these 'soft people skills' while on the job and specifically to enhance our capacity to:

▶ collaborate and work well as part of a team;
▶ interact smoothly with other people (including colleagues, clients from different groups/cultures);
▶ regulate behaviour/knee-jerk responses and think and reason clearly under pressure;
▶ communicate, listen and empathise in a lucid and compelling manner.

Sure, we can measure team success through the analysis of company metrics, but in order to improve this success we need to attend to the components that make this possible – our colleagues, clients, customers and ourselves. In fact, we need to attend to our colleagues, clients, customers and ourselves with great care. This is often a very challenging area, however, because most of us have very little knowledge about team dynamics, very little time to analyse them in any depth and a dearth of skills in how to manage them well. Furthermore, and sadly, while many of us are taught from earlier and earlier ages to use technology such as tablets, televisions and smartphones, we still have very poor education on how to actually communicate well with each other. This becomes particularly challenging when we find ourselves faced with 'difficult' clients, sensitive colleagues and awkward personalities that we simply must win over, give critical feedback to or simply get on with in order to get the job done well. Rather than being passive and hoping a problem will go away or resolve all by itself, or, alternatively, being bullish and inconsiderate, we need to find an effective means of breaking through our communication barriers. We can all benefit from enhancing these skills. As psychologists we make a lifetime practice of it, and still have plenty to learn! By developing skilful, empathic and insightful communication, work can become a pleasant, enriching and productive place – and mindfulness is one of the most profound and accessible tools for achieving this.

There are many ways of communicating without words – art, body posture, facial expression, eye contact, touch, dress, music, physical proximity, to name but a few – but by far the most common method of communication is verbal communication. The complexities and intricacies of the spoken or written word in human interactions are perhaps what most sets us apart (as far as we currently know) from other animal species.

While these amazing talents in all their myriad manifestations are so central to our ability to connect to our fellow earthlings, they are also central to endless misunderstandings ... and mishaps.

We will now turn our focus on how to use our mindfulness skills to improve our verbal comoonikashun.

The gossip mill

In all honesty, how often do you find staff (including yourself) gossiping, replaying the 'if only' conversations you never had, wishing so-and-so wasn't so f***ing difficult to work with or that such-and-such would just get on with their job properly and stop slacking off?

Vivian Scott, author of *Conflict Resolution at Work for Dummies*, says that employees spend about three hours per week dealing with conflicts. Employees are engaged in gossip, ignoring work, and even sabotaging as a means of resolving everyday conflicts. 'These all lead to a hefty loss for companies,' Scott says. And profit is not the only loss; staff morale is severely damaged by passive means of expressing discord (such as gossiping rather than directly speaking with the individual(s) concerned); conflicts are often also escalated, mishandled or suppressed and an environment of hostility, oppression and insecurity ensues, adding to the already high stress and pressure of the workplace and leading to high job dissatisfaction.

In their survey of 800 managers and employees working across 17 different industries, Christine Porath and Christine Pearson (you can find a link to their article first published in the Harvard Business Review in 2013 in the 'Useful resources' section at the end of this chapter) learned that there is a huge bottom-line cost to businesses that can arise from rudeness (including many forms of incivility: say, gossiping) amongst workplace teams. They found that among workers who had been on the receiving end of incivility:

▶ 48 per cent intentionally reduced their work effort;

▶ 47 per cent intentionally decreased their time spent at work;

▶ 38 per cent intentionally decreased the quality of their work;

▶ 80 per cent lost work time worrying about the incident;

▶ 63 per cent lost work time avoiding the offender;

▶ 66 per cent said that their performance declined;

▶ 78 per cent said that their commitment to the organisation declined;

▶ 12 per cent said that they left their job because of the uncivil treatment;

▶ 25 per cent admitted to taking their frustration out on customers.

(Porath and Pearson, 2013, p. 96)

Further findings from a study, reported in *Fortune,* highlighted how managers and executives working at Fortune 1000 firms spend an average of 13 per cent of their time at work (the equivalent of seven weeks per year) trying to resolve and settle conflicts at work. Yes, the costs of an unchecked gossipy and hostile work environment are severe. However, the flip side is that having a good gossip can help us feel part of a group, united in a common cause (or enemy); we can feel included and less bored with the daily grind.

And, no, gentlemen! Don't dismiss this all as a women's thing! Recent research has found that men spend an average 76 minutes a day nattering with their friends or work colleagues, compared to just 52 minutes for women. The poll of 5,000 people, conducted by a global research company, found that men prefer to do this gossiping in the office (rather than at home, like the ladies). *The Telegraph,* reporting on the study, adds:

'A spokesman for Onepoll said: 'It is commonly believed that women are the ones who love to spread rumours, and gossip about their friends behind their backs. But this poll proves that men aren't as bad as women, they're worse! Men just love a bit of scandal, and will do anything they can to be centre of attention with their colleagues and peers. At the end of the day, hot gossip spices up what would otherwise be another boring day at the office.'

Retrieved from: www.thetelegraph.co.uk (See 'Useful resources')

Spicing things up is all well and good until that turns into behaviours and consequences that start to hurt ourselves or others, whether intentional or unintentional. If you have ever been caught out or been on the receiving end of spreading rumours, you will no doubt still feel this sharply. It isn't pretty. There is a delicate balance between friendly banter and something with a more sinister edge that actually hurts and undermines your colleagues and your team as a whole.

Interestingly, it would seem that social exclusion does actually really hurt and our experience of emotional pain arising from perceived rejection at work can be similar in many ways to our experience of actual physical pain. MRI scans of our brain show us that rejection triggers the same brain pathways that are activated when we experience physical pain. In fact in one study[4] the researchers found that the posterior insular cortex of the brain was activated during a social exclusion experiment (participants being excluded from a simulated game of catch), just as it was during physical pain experiments (administration of a mildly painful stimulus – ouch!). The posterior insular cortex is *'traditionally associated with the sensory processing of physical pain,'* concludes one of the researchers. This study also found that the same part of the brain was activated in participants that witnessed the experience of pain in another participant, which highlights our natural tendency to empathise with one another and how our emotional experiences at work can be somewhat 'contagious.'

Communication outbreak

One way to consider the effect of your communication on your team is to understand the phenomenon of 'emotional contagion' a little more. Our emotional state at work has a measureable 'ripple effect' on our team, with leaders naturally being most influential because of their hierarchical position – most of us watch and take our emotional cues from the big cheese, don't we? But whether you're a team leader or not, it would seem that the old adage, 'smile and the whole world smiles with you', may hold some weight at work, and acting on this may really benefit the performance of your team (and the good news is that someone can notice your smile from 100 metres away, apparently). Smiling stimulates our brain's reward mechanisms in a way that even chocolate, a well-regarded pleasure-inducer, cannot match. In a study conducted in the UK (using an electromagnetic brain scan machine and heart-rate monitor to create 'mood-boosting values' for various stimuli), British researchers found that one smile can provide the same level of brain stimulation as up to 2,000 chocolate bars; they also found that smiling can be as stimulating as receiving up to 16,000 Pounds Sterling in cash! (Lewis, 2013).

Vanessa Druskat, who studies teams and productivity at the University of New Hampshire, found in many different studies that the most highly productive teams have the greatest harmony and positivity (see 'Useful resources'). When team members like one another and the team has fun and enjoys activities together, work becomes more pleasurable and people are not only more dedicated, but also less stressed and happier. In addition, a happy workplace makes disputes easier to resolve because of a general culture of respect and care, in which communication can be more honest and solutions-oriented (i.e. there is a genuine desire to resolve conflict and maintain harmony). Of course, all of this continues to foster a productive and healthy team which functions at its optimum. The good news here is that cheerfulness and positivity are easy to spread (more so than other emotions) which may be to do with the way our brains are hardwired. Scientists postulate that in times long, long ago, smiles and laughter helped to cement alliances and were therefore crucial forms of communication, aiding the survival of our species (maybe you've also noticed that when you see someone else smile, it's really difficult not to smile too!). Now we are not suggesting that you slap on a fake smile and do ten laps of the office each morning while grinning like the Cheshire cat (that wouldn't work and is bound to backfire). No, your cheeriness needs to be genuine and relevant. But all this does have implications for self-awareness and self-regulation (mindfulness) of our moods and emotions and also how we communicate these with one another at work.

Mindfulness of our communication and interactions (speech and listening) with our colleagues is essential for the nurturing of strong and healthy team dynamics, giving rise to greater team performance and success. As we rush about anxiously through most working days, we understandably have, and therefore give, little time and attention to our communication and relationships with one another. As we have already mentioned, the quality of our relationships and interactions at work can impact on our sense of well-being (which we will come back to again later on), which can in turn affect our performance on the job. So taking the time to attend to your interactions with your colleagues can have positive outcomes for all and the team as a whole. Think about it: when you bump into a colleague (say, in the elevator travelling down to the ground floor) are you really present, attending to the interaction and listening well? Although when two people are speaking we tend to assume that one is speaking while the other is carefully listening, in all honesty the reality is that while one is speaking the other (and this may sound a bit like you at times) is actually just waiting to speak themselves.

Being fully present in your communications by noticing your thoughts and feelings as they arise and really focusing on listening and the bodily cues and non-verbal behaviour of others can really improve the quality of your interactions at work.

So, in the spirit of enhancing our communications and supporting our own mindfulness practice in the process, the following exercise will help you develop awareness of speech, listening and interaction with your colleagues, for success as a team. Try this exercise regularly and as often as you can.

Exercise 5.2: Mindful on the job

Hello, and how are you? (mindful speech and listening)

Try the following exercise in a variety of interactions. You may wish to start with something pretty simple, like the example used here, but with practice this can be used just as well with more complex interactions. Here are a few points to consider first off:

▶ Start with someone you find relatively easy to get on with, and as your confidence grows you can start to move on to more challenging individuals!

▶ The key is to introduce more pauses within the dialogue, to give yourself just a little more space within an interaction to be present and to reflect. This way you can notice what others are actually saying to you. Mindful pauses will also help you to notice what you really think and feel, and what would be the most appropriate response, rather than just saying whatever pops into your head straight away and cutting your colleague off mid sentence! When you feel relatively comfortable with someone, this will be easier to do.

▶ Notice any distractions (i.e. sounds, sights around you, thoughts about what you should say, what else might be going on in your work/life that isn't in this moment) that pull your attention away and then bring your attention back to the conversation you are having right here and right now.

▶ Be aware that if you speak with good eye contact, a little more slowly than usual and in a calm tone, this will help to infuse the dialogue with ease and reduce the office stress levels (but you don't need to go all breathy and mystical here; keep it natural and honest).

▶ Although this exercise might feel a little odd and silly at first, remember it is likely to have a positive impact on your interactions and relationships with your teammates. Each of us likes to feel valued, and taking time to listen, respond and connect with a colleague in this way can have a dramatic effect on how appreciated they feel, which quickly translates into more camaraderie and team productivity:

1 Pick a person to greet with a 'Hello, X.'

2 As you speak, notice your body posture and eye contact.

3 Notice, too, if that person responds and how (smile, snub, surprise, etc.).

4 Feel your feet on the floor and notice a general sense of your body; this will help you stay present and connected.

5 Ask X: 'How are you today?' Notice your tone, gestures or posture as you speak.

6 They may well respond with the usual 'I'm OK, how are you?'

7 Pay good attention to their answer; see if you can attune to them/ their mood in this moment.

8 Take a (mindful) breath and notice it. This way you can be fully present.

9 Notice any impulsive urges to interrupt before they finish responding.

10 Notice too any thoughts, judgements or opinions in your mind and let them pass by.

11 Pause before you answer to give a considered response; know if you are being honest, giving a rote answer or trying something different.

12 Give your response, and know that this is as authentic as you can be right now (even if it is reactive, automatic or a plain lie).

13 You may now wish to smile and continue on, or to carry on your dialogue, but keep checking in with yourself periodically, observing your mood, body and breath.

14 Also periodically check in to notice how your colleague finds you/ how your speech lands with them. You may even like to ask them how they are finding the conversation, i.e. 'What is it like for you having this chat with me right now?' 'What are you thinking, feeling about what we are saying/doing right now?'

Over time, using this practice with some careful observation and reflection, you may come to notice all sorts of qualities to your interactions which may have been previously unnoticed. You are now empowered to consciously shape these interactions with your intentions (such as harmony, clarity, care, compassion, etc.).

> ## Jacob
>
> Jacob, a senior recruitment consultant, used the above exercise to improve his communication with colleagues at work. What he had taken as playful, jokey remarks were actually causing others to feel uncomfortable and alienating him from his team. He noticed subtleties in the body language and speech of his colleagues in response to his comments which he was then able to reflect upon and consider. By developing greater awareness and sensitivity within his interactions, he could observe others and himself and gain insight into what he wanted to be different. Jacob decided to try to be more caring, thoughtful and respectful in his speech, and as a result developed a greater sense of connection and ease with his fellow teammates.

Exercises like the one above should not be underestimated and should ideally be practised regularly. Then, when we do find ourselves forced into an awkward moment of communication (maybe with one of those uncomfortable silences), we may find that we don't feel so deskilled and uncertain about how to react or what to say. Instead we may find that each moment of interaction is an opportunity to connect in a meaningful way. Taking a genuine interest in the people around you at work will pay great dividends in terms of your team's productivity and overall effectiveness.

Team Success = Care = Mindfulness

Okay, it's time to hit some more research to help you understand just how much the impact of giving a sh*t about your colleagues really makes good sense for you and your team.

> ## Proven in science, smart for business
>
> ### *Mindfulness generates more empathy for others*
>
> Firstly, you might find it interesting to know that practising mindfulness does actually lead to changes in the brain that are associated with empathy for others. In one study[5], researchers found such brain changes after reviewing the MRI scans of participants' brains. It was found that both experienced and non-experienced meditators who practised mindfulness with a particular focus on compassion showed more brain activity in brain regions linked with empathy while meditating compared to when they were not meditating. So, it would seem that practising ➤

compassion-focused mindfulness (more on this later) will in fact help both you and others in your team to cultivate a more understanding, caring and empathic environment to work in.

Mindful managers can make for a happier, more caring and productive team

In a series of (two) studies[6], researchers were eager to investigate the effects that team supervisors (with a high rate of trait mindfulness) could have on team members' job-related performance and well-being. A total of 96 supervisors and their team members working across a variety of industries took part in this study and the results were really quite interesting. The researchers found that the more mindful the leader, the less emotional exhaustion was experienced by team members. Along with this, higher measures of mindfulness among leaders were also associated with better work–life balance and overall job performance ratings of the employees. In a replication of this study, the researchers also found that the more mindful the manager, the more likely employees were to engage in acts of *good citizenship*, such as showing concern toward their colleagues and other team members and expressing opinions honestly even when others may disagree. But this second study also included a proviso: when basic psychological needs like feelings of autonomy and connection with other people are not met, the employees can lose the benefits of having a mindful supervisor. Hmmmm, interesting! So how about employees who feel as if they have less autonomy on the job; can mindfulness help them? Well, yes it can.

Mindfulness promotes employees' well-being in less autonomous teams

In a recent study[7], researchers continued to explore this link between mindfulness and workplace autonomy. A total of 259 participants were assessed for their ability to pay attention for long periods of time, and similar traits associated with mindfulness, as well as how much autonomy they perceived themselves to have within their team work (as opposed to facing a more controlling managerial style). As in the previous study (above) feeling less empowered at work was associated with lower levels of well-being and health amongst team members, but the researchers found that these effects were moderated by mindfulness. In other words, the more mindful employees were, the less they felt frustrated even when their managers were more controlling and less promoting of their autonomy while on the job. The researchers conclude, '*mindfulness thus appears to act as a protective factor in controlling work environments.*' So it would seem that along with enhancing the well-being and performance of members in a work team, ➤

mindfulness can also buffer against the negative impact of certain undesirable team dynamics.

Warmth equates to loyalty within work teams

Positive relationships and feelings of warmth at work have also been shown to have a greater effect on employee loyalty than the size of their pay-cheque. In particular, a study[8] by Jonathan Haidt of New York University and colleagues shows that the more employees look up to their leaders and are moved by their compassion or kindness (a state he terms *elevation*), the more loyal they become to him or her. So if you are more compassionate to your fellow teammates (cultivated through the practice of mindfulness – more on this to come), not only will they be more loyal to you, but anyone else who has witnessed your behaviour may also experience elevation and feel more devoted to you.

Taking care with our co-workers makes our working lives more pleasant and enjoyable but it is also great for business. Cultivating a more caring environment leads to improved health benefits, greater loyalty and increased productivity. And the great news is that mindfulness and care are synonymous.

This is because skilled mindful attention IS caring (towards ourselves and others), simply by its nature (read here: open, accepting, non-judgemental and compassionate). Mindfulness increases our ability to be present, to have and give good attention and therefore to find calm, clarity and focus, and we also begin to gain insight into the impact of our choices, our emotions and our shared humanity. Care for self and others, cultivated through mindfulness practice, is necessary for community-building and is an inherent aspect of basic survival. As such, simply being in a harmonious (and mindfulness-practising) community relieves stress, as we are more secure and confident even on a most primal level.

The compassionate way to team success

We have already seen how self-criticism negatively impacts our own level of self-confidence (revisit Chapter 3 to refresh yourself on this if you wish) and resultant performance, and talking to our colleagues with the same harsh criticism can have exactly the same detrimental effects for them. Compassion is a strong driving force for team and business success, as the research above indicates (more on this in Chapter 7). So how can we develop more compassion at work and exactly what does being more compassionate look and sound like?

Well, as compassion is fundamentally concerned with alleviating suffering (for ourselves and others), our responses to our colleagues' mistakes, errors and inevitable human limitations naturally become more nurturing and motivating, which in turn is more likely to help them improve and grow (whereas a harsh critical response might do the exact opposite) and our teams flourish. Let's take a quick look at all this in action with the following example.

Just imagine that one of your teammates, let's call him 'Scott', failed to deliver the project he promised to you on time. Let's say you responded to this failure by saying something along the lines of: 'You're totally incompetent, what a loser! You've f***ed up big time, on this one! Everyone is going to suffer because of you! If you think you are going to make it here or in any company you are deluded!' Now, what do you reckon? Is this response (or something equally harsh and critical) really going to help motivate Scott? Nope, you guessed it, probably not. In fact he will probably experience a huge dent to his confidence and feel depressed and anxious as a consequence and his performance will suffer. He might never want to take the lead on that or any other similar project ever again. He'll no doubt be petrified about losing his job and ever being able to find another. So what difference, if any, would a more understanding, kinder and supportive approach have for Scott? Maybe something like: 'I know you're disappointed. I know how important this project was to you; you probably tried your best to get it to me on time. There seems to be a time-management issue here that I'm sure we can resolve together. How about we take a look at that next Monday over a coffee?' Taking this more compassionate approach is probably going to help Scott manage the strong feelings of failure, disappointment, frustration and anxiety he might have, which will clear the way to helping him gather up the confidence and motivation to try to manage his time better on the next project. Surely, your objective in this scenario would be to maximise rather than undermine the confidence in the dynamic with Scott and promote the motivation that Scott needs to succeed at his job, to bring about greater teamwork and success. What do you reckon?

So next time, before you respond with a knee-jerk reaction to someone in your team, try to first stop and think about what impact your words might have. Consider:

▶ how you might feel if someone were to say those words to you;

▶ how your behaviour would be affected if someone talked that way to you.

'When you are offended at a man's fault, turn to yourself and study your own failings. Then you will forget your anger.'

Epictetus

To increase your chances of responding to a colleague with more compassion (rather than performance-hindering anger and criticism), try to follow the steps below (as outlined in our acronym here) and remember to remain as **WARM** as you can be:

Wait a moment (or more!) before you respond, to take a mindful breath (or two!). Instead of responding impulsively, take a step back (which may even look like explaining that you need some time to think). Breathe mindfully, observe your thoughts and feelings, letting them come and go as they naturally will – this practice of self-awareness via mindful attention will help you to regain some control over your emotions and any impulsive, knee-jerk response.

Accept that mistakes happen and that your colleague is only human with limitations, after all. Nobody is perfect.

Relate to your colleague and empathise with them: 'put yourself in their shoes'; after all, you too are human and can make mistakes. Bring to mind a time when you have made your own or, better still, very similar mistakes. Empathising in this way will help you to forgive, which will help you to regulate your emotions and feel less stressed too (remember the wise words of Epictetus, above).

Mirror what you understand and what you have heard/seen/imagined (i.e. you can't mind-read or assume you know how they feel/think) about their predicament/position – so when you feel ready (less angry), respond with something like, 'I can see/hear/imagine that you are upset/disappointed, etc.'. You can then both think of a way to move on from the problem together.

In Chapter 1 we mentioned how Compassion Cultivation Training (CCT) programmes developed at Stanford University's Center for Compassion and Altruism Research and Education have become of interest within corporate organisations. This is no surprise when we consider some of the research around the impact that a more compassionate workforce can have on team cohesion, productivity and business success. In their aim of bringing compassion training to the workplace, Dan Martin and Yotam Heineberg have designed a program which they call Compassion Development Dyads (CDD) (based on the excellent work of the leading expert in the field and founder of Compassion Focused Therapy, Professor Paul Gilbert OBE, from the University of Derby, UK) and they are hopeful that their CDD will help to revolutionise the workplace (you can read more about their work in Suttie's article, (see the 'Useful resources' section at the end of this chapter). Essentially a CDD involves two employees meeting online via videoconference for an hour a week for eight weeks to have structured discussions on relevant research-based topics relating to personal and social well-being, such as mindfulness. The process helps workers to become aware of how they typically respond to stress and threat in work situations, and then trains them to respond in more appropriate ways using tools like self-management of feelings, empathic listening, and compassionate responses. To date, there are some promising results from this programme which has been tested in a pilot study, including a sample of business students. The researchers found that participants increased their compassion for others, their subjective happiness, and their leadership skills, among many other benefits.

This is all very promising stuff, as the more we demonstrate compassion within our teams at work, the more we move away from shame and fear and instead closer to empathy and connection. With more compassionate responses we start to cultivate a culture of trust within our teams and from this trust comes increased team performance. It is easy to see how a kinder and more positive work atmosphere will engender a safer environment within which to work, and in turn people's willingness is freed up, giving rise to greater creativity and overall improved performance. In bringing compassion and kindness (as trained via mindfulness practice) to our interactions with one another at work, we can help to strengthen team bonds and enhance team productivity and effectiveness.

Dealing with psychologically vulnerable colleagues

The success of our team also depends on the emotional support that we can offer one another at times of high distress. Sometimes we need to console a colleague in their time of need, or at other times we ourselves could do with a solid and caring 'shoulder to cry on.' In the demanding, cut-throat culture in which many of us work, it is likely that you have experienced a colleague feeling stressed or much worse, at some time or another. You may even have a specific 'people-supporting' role at work; maybe you work in HR or are a manager and can often feel stuck about what to say and how to say it when someone approaches you in distress, which is completely understandable. These moments can feel very scary indeed, particularly when we can't find the right words to use. We can feel deskilled, and in our hope to not exacerbate the situation we can cut these conversations short or, worse still, ignore this colleague altogether, even though they're sitting at their desk clearly distraught, in floods of tears. Either of these responses is likely to aggravate the situation and upset your colleague even more, as they may feel increasingly alone, shunned and ostracised by your apparent lack of warmth (although, of course, this was not your intention). We are not here to increase your anxiety in these tricky situations but we do want to remind you that how we talk and respond to our colleagues in distress does make a large difference – what we say and do as well as what we don't say and don't do can be helpful or unhelpful. Also, very subtle differences in how we say something can have a huge impact and make all the difference to how someone is feeling.

Language can be the problem as well as the solution

'Too often we underestimate the power of a touch, a smile, a kind word, a listening ear, an honest compliment or the smallest act of caring, all of which have the potential to turn a life around.'

Unknown

By its very nature, work is an understandably highly goal-oriented environment and within this context our brains are continuously trained to jump to solutions for each and any problem we may encounter. Couple this with our hardwired motivation to control, eliminate and avoid pain and discomfort (more on this to come in Chapter 6 and also please revisit Chapter 2 for a reminder on the function of our problem-solving mind as a tool for survival), and it is likely that we will try to help a distressed colleague by attempting to problem-solve their emotions away. Yes, this is the approach which we usually and habitually adopt in response to our distressed colleagues, but please note this is not always the best approach as it can shut the communication down and your colleague can be left feeling hurt, rejected and invalidated. Remember that emotions are not a problem to solve but they are a condition of life (if you could just push horrible feelings aside, don't you think your colleague would have done that already?). It is not easy to move out of this autopilot mode because, as we know, it is an innate human impulse to problem-solve, fix and therefore reassure in highly emotional and 'problematic' situations such as these. Instead of this, though, we can help our colleagues to trust and open up more. We can do this via mindful speech and listening (please remind yourself of Exercise 5.2 above) and try also to include more YESes and fewer NOs or BUTs in our responses to our distressed teammates.

With more mindful attention, we can notice the dramatic difference that an intentionally (but invalidating!) supportive response such as:

'There is no need to feel that way'

might have, compared to a more *accepting* response such as:

'It's normal to feel that way.'

What do you think the difference might be, in the way that these two slightly different responses are experienced by your colleague? Have a think, right now, before you read on.

Exercise 5.3: Work in progress

Yeah but, no but, yeah but ...

Try to think of how you might respond to the following five statements from a distressed colleague. Consider your response for each one, one at a time. You are not allowed to use the words 'No' or 'But' (or any variations of these that attempt to problem-solve their situation or convince them otherwise, such as the words 'not', 'yeah but', 'although', etc.). If you use one of these 'forbidden' words or sentiments in your response, start again. See if you can notice the natural impulses of your mind to try to problem-solve the situation for your colleague and how the mind may automatically go to 'NO' and 'BUT' when trying to respond:

1 'I've had enough, I just can't cope with all this work. I should just resign from my job right now, today, shouldn't I?'

2 'She's right, I can't do anything well, can I? I've let the whole team down!'

3 'No one gets how much I have to do. You don't understand either, do you? You're just here because it's your job to offer support. You don't really care!'

4 'I bet you think I'm a total loser also, just like everyone else in the team, don't you?'

5 'I've had it up to here. I failed again. I have nothing left to live for. I just want to jump out of that window!'

So how did you do? Easy? It's pretty difficult isn't it? This is because our minds are so well conditioned to avoid discomfort and to try to resolve any problems. However, the real problem is that when we try to solve emotions as if they were problems, it usually just backfires and exacerbates these unwanted feelings (both we and our colleagues can feel more upset and stuck) and we can get caught in a circular communication trap (or, worse still, an argument)! So, instead, consider how we can bring mindfulness to our interactions, and in doing so embody a more open and accepting response to our distressed colleagues.

Below we have summarised three aspects to a more helpful response to a colleague in distress. These refer to preferred and more helpful ways of being, which you would do well to embody when interacting with a colleague who is upset. They are:

1 **Be simple:** be a sounding board and offer signposting (depending on your role. Don't complicate things, no solutions, problem-solving, reassurance, judging, analysing).

2 **Be present:** direct exquisite, focused attention on the here and now (track your thoughts, sensations, emotions, and sights, sounds, urges and impulses – notice judgements and let them drop away, rise and fall. Pay attention to what you see/hear, your colleague's body, expressions, response to you).

3 **Be compassionate:** offer acceptance and validation of their experience; be kind (be aware of appearing judgemental, dismissive, minimalising, or patronising through unhelpful reassurance). To prime your brain for compassion, bring to mind the feeling of being with someone who loves you, while calling up heartfelt emotions such as

gratitude or fondness. Bring empathy to the difficulties of the other person. Opening to their suffering, let sympathy and goodwill naturally arise. In your mind, offer explicit and genuine wishes such as 'May you not suffer. May you find rest. May it go well with the doctor/your colleague/manager/client etc.' Show empathy by trying to understand how your colleague might feel, via curiosity and openness. Bring acceptance of what is – remember that what you experience is not universal – acknowledge, make room for your colleague's experience, accept their feelings and own your own experience. Don't just SAY you accept – TRULY accept (be accepting).

"Mindfulness allows us to truly and actively listen to our colleagues."

What to say, specifically

As we've begun to highlight, at the heart of effective communication is mindful attention, which includes the ability to remain aware and to regulate your own emotions and knee-jerk impulsive responses. Mindfulness allows us to truly and actively listen to our colleagues (to ensure that they feel heard, understood and validated) in an accepting way and to reply with the most considered and helpful response in a compassionate way. We have included a few of our top tips and ideas for specific responses (that might help you out in a tricky situation) below:

General pointers:

▶ Listen carefully (remember, listening is not just being silent while you're actually waiting to speak!) to what your teammate is saying to you and repeat what they have said back to them to ensure you have understood it. Show that you are listening: stop what you are doing (phone down!), paraphrase and clarify your understanding.

▶ You don't have to agree with what your colleague is saying. But by showing you understand and accept how they feel, you are letting them know that you respect their feelings – this way they will then open up to you more and trust will build.

▶ Use appropriate body language. Help the person feel comfortable. To show you are listening, try to maintain eye contact and sit in an open position.

▶ Don't diagnose or tell them to not worry, snap out of it, pull themselves together, get over it, keep busy.

Active listening/validating:

Non-verbal

▶ Nodding head, meaningful eye contact, silences, physical contact.

Verbal

▶ 'I understand', 'I see'; *with more* 'Yes' *rather than* 'No', 'yeah but'!

▶ 'I can hear you sighing. Is everything OK? Do you want to talk about it?'

▶ 'I can see that it makes you very unhappy when ...'

▶ 'I understand how you would feel that way' (remember: you don't have to agree).

▶ 'If I understand you correctly, you feel (X) when (Y). Did I hear you correctly?'

▶ 'Can you tell me more about how you feel in this situation?'

▶ 'I can see/understand how difficult that must be – it makes sense to me as your colleague/another human being.'

▶ 'I can imagine and see just how painful this is for you.'

▶ 'I feel touched/moved/upset by what you are saying.'

▶ 'I know how vulnerable it may feel to do and say what you just did and I want you to know that you are safe with me and what you said is sacred.'

Moving the conversation on:

▶ 'What are you afraid will happen if this situation continues?'

▶ 'What do you think the options are in this situation? What do you think you should do?'

▶ 'What do you need right now to make this situation work for you?'

▶ 'How do you see my role in this situation?'

▶ 'I would like to suggest how you might consider helping yourself with this difficult situation; would that be OK?'

▶ 'I would feel privileged to help you with this in the best way I know how.'

▶ 'Would you be willing to ...?'

We hope that the above tips and pointers will be of use to you. If you take your time to use them, along with the practice of 'mindfulness of listening and speech' (as described in Exercise 5.2 above), you may find that even in the most emotionally charged interaction, you can still help your distressed colleague along while also strengthening a sense of trust and camaraderie for the sake of greater team cohesion and effectiveness.

If you'd like some more tips on how you might interact with a distressed colleague, check out the relevant *Harvard Business Review* article, listed in the 'Useful resources' section at the end of this chapter.

So far we have covered ways that may help you manage challenging inter-actions with distressed colleagues as and when they arise. However, to really make a difference to the overall well-being of your teammates and team as a whole, we advise that you practise mindful interactions regu-larly, not just reactively when you see a colleague is upset. You may also want to introduce regular one-to-one meetings with colleagues or even small group meetings where you can check in with one another about how you are each feeling, and discuss any concerns you may have. It is important to leave any discussion about work projects, objectives or to-do lists outside of these conversations and instead preserve them as an open forum to support one another with general concerns, feelings of stress and issues of work–life balance. If you are not a manager or leader yourself, then you might also like to invite them on board with this too. If managers and senior leaders are able to model this supportive commu-nication culture, then in our experience it is more likely to take effect as, in doing so, they will reinforce the message that it 'really is OK to talk.' By sending a supportive message from the top, senior leaders and manag-ers can really help promote a culture of acceptance around mental health within a team and/or the wider organisation. In our own work we have been lucky enough to witness this first-hand while assisting in the devel-opment and implementation of 'mental health champion' programmes and other similar initiatives within companies. These programmes have involved training a number of employees and team members, includ-ing senior people, in mindfulness and mindful communication skills (among other competencies), so that they can effectively serve others who may be experiencing mental health conditions by offering them informal support and guidance. When implemented in this way, mind-fulness can seep into the very culture of any organisation, helping the company to transform (in a good way). Stress no longer is viewed only as a 'personal problem' that an individual employee must cope with alone, but as a wider concern which everyone can help to prevent and manage at an organisational and cultural level (more on this in Chapter 7).

When things get heated

Of course, there are times when we are all challenged, either by the office bully (which may even be you), a conflict of interests, or a personality clash. We might be faced with having to give or receive difficult feedback, make redundancies or deciding to take a stand about an injustice. There are many other times when many of us feel uncomfortable, out of our depth or overly emotional. When we are faced with the stress of being unable to communicate effectively (or at all) with someone at work, especially someone who has a significant impact on our job and experience at work, we can be left feeling angry and disempowered. It might not matter how careful or considerate you have been, how much you have planned and rehearsed a conversation and taken care to word yourself well, if you are met with a brick wall. Take Matthew's predicament, for example.

Matthew

Matthew, an ambitious vice president working in mergers and acquisitions at a large financial institution, had recently returned to work after a month of compassionate leave to care for his severely ill wife. On his re-entry into work he was feeling pretty anxious about all the work that he had missed, and whether he would be able to catch up and successfully reintegrate back into his team. Unfortunately, his anxiety seemed to get the better of him and despite a graded return to work he was finding it hard to reconnect with his teammates, concentrate on his work and keep up with his workload. He felt that his team, including his manager, had not welcomed him back with any warmth, and in a rather reactive and defensive way he tended to keep his head down, just get on with his work and not warm towards them either. He felt that others were pushing more and more work his way and he started to feel alone and overwhelmed. Following a number of review meetings with his manager, he was placed onto a performance improvement plan (PIP). Matthew felt aggrieved and as if management hadn't been considerate of his predicament. He felt that it was not humanly possible to meet the targets of his PIP and he became increasingly stressed, angry and worried about the security of his job. Matthew's distress escalated and he found it very difficult to keep it under wraps while in the office, on the job and also when meeting with his manager for fortnightly reviews on his progress in meeting his targets. He became angry, defensive and aggressive towards his manager, which obviously did him no favours at all. He found his manager would not listen to him and simply persisted in telling him his work was not up to scratch and that he needed to do better. He found it very difficult to even think about how his manager or others in his team may be feeling about his departure and return to work. The tension was high in the office and he and his manager were locked into a fraught conflict that HR needed to step into to try to resolve.

In highly tense interactions like those between Matthew and his manager described above, the common misperception is that having a sound, logical and clear argument will win you over – it certainly will help – but it is not enough alone. It is equally important to notice the unspoken dynamics of the relationship and to pay particular attention to defensiveness and reactivity. The same skills outlined in the exercises above for pausing and centring attention on the breath and body are once again invaluable. This balance of attention is sometimes referred to as a golden balance of 80/20 per cent attention: that is, 80 per cent attention on yourself (your body sensations, breath, emotions, thoughts, behaviours, etc.) and 20 per cent attention on the other person. Of course this is strictly speaking absolutely subjective and unquantifiable; however, the balance is strongly in *your* favour. You can then stay embodied, centred, present, focused and caring towards yourself, while sustaining enough attention to be engaged and receptive to another. It is also useful for containing enough balance to be emotionally resilient (see Chapter 6 for more on this) and to keep the perspective necessary to recognise when we are being reactionary, defensive and/or simply making the situation worse in some way.

Along with practising mindfulness while interacting with his manager, Matthew also found that spending time to practise mindfulness outside of these interactions was also tremendously helpful to regulate and manage his rising anger and frustration. He would spend 10 minutes or so running through the following exercise when he felt tension arise in his body and just before going into any meeting with his manager and/or HR around the issue. This way he was able to ensure that he stayed aware of his emotions and regulated them – and also any reactive, knee-jerk responses – as best he could. You might also like to try this exercise when emotions are running high for you at work. Along with anger, it can be equally effective for the whole range of intense feelings you might experience on the job, such as anxiety and/or sadness. So why not give it a go to protect and care for your relationships with teammates, the best you can.

Exercise 5.4: Mindful on the job 🎧🎧

Taming the mind

▶ Firstly find a place to sit down, where you won't be disturbed for ten minutes or so.

▶ Before you begin, you might like to close your eyes to limit distraction, or simply rest your gaze on a still spot or object in front of you and droop your eyelids.

1 To begin, first gently push your feet into the floor a couple of times; then as you let them come to rest, notice the sensations in your feet.

2 If you are sitting down, now also notice the sensations in your body where your body makes contact with the seat that you are sitting on.

3 Take a few mindful breaths. Notice the sensations of air flowing into your body tracking the air flowing down into your lungs, filling your lungs. Track the out-breath as your lungs empty and the breath flows out of your nostrils/mouth. Practise centring yourself in this way for at least two minutes.

4 Once you have become aware of yourself, right here and right now, begin to scan your body for any sensations of stress or discomfort you may feel.

5 See if you can locate a specific sensation in your body where you feel your stress the strongest; maybe there is discomfort in your stomach, tightness in your chest, tension in your head or shoulders, or some other place.

6 Hold this sensation at the forefront of your awareness, right now.

7 Notice any struggle that you may have with this sensation, any urges to push it away, or to stop the exercise or any thoughts about not wanting it there or how others have caused you this upset. Leave these urges and thoughts alone, you don't have to follow them; you don't have to problem-solve or struggle with this particular unwanted experience. Leave it be, just there, just as it is.

8 Return to noticing this sensation in your body as best you can; you don't have to like it, just notice it, just as it is, just now.

9 Now, with the utmost curiosity, begin to explore this sensation.

10 Notice what shape it has. Is it round, square or some other shape?

11 Notice if this sensation has a colour. Is it light or dark, perhaps?

12 Is it rough or smooth in its texture?

13 What about its temperature; does it seem hot or cold, maybe?

14 Notice if it is moving at all. Is it vibrating, pulsating, spinning or motionless?

15 What about its weight; does it seem heavy or light?

16 Now imagine that this sensation was able to float out of your body. Then picture it suspended in mid-air, and see it sitting there, right

in front of you. Just take a few seconds to really observe this sensation and all its properties as it suspends in mid-air in front of you right now. Notice its shape, colour and texture again.

17 Now, imagine this sensation floating back into your body and reclaiming its rightful position just where it was before, just where it belongs.

18 Keep noticing any thoughts and/or urges as they arise. Maybe there are thoughts to rid yourself of this sensation or not wanting it to return into your body, or wishing it gone – or any other thoughts about the situation or person causing you this upset. Leave them alone and return to noticing this sensation in your body.

19 Now, as the sensation sits back in your body, with all its properties, take a few more mindful breaths.

20 This time track each in-breath as it flows into your body, and imagine it flowing into the exact area where this sensation sits. Now imagine your breath flowing around this sensation, opening up the space around it.

21 As you breathe out, track each out-breath as it flows out of your body, and with it release any struggle that you may have with this sensation.

22 Repeat the above a number of times, for at least two minutes.

23 As you make space for this sensation in your body, remember the purpose of this exercise is not to get rid of the sensation, but to make room for it; make peace with it. Just allow it to be there.

24 You don't have to like the sensation; you just want to accept it.

25 Whenever you feel ready you can begin to open your eyes again, feel your feet against the floor and notice any objects around you, as you ground yourself back into the environment that you are in.

Repeating this exercise a number of times may help to decrease the intensity of any strong emotion and associated physical discomfort. If, however, you find that the emotion/sensation is just as strong following this exercise as when you began, then don't fret, as the purpose of the exercise was not to change the emotion but to accept it. In doing this exercise, you may have noticed many automatic urges or thoughts showing up which are designed to problem-solve or rid yourself of any strong unwanted emotion and sensation; there may be thoughts about the injustice of the situation that you feel is causing your upset or worries about some impending doom. Engaging in these urges and thoughts as you usually might is likely to intensify the emotion and lead to knee-jerk reactions also. So remember: in choosing not to follow or react to them, like in a practice such as this, you are participating in a worthwhile exercise of self-regulation training which will serve you well if you want to preserve and nurture any stressful relationships within your team.

Whatever the strong emotion you experience is, it is important to notice that it, along with all the associated urges, thoughts and bodily sensations, may conceal an underlying deeper sense of vulnerability. Our anger and/or anxiety can be seen as a suit of armour that we might wear to protect a sensitive wound underneath, before we go out into the battlefield. Sometimes it is important to take off our heavy suit of armour, even for a short time, to allow the air to help our wound heal, even if it's just a little at a time. As we drop the urges to protect ourselves, such as these anger- or anxiety-fuelled defensive positions, within an exercise just like this, we allow ourselves to make contact with our own deeper sense of vulnerability, our humanness, and instead of hiding it away, we can begin to offer it some kind, mindful attention.

Taking feedback on the chin

In all our years working with corporate executives, we can confirm that we have never yet met one that has been fully at ease with performance reviews. It seems that although work appraisals are an accepted part of the deal and everyone needs to do them, everyone still seems to fear them: team members are terrified that they will be pulled up, criticised, and given a bad review, and managers worry that even the mildest piece of constructive criticism will be received in the worst possible way resulting in either a full-blown temper tantrum or uncontrollable tears. The result is that these potentially highly valuable interactions are often avoided for a long time, there is an air of procrastination around them, and then when they do eventually occur they are often filled with high anxiety and tension. The truth is that authentic feedback is essential to the overall effectiveness of a team and any group endeavour. Although it can feel difficult to give and receive, feedback provides us with greater self-awareness, which is crucial if we want to have better relationships with our colleagues. From this self-awareness we can then choose to consciously change our behaviours for the greater good of the team. You can find a link to a short video with Daniel Goleman and Bill George discussing how best to give feedback as a manager, listed in the 'Useful resources' section at the end of this chapter. Here, however, we are going to turn our attention to how we can best increase our willingness to be on the receiving end of feedback for the sake of good teamwork and group success.

In their paper published in the *Harvard Business Review* (there is another link to this paper in the 'Useful resources' section at the end of this chapter), Jay Jackman and Myra Strober outline a number of steps that foster a more helpful response to feedback and the changes that it demands. Specifically, they advise that it is wise to first recognise your emotional relationship and response to feedback. So if you have been putting your appraisal meeting off and avoiding your boss (just praying that he/she will leave you out of the process this time around), then notice that there might be a degree of vulnerability and associated fear motivating your avoidant behaviour. This might be an understandable fear within the context of wider redundancies and job insecurity: about losing your job, for example. Secondly, whether it's fear or anger or some other emotion that keeps you running for cover at appraisal time, you may want to then seek some assistance to help you manage this, maybe from a coach or psychologist – your mindfulness practice (and particularly Exercise 5.4 above) will of course help you here too. Once you receive feedback it might be helpful to reframe it. So instead of ruminating on how unfair and outright ridiculous the criticism is, notice this circular, unproductive thinking pattern and recognise its outdated function (i.e. problem-solving/protection) and the impact that it is having on your mood and confidence (you might like to revisit Chapter 3 to remind yourself of the different forms of self-criticism and how they affect our confidence level, mood and performance). If you are able to gain perspective on your thoughts, by taking a step back to notice them in this way, you are then free to learn from the feedback, and then choose to use it to your advantage. For example, if you view the larger picture and what really matters to you, which might involve you keeping your job, or maybe you want to play a more pivotal role in propelling your team to greater success, then maybe you can take some mindful breaths and 'make room' for implementing the advice that you have been given: perhaps, working on your assertiveness skills with clients or colleagues. Then when incorporating this feedback into proactive action, it might be helpful to break it down into measurable and realistic goals and targets (please see Chapter 6 for how to set SMART goals); your manager, mentor, coach or a colleague can help you with this too. To ensure that you stick to your targets, you can use incentives and give yourself rewards along the way. So, you might like to treat yourself to your favourite meal if you complete that online training module in assertiveness skills, for example.

Feedback is a necessary component to collaborative endeavours at work and can actually be a really rewarding experience. If you want to improve your relationships with your colleagues and if you want to help your team to succeed, then you'll need to increase your self-awareness; your willingness to receive feedback (in an authentic way) is an excellent vehicle for doing just that. It is helpful to open ourselves up with more flexibility around the uncomfortable feelings that feedback is bound to trigger, for most of us anyway. Remaining mindful of the thoughts, emotions and behaviours that might get in the way of truly opening up to feedback can help each of us to face this daunting part of our work, and in doing so take proactive steps towards self-improvement which can positively strengthen team dynamics and benefit our team as a whole. So when the next batch of appraisals come around, make sure you're first in line, remain mindful and act boldly in the service of bettering yourself and, as a consequence, your team.

One for all and all for one – delegation

Many people we meet tend to struggle with delegation at work. In their personal lives they find that they can easily ask their partner, kids, parents or friends to do stuff for them, but when it comes to work they seem to find the act of asking for help impossible to do. This is unfortunate, as delegating work, if done well, can have a really positive impact on team dynamics, enhancing a wider sense of team trust and confidence. It can lead to greater levels of group creativity, productivity and an overall higher team performance. A successful team is one that feels comfortable delegating work among its members.

Despite the benefits of delegating work, there are many reasons why we may choose not to delegate to our colleagues. For example, we may fear that if we lose control of our work, then everything is bound to go horribly wrong; we fear that others will mess it up and that will reflect badly on us or, conversely, that the other person might do a better job and pass us by on the career ladder. In the cut-throat and competitive environment in which many of us work, it is completely understandable that we would have some of these fears. Alongside these obstacles to streamlined delegation come others such as how some of us may derive a great sense of satisfaction from being a 'martyr' – i.e. feeling good about ourselves because we don't need any help, and, as no one else could do the work quite as well we are, very happy being the one that saves the day for everyone else. This tendency could be easily linked to a lack of interests outside of our work (i.e. 'who would I be if I'm not needed here?!'). Commonly, however, many of us just don't trust anyone else to do the work properly and we might see delegation as a sign of weakness and as an admission to everyone else that we are not coping very well. Alternatively, some of us may feel guilty about asking our colleagues to take on more work, especially if they already appear overloaded. Whatever the reason/s for your lack of delegation might be, remember that a team that doesn't delegate appropriately erodes the strength in its own dynamics and any trust that it may have and ultimately impedes its own levels of productivity and effectiveness.

If you're now starting to think about how you might try a bit more delegation, it might be helpful to remember that delegating is not simply about offloading the boring work to someone else (because you simply can!). Instead, it is about giving others in the team the opportunity to do work that will help them to develop their skill set and grow in confidence, which will also be for the greater good of the team as a whole. For a team to function at its optimal level, it is helpful for each member to have as many skills as possible in order for the work to be done efficiently and to the highest standard. Further, the absence of any form of delegation within a team would easily equate to team resentment and a breakdown of trust and healthy relationships. Effective delegation builds trust, healthy team dynamics and a sense of a shared purpose and group identity, making success more likely when working towards common goals.

Effective delegation can have the following benefits:

▶ frees up time to focus on other important tasks: i.e. it saves time;

▶ encourages healthy interactions within a team;

▶ helps individual team members to learn and develop new skills and build confidence;

▶ gets the group working as a team more effectively;

▶ brings creativity, new ideas, greater productivity and profitability to your business.

Make no mistake about it: when delegation is done very badly, it can be detrimental to team dynamics and confidence, decreasing the productivity and bottom-line profitability of that team. All delegation is not good delegation. For example, micromanaging is not the way to delegate, as it comes from a place of fear and will likely backfire in terms of any of the benefits listed above. So if you are going to delegate, ensure that you do it mindfully and as fully as you can; remember, micromanaging is likely to squash any team morale, confidence, creativity and growth and become a real time consumer (rather than saver!). If you delegate a task to someone in your team and they fail at that task in some way, it is most likely down to your own poor delegation skills (no doubt you have been micromanaging). To delegate successfully, it is wise that you invest time and effort into the communication and handing-over processes. Think about how often you delegate, if at all, and when you do, how you go about it.

▶ Do you invest time into the process?

▶ Do you end up micromanaging your colleagues?

▶ How does that all work out for you? Your team relationships? The successful outcome of that task?

Interestingly, *The Oxford English Dictionary's* definition of the word 'delegate' is: 'Entrust (a task or responsibility) to another person, typically one who is less **senior** than oneself.'

So do you really and truly 'entrust' tasks to your team members when you hand over some work for them to do? If not, you might like to follow our steps to effective *mindful* delegation as outlined here in our acronym, **ENTRUST**, below:

Enlist the person that you want to take on the job. Now, this first step involves both choosing the right person and meeting with them to impart the instructions for the job. Although it is tempting to give the job to someone that you know can do it very well, you might like to push both yourself and a less experienced team member (if they are willing!) outside of your respective comfort zones. See this as an opportunity to improve team dynamics, to build trust in someone, and to help a colleague, yourself and the team to grow in confidence. When you have chosen the 'right' person, sit down with them and clearly explain what the job is and what it involves, what the end result should look like and how much time they have to get it done. Clearly outline the desired outcome and how the results of the job will be measured with facts, figures and deadlines, to avoid any grey areas and confusion.

Negotiate the rules and limitations of the delegation. To build trust, allow your colleague to take on the entirety of the job; give them full responsibility, as only giving them part of the job might break down some of the trust that you are trying to build. End this discussion with an agreement on very clear instructions on what they can and can't do, i.e. whether they can or cannot and how they might return to you for clarification or further advice along the way.

Tackle the job at hand. Ask the team member to outline a plan of action around how they propose to tackle the job, step by step. Give them free rein to come up with this plan.

Review the team member's proposed plan of action with them. If you are not certain that their plan is going to bring about the desired outcome in the time specified, then say so (compassionately) and help them to refine this plan. Be mindful of micromanaging them at this stage and making this *your* plan; ensure that you give them space to rethink through how they may do the job differently so they retain a sense of ownership.

Understand that the proposed plan may not be your preferred way, but if it seems like it might work then just go with it. Remember you're helping someone grow into a more productive member of the team (this may apply equally to you as you mindfully allow feelings of anxiety, potential failure, etc. to just come and go, rather than trying to micromanage them away!).

Set a start date and also regular update meetings to monitor progress and redefine objectives. Pre-setting a start date and 'catch up' times like this in advance will help you to not continuously look over your team-mate's shoulder every five minutes (undermining their confidence).

Tactfully provide feedback at the end of the task. Take time to go through it with your colleague; give praise on parts that were completed successfully; if there were aspects that could have been done better, make sure your comments are constructive and clear, and compassionately delivered (use the acronym WARM as outlined earlier in this chapter), so your team member can learn from them.

Part of working successfully within a team is accepting that you can't do everything perfectly by yourself. This might mean that you need to make room for uncomfortable and anxious feelings and pass work on to someone else who can dedicate their time, energy and resources to it. Remember to use mindfulness practices and breathe alongside these feelings. This opening up to feelings (even if we don't like them) can help with breaking work stressors down, as Ellen J Langer says:

'Events are less stressful when considered from multiple perspectives, and speaking to different people helps with this.'

(Langer, 2014)

Effective delegation that results in quality outcomes depends on the right type of mindful attention to the handing-over process and the communication with which it is delivered. This can significantly enhance a sense of mutual trust and confidence as well as shared goals and group identity within a team, giving rise to greater team productivity and success.

Taking care of conflict

Feelings of hostility and conflict are common among teams. Whether these arise from scenarios like performance reviews, colleagues not meeting expectations, office gossip or other acts of rudeness, it is imperative that we practise ways to manage our feeling of resentment and effectively resolve conflicts, to preserve a more harmonious team vibe and all the benefits that will result from that. In a time of cutbacks and understaffed teams, a very common bone of contention that we often hear about relates to a strong feeling of injustice around teammates' apparent lack of shared responsibility to help out when the pressure is on. Of course in some cases it feels as if the pressure is always on, and teammates consistently leaving the office 'early' without any obvious consideration for the others left behind (to manage the excessive workload) can really get our hackles up! Whatever your bone of contention with your fellow teammate(s), along with the exercises above, you might also like to try the following exercises to lessen your anger so you are then in a better place to work towards team cohesion, negotiation and problem-solving around these rifts.

We are going to cover two specific and practical mindfulness approaches (one intrapersonal and another interpersonal) to dealing with conflict at work. The first is a traditional practice known as the *metta bhavana*: this is commonly translated as a 'loving kindness' practice that cultivates the naturally kind and caring qualities of the heart (by the way, this is the same practice that led to increased brain activity associated with empathy in the study listed earlier in this chapter, so brace yourself for seeing your arch-rival in a very different light indeed!). The intention of this practice is to actually free *ourselves* from the tyranny of judgemental, angry and harsh thinking. The impact on others may or may not be noticeable, but we ourselves become less entangled in the toxic dynamics of the conflict and thus cease to act out the necessary other half of a conflict relationship. This often disarms our 'opponent' and we are left to perceive them as they are rather than as the meaning we are making of them – more a windmill than a giant.

> 'Just then they came in sight of thirty or forty windmills that rise from that plain. And no sooner did Don Quixote see them that he said to his squire, 'Fortune is guiding our affairs better than we ourselves could have wished. Do you see over yonder, friend Sancho, thirty or forty hulking giants? I intend to do battle with them and slay them. With their spoils we shall begin to be rich for this is a righteous war and the removal of so foul a brood from off the face of the earth is a service God will bless.'
>
> 'What giants?' asked Sancho Panza.
>
> 'Those you see over there,' replied his master, 'with their long arms. Some of them have arms well nigh two leagues in length.'
>
> 'Take care, sir,' cried Sancho. 'Those over there are not giants but windmills. Those things that seem to be their arms are sails which, when they are whirled around by the wind, turn the millstone.'
>
> **Don Quixote**

Practising loving kindness helps you to become much more aware of yourself and of how you relate to other people. It also helps to cultivate greater awareness of and compassion for yourself and others. This is especially crucial in relationships marked by frustration, resentment or anxiety because those emotions narrow our perceptions and make our interactions more clumsy, rigid, and prone to failure.

An article from the *Harvard Business Review* on how to solve conflicts at work (which you can find a link to listed in the 'Useful resources' section) describes the narrowing of our views in challenging relationships as being like caricaturists who exaggerate their subjects' most prominent physical features: we mentally distort our perceived opponents and ourselves, reducing them to a narrow collection of traits and behaviours (a giant or a hero, for instance). Then we interact with that caricature rather than with the whole person. This may mean relating to ourselves as a victim and the other party as an aggressor, for instance, and entering into co-dependent relationships at work where we struggle to gain a healthy perspective and conflicts simply endure.

Mindfulness opens up our view to include many facets, roles, and the experiences that may have shaped our patterns of thinking and behaviour. The practice also helps us see how we engage in ways that break down communication. With awareness and compassion, it's much easier to find common ground.

Exercise 5.5: Mindful on the job 🎧

Loving kindness for conflict

Before you take on your next challenging interaction, or whenever feelings of conflict arise, take ten minutes to clear your mind and tune your brain for interpersonal effectiveness. Here's the practice:

▶ Find a quiet place to sit, walk or stand comfortably.

▶ Close your eyes if you wish.

▶ Breathe in, filling your lungs with oxygen and alerting your senses to the aliveness of this moment.

▶ Breathe out slowly, experiencing the natural release of tension that you may be holding.

▶ Let your mind settle gently on the rhythm of your breathing, paying attention to the feeling of air flowing in and out of your body.

▶ When your mind wanders off, gently bring it back to your breath.

▶ Continue this mindfulness meditation for two minutes

▶ Loving-kindness meditation begins with a focus on the self. Without self-compassion, it is difficult to cultivate compassion for others. Continuing with your breathing, slowly repeat all or any of the following phrases to yourself multiple times: 'May I know safety, may I be happy, may I find peace, may I know ease and well-being, may I be free from suffering.'

▶ As you repeat the phrases, settle into the intention of goodwill they convey. Connect your breath to the positive intentions you are directing toward yourself. Smile if you wish to.

▶ Sense in the body any residing ease and breathe into this.

▶ Don't worry if it is difficult; the setting of intention will bear fruits with time and patience.

▶ Now bring to mind a person who has cared deeply for you, such as a mentor or close colleague or friend. Focusing on that person and, continuing with your breathing, slowly repeat the following phrases (or whatever ones work for you) multiple times, settling into the positive intentions you are directing to this person: 'May you be safe from harm and danger, may you be well and happy, may you experience health and strength, may your heart know release.'

▶ Next, repeat the same above phrases and positive intentions while focusing on a person with whom you are acquainted at work, but don't know well.

▶ Finally, focus on a person with whom you have difficulty. Notice what sorts of thoughts and emotions arise. If they are negative, it may help to repeat a few phrases such as the following:

'You have hopes and dreams, just like me.'

'You have anxieties and fears, just like me.'

'You have known suffering, just like me.'

'You wish to be happy, just like me.'

'You wish for forgiveness, just like me.'

▶ Then, continuing with awareness of your breathing and focusing on the person, repeat these phrases several times: 'May you be safe, may you be happy, may you be healthy, may you be free from suffering.'

▶ If this is too hard to do, that is OK. You can try changing the words to: 'I am inclining my mind towards wishing you well and will get there when I am truly able to.'

▶ You may like to expand the practice to include your team, colleagues and co-workers within your business, and then all others, like your customers and even competitors, as you wish.

▶ Conclude your meditation practice and continue with your day, carrying with you the intentions of goodwill for yourself and others.

With the intention set in these practices, we can gently free ourselves from our limited views and entrenched positions; we are able to remember our basic shared humanity. There is no need to especially 'like' someone or be their new BFF, but we can relate in a more equanimous manner which liberates us from our fixed position without denying our own emotional reality. As such, we are freed up to make caring (for ourselves and others) choices, to interact with effectiveness and to model to our team a truly beneficial way of relating to others.

Effective confrontation

Done well, confrontation can be experienced in a very positive way; it is a way for any team member or the team as a whole to say to another member, 'We want you in, we value and need your contribution.' Without productive and effective confrontation, disruptive behaviour can fester and erode any established sense of trust within a team. So when someone is continuously arriving late for team meetings or leaving earlier than anyone else (assuming that's not the boss and you want to keep your job!), you might like to use the following as a guide for effective confrontation.

The second technique for conflict that we would like to impart, which also works equally well whenever we hope to maximise the chances of an effective outcome in any communication, is adapted from Dialectal Behavioural Therapy (thankfully usually shortened to DBT). This is a complex therapy designed specifically for people who often really struggle to interact well with others. The techniques, which all use mindfulness, require us to first discern the intensity with which we wish to pursue a line of communication, from understanding whether we decide we want to change a situation or whether we work on accepting it as it is. It is sometimes very helpful to clarify our actual position regarding an interaction, to ensure that we aren't just habitually avoiding conflict or entering unnecessarily into the fray.

Exercise 5.6: Work in progress

Clarifying the intensity of communication

Ask yourself the following to establish the intensity you need and then the appropriate level of persistence required for that interaction:

High intensity:

▶ Do I have a clear desire for change?

▶ Is there a high level of urgency to the situation?

▶ Is there an identifiable 'need' for change?

If you have two or more 'yeses' then you can establish that you need to:

1 **Be clear** (use precise language, state goals and objectives succinctly)

2 **Be persistent** (repeat yourself, keep making your views known)

3 **Be firm** (don't take no for an answer, stand your ground)

If you have one or no 'yeses', try dropping down a level.

Medium intensity:

▶ Does the situation need further clarification?

▶ Am I open to alternatives?

▶ Am I experiencing any ambivalence or uncertainty?

If you have two or more 'yeses' then you can try to:

1 **Be open** (keep an open mind and seek clarification about goals)

2 **Be questioning** (explore alternatives, ask questions to generate possibilities)

3 **Be tentative** (be prepared to compromise, back down or change your mind)

If you have one or no 'yeses' consider the level of intensity either above or below.

Low intensity:

▶ Am I content to accept the situation as it is?

▶ Do my needs and desires align with the interaction as it is?

▶ Am I willing to acquiesce, comply and/or consent?

If you have two or more 'yeses' then try to:

1 **Be accepting** (be present and mindful of the communication just as it is)

2 **Be temperate** (be fair, moderate and balanced)

3 **Be accommodating** (stay cooperative, tolerant and willing; do what is asked)

If you have one or no 'yeses' move up a level.

Once we discern which level of communication best serves us at this time, we can then enhance interpersonal effectiveness further by prioritising which of three different scenarios best meets our priorities in the interaction (we'll work through these in the following exercise):

1 **Objectives effectiveness** (ways of maximising the chances of getting what you want)

2 **Relationship effectiveness** (ways of maximising the chances of keeping the relationship)

3 **Self-respect effectiveness** (ways of maximising the chances of keeping respect for yourself)

Exercise 5.7: Work in progress

Which effect to perfect?

1. Objectives effectiveness: I want that one ... and that one ... not that one

In her therapeutic skills manual, Marsha Linehan uses the acronym DEAR MAN for this particular set of techniques. Consider a work situation where you want specific results from a person or your team, then use the following steps:

Describe the situation using facts.

Express your feelings and opinions using phrases such as 'I want ... ' or 'I don't want.'

Assert yourself by asking for what you want or saying 'no' clearly (refer to the intensity scale if necessary).

Reinforce your position by explaining the positive consequences.

(Stay) **M**indful, focus on your objectives, repeat your opinions, keep your intentions clear by mindfully detaching from reactivity.

Appear confident, use an assertive tone of voice and posture, and keep good eye contact.

Negotiate by offering alternatives and solutions; you could ask them, 'How can we solve this problem?'

2. Relationship effectiveness: I want you, you, you

When you decide that the quality or intactness of your relationship is paramount, there is another handy acronym, this time GIVE. Now consider an interaction with another person or your team and how you would like them to feel about you after that interaction (remember, you cannot control the outcome but these skills will help you maximise the potential to get the results you want). Try these steps:

(Be) **G**entle, be courteous, kind and polite. Leave aside the threats, the judgements and the attacks. Make your speech kind.

(Act) **I**nterested by listening well, with patience and good attention.

Validate and acknowledge the other person's viewpoint using phrases like 'I understand', 'I realise this is hard for you', 'Thank you for clarifying that' (without sarcasm if you want to keep things chirpy).

(Use an) **E**asy manner and smile. Soften your hard shell with a little light-heartedness and diplomacy.

3. Self-respect effectiveness: R.E.S.P.E.C.T – find out what that means to me (yeah)

And you could always benefit from this set of skills. Try weaving this in with the others, because even if you don't get what you want and you have a shouting match with the boss, you are the only one who is going to have to put up with yourself for the rest of your life – so treat you well.

The acronym this time (Marsha L really loves them) is FAST. Bring to mind how you want to feel about yourself following the interaction and then follow these steps:

(Be) **F**air, be balanced in your communication and treat yourself and the other person with fairness and even-handedness.

(No) **A**pologies. You do not need to apologise for any of the following, ever: having an opinion, making a request, disagreeing or being alive.

Stick to your values (we will come back to how we might begin to clarify our values in the next chapter). Be clear about what matters most to you and how you want to be as a person, colleague, employer, employee, etc. Keep your morals, ethics and integrity in mind and act in alignment with all this.

(Be) **T**ruthful. Drop the excuses, lies, helplessness and exaggerations. Firstly, you will be more likely to be heard without the drama. Secondly, if you use these things you undermine and disempower yourself in the long run.

Mindfulness within and between teams

Mindfulness practice, as we have seen, increases our awareness of thoughts and emotions and our ability to regulate them, often referred to as *'emotional intelligence'*; this can lead to a greater level of personal effectiveness and performance in our work (which we will discuss again and in further detail in Chapter 6). Research into 'group emotional intelligence', conducted by Vanessa Druskat and Steven Wolff (please see a link to an article about their work listed in the 'Useful resources' section at the end of this chapter) has found that beneficial team skills such as collaboration, cooperation and shared group objectives are more likely to emerge when there are three basic conditions in place within a team; these basic conditions are:

▶ mutual trust among team members;
▶ a sense of group identity;
▶ a sense of group efficacy.

Without these fundamental conditions in place, team members are likely to only go through the motions of participating, cooperating and committing, and as a result the team may not be as effective as it could be. In order to fully engage and give their all, each team member needs to experience the sense of trust, identity and efficacy that exists within the group as a whole. This is more likely to occur when a team makes efforts to practise mindfulness such as the mindfulness-based exercises for effective interaction presented in this chapter. With these ways of interacting, a team can build its capacity to respond constructively in stressful and emotionally charged situations, resulting in a fuller engagement in tasks and greater team effectiveness. For sustained effectiveness, a team needs to remain mindful of the emotions of its group members and the team as a whole, as well as others it may be interacting with outside of the group.

Mindful of team members

A team's ability to regulate the emotions of its members is crucial for its overall effectiveness. As we highlighted earlier on, the most constructive way to do this is by establishing ways for dealing with confrontation, as well as with distressed individuals in the team. Although it may sound counterproductive to engage in confrontation, when it is done well, confrontation can be very positive and really help to boost a team's sense of trust and efficacy. Most team members will inevitably engage in behaviour that falls out of line from time to time, and a team that feels comfortable to pull a member up on that behaviour is more likely to address emotional issues promptly and nip them in the bud before they fester and escalate and then become detrimental to the team's overall performance. Even in the absence of any obvious moody or challenging team members, it would be wise in any team meeting to check in and ask each other questions in a genuine and curious way, such as, 'Has anyone got any other opinions that we have not yet heard or considered fully?' Equally, caring for team members who may be upset may make all the difference to team cohesion and effectiveness. Offering one another support via mindful communication including validation and compassion (as outlined in the exercises in this chapter) is likely to strengthen a team culture of positive regard, respect and appreciation, giving rise to a greater sense of trust, identity and efficacy which soon translates into greater efforts and commitment to common goals.

Mindful of the group

It is important for any team to be aware of its overall group emotions and also to feel skilled in regulating these emotions. For example, negative feedback from clients, management or other teams can really deplete team morale and lead to the team losing sight of all its good qualities and hard work. This in turn can negatively affect team confidence and therefore the team's effectiveness. Similarly, group emotions can run high at times of change, redundancy and restructuring, and also in the face of 'bad news' generally. It can be helpful to set time aside to check in with one another at regular intervals and/or foster an environment where it is OK for any team member to bring attention to the rest of the team if they notice that the group mood is low, fearful or irritable. Any conscious effort to build team spirits, such as team-building events or away days can help to increase the team's emotional capacity and its ability to respond to the inevitable emotional challenges it faces. Actively seeking feedback from other teams or customers can also increase group awareness of its emotions, and scheduling problem-solving sessions as well as reframing negative feedback and cultivating a 'can do' group attitude within the team can also help regulate the team's collective emotional state.

Mindful of others outside the team

Successful groups should also be mindful of others' emotions and regularly and consistently look outwardly towards other individuals and teams or organisations. Developing other standard practices that increase team awareness of the broader organisational context can be very helpful in enhancing its effectiveness. Looking outside of the group is especially important in situations where a team's work will have significant impact on others in the organisation. For example, an HR or IT team serving others' needs would do well to become aware and listen to the perspectives, emotions, priorities and needs of other groups in the company which it may be offering services to. Certain team members can take the role of 'go-between' with other teams to gain greater insight and awareness rather than blissfully ignoring others' needs and becoming lost in blinkered perspectives. With this awareness, the team can increase its chances of success by then using its skills to offer tailored services that directly respond to the needs of other teams to help regulate the emotions in these other teams and win their positive appraisal.

Mindfulness and team work

In summary, to develop a more mindful and therefore effective team, team members will need to be willing to talk openly about their emotions and have an understanding about how emotions affect the team's work. The team needs to take proactive steps to increase its awareness and regulation of emotions in the service of strengthening its relationships both inside and outside of the group. In developing mindful attitudes (i.e. openness, acceptance, curiosity, compassion) and bringing mindfulness to their interactive behaviours (i.e. active listening, validation, effective confrontation, feedback and delegation processes), as described in this chapter, a team can increase its chances of becoming the most effective it can be. A mindful team will become a deeply human team by nature.

Unfortunately, for many teams it can remain difficult to implement the mindful attitudes and interactive behaviours described in this chapter. This is because many company cultures still do not seem to welcome employees' emotions and instead encourage emotions to be checked in at the front door, before the work day begins. We are, however, witnessing a positive trend in the opposite direction. More and more teams are recognising the benefits of more mindful interactions to more effectively manage the thoughts and emotions that can impede group processes and the impact this has on team performance and overall effectiveness. More companies seem to be willing to make efforts to develop and establish these mindful ways of operating in a team into their company culture via leadership development training and more general communication and stress management workshops across all levels of staff. This is all very promising to see, as in our experience any team that lacks mindful attention in team interaction is likely to fail. A team's commitment to mindfulness practice is the key to its success.

As always, here are your salient take-away points from this chapter:

Mindfulness top tips to go

▶ Spend time each day, five minutes or so, practising mindfulness to reconnect with yourself and notice the inevitable connection you have with everyone and everything else around you too. This will help you to strengthen your sense of interconnectedness and the importance of recognising it for both you and your team to flourish. Invite colleagues to practise with you.

▶ Proactively seek out colleagues to practise mindfulness of your communication (mindful pauses, speech and listening). This way, you can ensure that you are doing your best to lay the foundations (less stressful environment, more trust and confidence) for effective communication and greater team performance. Let your colleagues know what you intend to do and invite them to do the same with you.

▶ Make a conscious effort to respond with more compassion when you feel frustrated (or worse) in response to a colleague's behaviour. Use the acronym WARM to help you to be compassionate in your response, and ensure you are doing your best to preserve the relationship and the confidence in your teammate, along with the overall team dynamics and efficacy.

▶

▶ Next time you see or even hear of a teammate in distress, make a proactive effort to approach them. Remember you are not there to solve their problems. Use mindfulness to listen, validate and respond compassionately. Simply being there with them, alongside them and their upset in this way (rather than shying away or trying to problem-solve their situation) demonstrates that you care and understand their distress, which will help to build trust and strengthen team bonds (remember that others witnessing you doing this will also likely increase positive regard for you among other team members). Rather than simply reacting to your colleagues' distress, create a culture of supportive conversations and get managers on board with this.

▶ If you are feeling high emotions such as anger or anxiety in relation to a colleague, use mindfulness practice for ten minutes or so, and certainly before you engage with that colleague in conversation, to help increase self-awareness and to regulate your strong emotions and any associated knee-jerk reactions. This way you can ensure you are better prepared to not let your emotional reactivity damage relationships with your team members.

▶ If you tend to shy away or want to avoid feedback and appraisals of your work, try to understand what your 'avoidant' behaviour is really about. Are you scared of losing your job, maybe? Practise mindfulness to help manage your fears and any unhelpful thoughts you might have about the feedback you have been given. Use the feedback constructively and take proactive steps to implement it so you can improve your performance as well as the overall effectiveness of your team. Remember, feedback is a necessary component of collaborative team endeavours.

▶ Seek out opportunities to proactively delegate work to your colleagues. Understand the fears that get in the way of delegating. When delegating, notice any tendency to micromanage and use mindfulness to help facilitate productive handing-over and motivating feedback processes. Effective delegation can foster trust, a shared purpose, identity and confidence within a team. It can give rise to greater team creativity, productivity and improved performance and profitability.

▶ When you experience conflict with a team member, address it through mindfulness practices, otherwise it can fester and go on to erode team dynamics and the functionality and efficacy of the team. Use the 'loving kindness' practice to foster greater feelings of compassion towards a ▶

teammate that you feel aggrieved by. This will help to untangle yourself from the unhelpful thoughts and behaviours that will simply aggravate the conflict. Then increase your interpersonal effectiveness by boldly approaching them with considered mindful communication, which will strengthen team dynamics. Although it may seem counterproductive, remember that when confrontation is done well (in this mindful way!), it can actually boost trust within a team, as people feel cared for and needed, and it can enhance the team's overall shared sense of efficacy.

So that wraps up this chapter. We hope that in reading it, you have been able to consider the practical ways that you might be able to increase your team's productivity and overall effectiveness via careful attention to mindful interactions and communication. Whether you invite other team members to consider joining you in implementing these mindful approaches or you simply begin to implement them yourself, you can be certain that you are offering your team some of the most helpful strategies to maximise its chances of being a great success. Next, we are going to turn your attention to how mindfulness can help us to manage work-related stress and also buffer against burnout and exhaustion so that whatever may come around, you can know that you are doing your very best to maintain your peak performance while on the job.

Useful resources

▶ Caan, James (2015, September 15). *James Caan: It's about time we close the soft skills gap* [article from hrmagazine.co.uk]. Retrieved from: http://www.hrmagazine.co.uk/hro/features/1153726/james-caan-it-s-about-time-we-close-the-soft-skills-gap#sthash.qACKmxM2.dpuf

▶ Davey, L. (2015, September 10). *Helping a coworker who's stressed out* [*Harvard Business Review* article]. Retrieved from: https://hbr.org/2015/09/helping-a-coworker-whos-stressed-out

▶ Druskat, V. U. and Wolff, S. B. (2001, March). *Building the emotional intelligence of groups* [*Harvard Business Review* article]. Retrieved from: https://hbr.org/2001/03/building-the-emotional-intelligence-of-groups

▶ Ford, B. and Kornfield, J. [shamash753]. (2013, February 24). *Wisdom 2 Bill Ford, Jack Kornfield* [video file]. Retrieved from: https://www.youtube.com/watch?v=9W0Wy8-06t4

▶ Goleman, D. and George, B. [MoreThanSoundnet]. (2015, March 26). *How to give feedback* [video file]. Retrieved from: https://www.youtube.com/watch?v=5YtLDVVGjEs

▶ Jackman, J. M. and Strober, M. (2003, April). *Fear of feedback* [*Harvard Business Review* article]. Retrieved from: https://hbr.org/2003/04/fear-of-feedback

▶ Porath, C. and Pearson, C. (2013, January). *The price of incivility* [*Harvard Business Review* article]. Retrieved from: https://hbr.org/2013/01/the-price-of-incivility/

▶ Suttie, J. (2015, February 16). *How to increase compassion at work: A new program tries to help business leaders to identify and alleviate suffering in the workplace* [article from http://greatergood.berkeley.edu/]. Retrieved from: http://greatergood.berkeley.edu/article/item/how_to_increase_compassion_at_work

▶ The Telegraph (2009, March 31). *Men Spend More Time Gossiping than Women, Poll Finds.* Retrieved from: http://www.telegraph.co.uk/news/uknews/5082866/Men-spend-more-time-gossiping-than-women-poll-finds.html

▶ Valcour, M. (2015, April 27). *A 10-minute meditation to help you solve conflicts at work* [*Harvard Business Review* article]. Retrieved from: https://hbr.org/2015/04/a-10-minute-meditation-to-help-you-solve-conflicts-at-work

6

Maintain peak
performance

'It's important to train your mind like you train your biceps in the gym.'

David Creswell PhD, Associate Professor, Director of Health and Human Performance, Carnegie Mellon University

In this next chapter we are going to take a look at a mindful approach to sustained well-being at work. We will consider how stress is impacting our working environment, the consequences of this and how mindfulness can not only help relieve stress in the short term, but also then translate into long-term benefits for optimum performance for you and your business.

Year on year, businesses continue to incur significant financial costs due to workplace stress and high rates of employee burnout. According to the Health and Safety Executive the total number of working days lost in the UK due to work-related stress, depression or anxiety was 9.9 million in 2014/15, which amounts to an average of 23 days per case of stress, depression or anxiety. And it's not just absenteeism that costs: a lack of productivity while workers continue on the job despite feeling unwell (i.e. presenteeism) also does. Employers are now recognising the exceptional benefits that mindfulness can bring in reducing health-care expenses as well as increasing the productivity and sustainability of their workforce in the face of inevitable daily workplace stress.

Therefore, in the following chapter you will develop:

▶ Insight into the modern-day stressors that we all have to contend with while on the job.

▶ Understanding of how our own behaviour plays a major part in creating our stress.

▶ Tools to help you manage daily stress.

▶ Strategies to ensure that you remain resilient in the face of inevitable future stress.

▶ Techniques to maintain your peak performance while at work.

▶ The foundations to enhance your sense of fulfilment and satisfaction at work so that you can increase your endurance and reduce your chances of burnout.

Getting the balance right

You will already appreciate the importance of assessing and maintaining efficacy and well-being in the workplace if you are working in business, especially at managerial or leadership levels. The constant balancing of our own and our employees' needs with company productivity is a fine art, much of which is learned through bitter experience rather than nec-essarily any coherent and useful training. This job skill has increased in challenge as the demands of modern fast-paced technologies, global communications and employee welfare policies have also exponentially increased and developed. Unfortunately, while businesses have expanded in these ways, many have been through tough economic periods, experi-encing challenging mergers and restructuring with the inevitable redun-dancies and cutbacks, adding even more pressure. This chapter will help you to learn some invaluable skills in dealing with these challenges, with-out the usual futile attempts to temporarily deny the reality of your work-ing life, without you having to make any extra demands on your time or requiring any major re-hauls in the office, and without you having to leave the country on an 'escape to the wild' to live amongst yetis and mountain goats just to try to eradicate the trauma. Help is at hand. You can have your cake and eat it; with mindfulness, you get to maintain peak performance *and* enjoy well-being while on the job.

Here's a quick exercise to help you settle into this chapter. You may choose to incorporate this short, simple, yet effective, practice into your morning routine (rather than starting your day by habitually running through your usual morning routine, checking your phone, etc., why not take a few moments to 'just be' instead?). Equally you might like to use this at any point throughout the day when stress feels high, or simply to refocus your attention on the task and/or day in front of you.

Exercise 6.1: Mindful on the job

Take a moment (or two)

1 Sit, stand – either is fine.
2 If sitting, rest your hands on your lap and notice the sensation of where your hands and lap meet. If standing, notice the sensation of your feet against the floor.
3 Take a breath in; feel the lungs fill with air.
4 As you allow the lungs to naturally empty on the out-breath, also sense the tension flow out of your shoulders.
5 Repeat steps 3 and 4 as many times as you like.
6 Now, with a new sense of calm, composure and clarity of mind, you can get back to work.

Downtime from stress is really what this chapter is all about; the benefits are enormous, and if they aren't immediately obvious then here is a quick summary of a few supportive research studies about the impact of stress (mental, physical and emotional) on well-being and performance at work and how mindfulness can help.

Proven in science, smart for business

Mindfulness eases aches and pains

Do you ever feel your stress in your body? Maybe you struggle with back, neck or other bodily tension, aches and pains? Well, if so, help is at hand. According to a 2011 study[1], just 80 minutes of mindful meditation can cut pain perception nearly in half. This study is backed up by another piece of research[2] conducted at the University of Montreal which found that a group of 13 Zen meditators (all of whom had at least 1,000 hours of practice behind them) had a significantly higher pain threshold compared to a group of non-meditators. The results of this study are really quite extraordinary and demonstrate how regular mindfulness practice can significantly lower the severity of our pain experience.

Mindfulness helps to get a good night's slee ... Zzzzzzz

Ever lie in bed wanting and wishing you could just fall asleep? Whether this happens for you regularly or just now and again, most of us can relate to this very frustrating scenario, and how our worry about not falling asleep just seems to get in the way. We all assume that having a good night's sleep can help buffer against stress, and without a fatigue-fuelled mental fog the next day at work we're better able to concentrate and perform at our best, right? The good news is that mindfulness can help to improve our sleep (including the worry about not sleeping). Recently, researchers[3] at the University of South California and UCLA recruited 49 older men and women to investigate the effectiveness of mindfulness to help with sleep disturbance. The participants were randomly allocated to either a standard sleep hygiene education program (weekly classes on education about sleep problems, stress reduction and relaxation techniques) or a mindfulness practice programme (involving two hours of practice each week). Following six weeks, those that participated in the mindfulness group showed significant improvements in their overall sleep quality, compared to the sleep hygiene group, showing reductions in their insomnia symptoms, as well as in symptoms of depression and daytime fatigue. The researchers propose that '*through mindfulness practice, people learn how to observe thoughts without having to*

➤

elaborate. It allows people to be present without further interpretation of their symptoms.'

Mindfulness makes us smarter and improves decision-making

In a study[4] published in the journal *Frontiers in Human Neuroscience,* researchers at UCLA found that participants who were experienced in mindfulness practice had larger amounts of gyrification, or folding of the brain's cortex, than people who didn't practise mindfulness. These extra folds in the brain help mindfulness meditators to process information faster than others while also reducing their tendency to ruminate on past events (a common feature of stress), which can distort our thinking and decision-making process. Even just one 15-minute focused mindfulness breathing practice can get you out of your head, remove the bias from your brain and help you think with more clarity.

Mindfulness-based training reduces burnout, particularly for distressed workers

Even when your stress levels skyrocket and it feels as if there is no returning to earth, mindfulness can help you to regain a sense of calm composure. In another piece of research[5], 311 local government employees were randomly assigned to either a mindfulness-based stress-management training group based on Acceptance and Commitment Therapy or to a wait-list control group. Those employees allocated to the experimental group underwent three half-day training sessions which involved the development of a mixture of mindfulness and values-based action skills. After a six-month assessment period, the intervention resulted in a significant reduction in employee distress, particularly for those employees with significant levels of distress at baseline. This study demonstrates how mindfulness-based stress-management training can help workers who are experiencing a high level of distress, which, if left unchecked, would likely to lead to burnout.

Online mindfulness training enhances employee resilience, energy and well-being

Do you ever feel drained, flat and as limp as a wet lettuce leaf? Well, the good news is that even a course of online mindfulness training could help you replenish your energy reserves and get you back on your feet, bouncing around the office again. In a study[6], 80 employees at a major chemical company were randomly assigned to either an online mindfulness program or a wait-list control group. In a six-month follow-up all 80 participants were administered the same measures for stress, mindfulness, resiliency and vigour that they had completed ➤

at baseline. The results showed that the experimental (mindfulness) group were significantly less stressed, more resilient and more energetic than the wait-list control group. The researchers conclude that '*this online mindfulness intervention seems to be both practical and effective in enhancing overall employee well-being*'.

Mindfulness-based apps can reduce stress in the workplace

Ever feel that your smartphone is a great source of stress? Well, it would seem that when we use our apps to practise mindfulness our phones can actually help us to de-stress while on the job. In another study[7], a total of 73 corporate middle managers working in medium- and large-sized companies across Sweden were randomised either to receive a six-week smartphone-administered stress intervention (ACT-based smartphone app) or to a wait-list control group. The results showed that those managers from the experimental group experienced a significant reduction in their perceived level of stress as well as a significant increase in their general health compared to the wait-list control group of managers. This study shows that although our smartphones and general advancements in technology can be a great source of anxiety (which we will come back to again later on), for many of us they can also serve us well when we use them wisely to manage stress levels on the job.

So with all the amazing research to back up the efficacy of using mindfulness at work to reduce our stress and enhance our resilience, let's now take a closer look at what we are up against (stress-wise) and just how we can implement mindfulness to maintain our peak performance, while on the job.

Running on empty

We're sure you would agree that the way we work has changed dramatically over the last few decades. Long gone are the days when there was a very clear dividing line between our working and personal lives – and when we were in either one of these contexts it used to be so much easier to focus on one thing at one time. These days we have an endless collection of mobile devices at the ready – one in each pocket and bag and others strapped firmly to any body part that can accommodate one – yes, wearable tech is all the rage these days, have you not heard? Now, don't get us wrong for one second; these advancements in technology are amazing, really quite extraordinary, actually, and very useful; we're just as sold on the next iPhone upgrade as the next person and we're also guilty of yelping like an excitable puppy, salivating in anticipation of the forthcoming release date for the latest strap-on technical device – yay! This technology allows us to order our shopping online while stuck in a traffic jam, and respond to work emails while we're sunning ourselves somewhere on a faraway tropical beach; now what could be better than that? Nothing (right?). Well, as you will recall from Chapter 2 there is in fact a large cost to all this. The pay-off is that while we're logged on, switched on and waiting for the next one of our limbs, bags or pockets to vibrate, we may find ourselves in a perpetual state of distraction, never really present, and our ability to sustain focus and remain productive on the job declines rapidly. But along with all this, as we are in a constant state of high alert, primed ready to respond to the next compelling ring, bleep, buzz or flashing red light, it would seem that we have actually created a great paradox in these modern times – the more we invent these smarter and faster ways of getting things done, the more it seems that we are actually caging ourselves in increasing levels of stress, using up more and more of our energy reserves, tiring ourselves out physically and mentally and ultimately risking psychological exhaustion and complete burnout.

Exercise 6.2: Work in progress

Feelin' the burn?

See how many 'yesses' you answer to the following ten sets of questions:

1 **Exhaustion:** Do you feel (emotionally, mentally or physically) tired all or most of the time? Do you lack energy after work to do stuff in the evening like cook, go to the gym or socialise? Do you find it difficult to fall asleep or stay asleep?

2 **Motivation:** Have you lost enthusiasm for your job, sometimes finding it hard to even get out of bed in the morning? Maybe you hit the snooze button over and over again, then frantically jump out of bed to avoid being late? Do you suffer the 'Sunday blues', dreading Monday mornings and the week ahead?

3 **Negative emotions:** Are you regularly struggling with feelings of: Impatience? Intolerance? Depression? Anxiety? Cynicism?

Pessimism? Frustration? Disillusionment? Have colleagues noticed this in you? Do you constantly feel overwhelmed, even by seemingly small stressors at work?

4 **Cognitive function:** Do you find it hard to concentrate and stay focused at work? Is it difficult to remember stuff? Do you find it difficult to write emails and/or articulate yourself generally?

5 **Performance:** Has your work performance declined over the past year? Is it difficult to remember the last time you felt satisfied or a sense of accomplishment at work? Do you often feel stuck or like you are not progressing?

6 **Relationships:** Are you often either in conflict with colleagues or feeling increasingly isolated and withdrawn? Do you avoid lunch events, after-work drinks or other work-related networking events? Have you stopped caring about others at work? Do you disregard how you interact and treat your colleagues, clients or customers?

7 **Self-care:** Are you neglecting your self-care by doing any or all of the following: Drinking excessively? Over/under-using medications? Not getting enough sleep? Eating too much/little? Spending all your time indoors? Neglecting personal grooming (laundered clothes, washing, hair care, etc.)? Becoming more sedentary? Using stimulants to get through the working day (nicotine, street drugs, caffeine, so-called 'smart drugs', etc.)?

8 **Work – life balance:** Are you spending increasing amounts of time at work and/or thinking about work to the deficit of your hobbies/relationships/leisure time? Are you constantly bringing work home and/or complaining about work to your partner, family and/or friends?

9 **Satisfaction:** Do you feel a lack of contentment with your life both in and outside of work? Do you ever fantasise about escaping or quitting work altogether?

10 **Physical health:** Have you noticed an onset or worsening of: Digestive problems? Skin rashes? Excessive sweating? Weight issues? Raised blood pressure? Lowered immune function? Heart problems and/or palpitations? Physical aches and pains? Sexual dysfunction?

If you have found yourself answering 'yes' to anything more than 1 (yes, that's 1!) of these questions, then you are probably already feeling the strain and experiencing some degree of impairment to your well-being and level of functioning at work, and it is likely that you are feeling pretty burnt out (or soon will be). Before you head for the nearest bridge (to admire the view, obviously), you may want to try some more of the exercises listed in this chapter and repeat them as often as you can, starting with this.

Exercise 6.3: Mindful on the job 🎧

Phew!

In times of stress, when breathing is less variable, a sigh can reset the respiratory system and help loosen the lungs, easing tension in the whole nervous system, which may be accompanied by a sensation of relief: this is according to research from Belgium[8]. So look at the list above and all your 'yes' answers. Then:

1 Take a moment to see where tension resides in your body right now – maybe your jaw is clenched, your leg is twitching or you have a tightness across your chest or shoulders.

2 Simply and silently if you wish, repeat to yourself: 'I am noticing tension in the jaw', 'I feel my leg twitching', or label whatever tension you do notice in your body right now.

3 Let yourself experience this perfectly understandable habitual response to stress, and your body's way of holding this physically.

4 You might now notice thoughts such as 'I haven't got time for this', 'I am overwhelmed', 'I have to get on', or whatever other thoughts your mind might be giving you right now.

5 If you notice any thoughts at all just let the thoughts come up, no need to add to them, dramatise them or push them away; just see them popping up and notice this.

6 Try repeating the following few words: 'I am noticing the thought that ...' before any thought/s that might be showing up. For example you might repeat: 'I am noticing the thought that "I haven't got time for this"' or 'I am noticing the thought that "I am overwhelmed"', or 'I am noticing the thought that "I've got to get on"' or whatever your thought/s may be.

7 See these as 'just thoughts' and recognise them also as a perfectly understandable, habitual response to stress, which you are mentally trying to manage right now.

8 Now allow the thoughts to recede from your attention and take a nice lungful of air; as you breathe out just gently say 'phew', or sigh slightly, allowing yourself the possibility of dropping a couple of inches off of the ceiling. Repeat this a few times.

9 You may notice emotions arising, or thoughts and sensations in the body, or you may become distracted from time to time. Don't worry about that; just come back to being present when you remember to, and use the breath as an anchor to this moment.

10 Allow your breathing to flow naturally for a few more in-breaths and out-breaths; you may like to close your eyes to bring your attention inwards, allowing yourself to be connected to the present moment.

Shooting yourself in the foot

The ability to soften and soothe the stress we are under daily is so often overlooked and/or traded for the time we imagine it might take. We somehow, counter-intuitively, insist that if we just do this, that and the other first, then we'll take a break. We simply do not seem to value our well-being until we crack and then, more often than not, there's no time to do this either, so we head to the GP for a quick fix and feel further frustration if this is not good enough, quick enough or enduring enough. In essence, we very quickly mirror the environment around us mentally. Our internal expectations align themselves with what our culture seems to demand and almost imperceptibly our sense of self is eroded; we feel lost and directionless and so strive even harder (using another quick fix) to 'get better'. It's so exhausting, and so utterly compelling to keep going. The striving to maintain our 'peak performance' then becomes the very thing which undermines it. Take Laura's case, for example.

Laura

Laura worked as a Managing Director for a large investment bank. She had been working long hours (often getting home from work around 11pm and returning to the office the next morning at 6am) consecutively, over many months. She also travelled frequently for her job, feeling the need to attend meetings in Europe (on a weekly basis) and Asia at least once a month, often catching the red-eye flight back into London to start work that same morning. It's no great surprise that this gruelling routine had started to take its toll on Laura's health. She had felt tired for some time but kept pushing through, ignoring her fatigue, and she came to rely on 'smart drugs' to keep her more alert and energised (as she described, anyway). This all seemed to 'work' for a while, until one day when walking into work she felt totally wiped out. She noticed tight cramps in her stomach and a rash down the right side of her torso. Over the next few days her energy level depleted rapidly; she found it increasingly ▶

---

difficult to concentrate (those drugs weren't working anymore and seemed to be making it more difficult for her to fall asleep at night) and began to worry about what all this would mean for her career. Despite feeling exhausted, her worry also kept her awake at night and got in the way of her much needed rest. Laura took herself off to the doctor, who signed her off from work, and what followed was a protracted period of medical investigation to understand what was wrong with her. She visited specialist after specialist, underwent test after test and became increasingly frustrated with the absence of any conclusive diagnosis. She was determined to get well and get back to work as quickly as possible; she feared others seeing her weakness, that she was not coping and ultimately losing her job. She felt that doctors could not understand what she was going through or how to help her. In losing faith in the whole medical profession, she turned to alternative remedies and began a course of Chinese herbal medicine which seemed to help a little with her tiredness for a day or two, but her stomach cramps and rash flared up aggressively as a result. She was determined to find out what was wrong with her once and for all so that she could eradicate these symptoms as fast as she could and return to her former self. She searched the internet day after day, looking for an answer and a cure which, again, just left her feeling exhausted and increasingly frustrated. Laura was at her wits' end and became increasingly anxious and depressed. Laura's behaviour was totally understandable but it certainly wasn't working for her. After coming for some mindfulness sessions, she soon realised that she needed to slow down a little, give up the struggle with her unwanted experiences and limitations, and instead begin to accept that this was 'just how things were right now'.

Mindfulness gives us a golden opportunity to see into the fallacy of these tyrannical compulsions, to recognise that they do not ease us, soothe us or bring lasting relief. In fact, the very insight into recognising that we are deluded if we think that constant pushing and striving will bring us peace and well-being, brings a relief that brings (at least a little) peace and well-being! So even the very act of seeing into the nature of 'how things are right now' can help us relieve stress and maintain our peak performance. It seems ironical and contradictory, but with just a sigh, we experience the truth of it.

This does take effort in a world increasingly filled with wondrous, rapid technologies full of tempting promises. Recognising that we can skil-fully weave peace into our modern lives alongside modernity helps us also not to crave and idealise a radically alternative world (the 'monk on the mountain-top', for instance) which is not our daily reality, and can just serve to further our sense of dissatisfaction. In essence we can instead embrace the contradictions that life presents and face these with equanimity, seeing life 'just as it is'. This does not imply that we might not skilfully discriminate, discern and take action when a situation is causing us harm, and maybe head off to that mountain-top (or to the doctor), but neither do we have to demonise our modern, hectic life. This skilful discernment is a tool which can be developed with mindfulness, when we come to rest in the reality of our present experience and not reactively try to zap it away.

For most of us it is common to act impulsively in the face of stress, and these actions are often the cause of greater distress for ourselves, whether that might be lying in bed worrying about not falling asleep or taking all kinds of medicines (licensed or not!) in the hope of staying awake and feeling more energised on the job. In a series of two large-scale studies[9] mindfulness was shown to strengthen the ability to refrain from unhelpful impulsive behaviour even in the presence of negative emotions and high levels of stress. So with that in mind, why not try the following exercise to ensure that when you are stressed out you don't continue to react in a way that just makes matters worse for yourself.

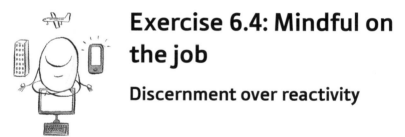

Exercise 6.4: Mindful on the job

Discernment over reactivity

For the following exercise we are going to offer a way of honing your skills of helpful discrimination. This will be useful in a multitude of ways and encourage the ability to tame the reactive, habitual mind. Pick a situation where there is a sense of urgency, but nothing to which a delayed response will cause harm. So, for instance, a time when you are hungry, thirsty or in mild physical discomfort would do well or, alternatively, when you are walking in a rush, speaking rapidly or waiting for something.

1 First notice your body. Scan for discomfort. Find whatever is alive in your body right now.

2 When you notice tension, hunger, stiffness, strain or any other unpleasant sensations arising in the body, do nothing.

3 If possible, still the body to increase the focus on the discomfort and allow yourself to explore the sensations with intentional curiosity for a few moments.

4 Alongside the unpleasant sensations, you will probably notice some emotions arising, such as impatience, frustration, anxiety, etc.

5 This is, at least partially, the reality of your experience right now; stay with it.

6 Now closely regard the mind's reactions to these emotions and sensations which may take the form of 'I must move', 'This is unbearable', 'I hate this', 'I want this to go away'.

7 This kind of response is reactivity. Behaviours stemming from this are reactive. These are not bad or wrong, but without discernment they are often unconscious and habitual.

8 Noticing any reactive urges, now use discernment to ask yourself, 'What am I choosing to do with this experience?'

9 Your response could be, 'I am choosing to now drink a glass of water', 'Oh, I'm not really hungry after all, I'll put the biscuit tin away', 'I am going to wait patiently and, instead of fidgeting, be still', or anything else.

10 These responses are discerning and they are now considered and 'known'. The behaviours stemming from them are conscious choices.

With practice, the above techniques can be developed further still and we can start to inquire into the underlying motivation for our actions and see whether, when we are not reactive, we instead can find room for greater self-care, sensitivity or self-control which can reap beneficial rewards for our well-being and ability to perform well at work.

Technology race

Advancements in technology have made for very positive changes in the way we work, not to mention opened up new opportunities for 24-hour global communication. But again, there is a cost. Being present in the office doesn't mean just being 'physically' there in person anymore. We're expected to be at work 24/7, as long as our employer has been kind enough to provide us with our very own work email account and mobile smartphone and tablet. There seem to be increasing demands on our time and attention and general resources. Emails, emails, emails (and more emails) – ARGHHHH! Will they ever stop? Well, we don't think so, and we can't rely on the world changing to suit our internal state. And what about our capacity to deal with these increasing demands – will that suddenly and automatically just start to improve? Again, we don't think so. So we need something to help us with all this or we're just going to become more and more swamped!

No doubt just like ours, your working day can feel pretty overwhelming at times. Some days we feel like we're one email away from exploding! Sound familiar? We have come up with an acronym (just in case you are missing them after the last chapter!) that we feel accurately reflects our experience of most days on the job and we wonder whether you too can relate to any of the experiences of SWAMP?

Exercise 6.5: Work in progress

Struggling in the SWAMP

Consider the following to open the inquiry into your present experience; is it one of being swamped?

Stress: do you ever feel a bit on edge, anxious, irritable, a bit flat or down sometimes? Maybe you find that you are short and snappy with people? Aches, pain and tension in the body? What about a few sleepless nights here and there?

Wandering mind: does it ever feel difficult to stay focused on one task at a time? Maybe you find it difficult to concentrate with all these compelling mobile devices demanding your attention?

Always 'on': what about feeling as if you are always on the go, switched on, on the move, wired? Maybe you tend to arrive at destinations without any recollection of how you even got there?

Multitasking: (yes, our old friend from Chapter 2) how about doing more than one thing at the same time, juggling many tasks at once? Do you tend to gobble down your lunchtime sandwich while glaring at your computer screen? Talk to someone while checking your phone?

Pressure: what about feeling pressured to perform, to deliver, to be on time all around the clock? And maybe it's not just in work that you feel this pressure. Maybe after a gruelling week at the office, when all you want to do is dive under your duvet for the entire weekend, your inconsiderate friend decides to throw his birthday party and you are expected to show up, put a smile on and look enthused?!

Any of this sound familiar? Good, it's not just us then!

Why are we so 'SWAMP'ed?

If we were to ask you 'what is the opposite of black?', you'd probably say 'white', right? If we were to tap you on your shoulder, what would you do? Well, we hope turn around immediately to pay attention. We are creatures of habit and often these habits run on autopilot and impulse. If you had a work email ping onto your phone – what would you do? Well, if we know your boss, s/he'd probably say 'CHECK IT IMMEDIATELY', and no doubt you often do just that. We are SWAMPED, not because the world is speeding up but because our minds are speeding up, mirroring the world around us in a frenetic attempt to keep up with ourselves. We have this endless collection of mobile devices demanding our full time and attention all day every day, and, sure, these do influence and can trigger our swamped experience, but they have nothing to do with how swamped we are or for how long we feel swamped at any given time. We seem to have forgotten one crucial element in the making of our realities – our choices and our own *reactive* behaviour. The reason we are so swamped is much more to do with the choices we make in any given moment, the choices that influence our behaviour. It's our own behaviour that keeps us drowning in the swamp. We are swamped because of our impulsive reactions towards the swamp. Our relationship with the swamp and how we behave and interact with it is the real problem here. We struggle, don't accept help, fight and flounder about and then wonder why we are sinking deeper and deeper into a gooey, smelly, stinking quagmire.

Our anxiety and overstimulation from technology fuels our compulsion to open and check our inbox for emails, our phone for messages, LinkedIn for connections, Facebook for invites, Twitter for retweets, Instagram for likes, Tinder for rejects, and probably loads of other apps and websites and things that we're not cool enough to even know about (yet!). We feel compelled to check and respond to them all. As if once we have successfully attended to each and every one and ticked them off the to-do-list, we can then kick back and relax – ah bliss, no more swamp for me!

The problem is that this is an endless pursuit, as the emails, messages and posts keep coming in thick and fast most days (along with all the other stuff), and as soon as we've just ushered the last pesky email along to the trash can icon, the next fresh, compelling one arrives, exclaiming a big 'ah hah – where do you think you're going? Not so fast sucker!' Doh! The thing is, no matter how fast we work to escape the swamp we never will: it's bottomless and a real struggle to get out of – in this way, anyway. We end up exhausted, stressed, with physical aches and pains in trying to clamber out and away from all this mess, and often lose touch with all the things that really matter to us in the process of trying: like choosing a more meaningful or productive work endeavour that may even further our careers in a direction that we really want, or even hobbies, leisure pursuits, family, friends, relationships and 'me time' outside of work!

In our desire to escape the swamp, we have checked our mobile devices time and time again, and this behaviour has become so reinforced as a result that even in the absence of a new message alert grabbing our attention we still continue to habitually check the damn things! The research tells us that the average person checks their mobile device every 6–7 minutes. We were both shocked to read that too – surely that's a very generous estimate and most of us are probably guilty of checking our emails more frequently than that (or is that just us?). Once you can acknowledge that you have a problem with this checking – that perhaps it is getting out of hand, dragging you away from present-moment focus in your life, maybe affecting your relationships, energy levels, etc. and at risk of taking over completely – then you can begin to tackle it mindfully and effectively, and still get the job done. Turning the tables on this obsessive and invasive technology influx are now various apps, for example 'Checky', 'Quality Time' and 'Moment' which summarise your daily phone use, and there is also 'RescueTime' for the computer. These sorts of gadgets could be just the help you need to keep a check on your digitally charged behaviour to ensure you cap it within reasonable limits and prevent a complete meltdown.

As we have mentioned, our obsession with checking and responding to messages on our digital devices is often an anxiety-fuelled behaviour, designed to escape the swamp and all the nasty stuff that goes with that (read here: fear of missing out, unworthiness, failure, being unloved). But, as we know well by now, trying to erase these unwanted feelings is a futile exercise, as they are part of our working realities, and trying to obliterate them will only lead to more stress and pressure for you.

Pressure cooker

Trying to escape your stress by clambering helplessly out of the swamp is like trying to dig yourself out of a hole – it's just not going to happen. The only place you're going to get is deeper and more stressed, tired and exhausted. Still don't get what we mean? Well, try this quick exercise right now and hopefully you'll see where we're coming from.

Exercise 6.6: Work in progress

Resistance is futile

1 Hold your hand, palm facing, up against the wall (if you can't do that right now, then make sure your feet, soles facing down are flat on the floor).

2 Imagine that the wall (floor) represents all the emails, stress and swamped feelings that you want to get rid of, that you want out of your life now and forever!

3 Now, as you would tirelessly attend to email after email to escape the swamp, right now push against the wall with your hand (floor with your feet) to try to get rid of all those nasty feelings.

What happens? Does the wall (floor) go anywhere? How does your body feel? Stiff, tense, tired, achy, we suspect? Now, hold that position for a bit longer and tell us, if you were to stay like that all day, would you get much else done? No, we presume not. So there it is: the more we try to eradicate the stuff that just simply is not going to vanish (completely, forever, anyway), the more we stress ourselves out in the process. In doing so we build up stress and tension, like a pressure cooker, ready to blow! Oh, and you can stop pushing against the wall (floor) now, if you haven't already; we wouldn't want you to explode on us right now, not before you finish reading this book, anyway.

Home work

As we know, advancements in digital communication have led to dramatic changes in the way we work as well as our work environments. Although, historically, working from home (or the local Starbucks!) was mostly done by a student, or say by a mother with small children, it is increasingly common for all of us to be working away from the office these days. But some of us may find that 'working from home' is not always what it's cracked up to be. Sure, a bit of flexitime might lessen unnecessary travel or allow for a greater sense of efficiency throughout the day (to be there for the delivery any time between 6am and, oh, never), but the expectations can extend to it feeling normal to answer work calls and emails in our kitchen at lunchtime, in the bathroom in the evening, or to Skype first thing still half-dressed in pyjamas (you do that too, surely!).

If you work from home a lot, or even only occasionally, you may find that it's all too easy to blur the boundaries between work and home, and to get caught up in stuff that distracts you from getting on with any work that you'd plan to get done, and before you know it, most of the day is already gone. If you are not careful, working remotely can reduce your performance on the job as well as being the cause of more stress. If this sounds like you, then here are our top five tips to ensure that you maintain your peak performance while 'working from home':

1 **Maintain a regular routine:** try to stick to the same schedule that you would do (and that your colleagues might be doing) in the office. Start and finish work at the same time each day (of course, there may be some flexibility in this, depending on what needs to get done, but do try to be as strict as you can with your clocking in and out times).

2 **Take regular breaks:** set times for a 5–10 minute break and a longer break for lunch (away from where you are working!) and stick to this schedule. Eat a proper lunch rather than just snacking irregularly from the cupboards and fridge throughout the day. Use your breaks to gather energy and refresh your focus for when you return to work. So, go for a walk outside (you might like to use Exercise 4.5 to use this break for a mindful walk) or do something else totally unrelated to work, but ensure that you return to your work as soon as your break-time is up. You might like to use your breaks and/or the time you save on commuting to and from the office to practise some other mindfulness exercises also.

3 **Design a designated office environment:** choose a spot where you will work from home and keep this space just for that and nothing else. Create an office environment around you so that it looks like work. File paperwork in folders and keep the environment tidy and that way it will also appear professional for conference calls when you need to do them.

4 **Create an environment that suits you:** this is your space and no one else's, so take advantage of that and set the temperature as you

like it, play the music (if that helps you work!) that you prefer, and get a chair and desk that you're comfortable with.

5 **Keep in contact with the office:** ensure that you remain communicative with your colleagues and manager, etc., especially if you think that your chances of promotion may be affected by working from home. Although they will be able to see the work that you are doing, it might be helpful to communicate more regularly with your team than you might do if you were in the office. So arrange daily/weekly catch-ups via email or conference calls to ensure that you remain visible. You might like to ensure that on some days you are physically present in the office.

Managing your accounts

Hopefully, you are now (if you weren't already) beginning to become more conscious of the reality of this working life and the consequences that trying to hold it all at bay are having on you. It is not the case that this does not need addressing on practical terms as in delegating (see Chapter 5), saying 'no', taking regular breaks, resisting the compulsive phone-checking urges or taking the weekend off to chill out for once. However, none of this can even occur until you decide to accept and acknowledge the pressure you feel. Janice Marturano, founder of the mindfulness programme for General Mills (the food company which produces Häagen-Dazs, Cheerios, etc.) said in a recent article in the *Financial Times*:

> 'There is no work–life balance. We have one life. What's most important is that you be awake for it.'

Janice Marturano

That's it. Your first step in rising out of the swamp, with the intention of improving and then maintaining your work performance is simply to acknowledge that you are in the thick of it.

Before we move on and investigate further the nature of how our minds tend to operate in ways which impair our performance at work, just consider this. Recent research (which you can read more about in an article by Stephany Tlalka listed in the 'Useful resources' section at the end of this chapter) from the University of Glasgow looked at London Power (a utility company) executives' use of emails and habits around dealing with in-coming messages. They asked employees to stop and think before they hit 'Send'. As a result, office email use was reduced by a HALF! (We know! Wow!) freeing up 11,000 annual working hours. In an article discussing these findings, researcher Karen Renaud offered three suggestions:

1 **Break the chain:** When people email you, consider who really needs a response. 'Only send to people who have to see the message and act on it,' says Renaud. 'If you keep blasting stuff into people's inboxes, they will just ignore you – like the boy who cried wolf.'

2 **Resist speed:** 'Email begets email,' says Renaud. If people realise you respond quickly, you'll get more emails. Carve out intentional times to respond. Four to 12 hours is an acceptable response time.

3 **Think outcome, not convenience:** If someone is in the office, meet face to face or call them. While you might think it's more productive to send a quick message and move on, an email chain inevitably follows. 'The task comes back and in the long run takes much longer,' says Renaud. 'Connecting personally saves time.'

Once you become aware of the swamp, perhaps tracking your own technology use/obsessions, you may like to implement the above steps and then re-track your computer/phone use so that you see tangible results for yourself (you can read a few further articles listed in the 'Useful resources' section at the end of this chapter, which contain some more tips and advice about how to take control of your tech habit, conquer inevitable digital distractions and manage your email inbox). With this new-found time, why not try reading more of this, or similar books, on mindfulness, practising the techniques (maybe revisit Exercise 2.5 to get 'Smart with your Smartphone') and taking some really beneficial steps to maintaining your performance and well-being at work?

You might find that even with the phone off (Heaven forbid!) or away from your technological devices for more than five minutes, you are left to observe your mind, searching, yearning or fixating on anything other than the present moment. Meetings, and especially boring ones, tend to bring up this habitual tendency. So let us now look at some of these ways in which, even if we aren't swamped by technology, the mind just keeps the chatter coming …

Get out of your head and back on to the job

Have you ever found your mind wandering in a meeting: you know, when someone is talking about this, that or the other, you have your very best listening face on, smiling and nodding away but really you're somewhere else entirely? Yes, us too.

Now, at times we've found that that mental escape might have been the very thing that has kept us from getting up and giving the person speaking a forceful shake, pleading with them, 'Oh do shut up and give it a rest, already!' Or at the very least keeling over in absolute boredom. But at other times, that wandering mind may have taken us away from listening to important information and the opportunity to connect meaningfully with some colleagues at work. It is not uncommon to have actually tuned out for entire sections of communication and have absolutely no idea what has just been said at all (your practice of mindful speech, listening and communication as outlined in the previous chapter will help you with this)! When we feel bored it is important to recognise and name it. Boredom arises out of a lack of attention. We get bored because we either don't like what is happening and/or we feel lost, confused, stuck or helpless in some way. Our boredom is often accompanied by a lack of enthusiasm and an increase in judgement and self-righteousness ('Oh, this is such a waste of time!'). Becoming distracted by boredom like this can really get in the way of meaningful experiences at work, so it's best to get to grips with it when it arises. So next time you feel boredom take its hold, bring your attention towards it, name it and explore it, curiously. Notice where you feel it in your body and what information your mind is giving you about the situation you are in. Notice how you feel beneath your boredom (confused, lost, maybe?) and what arises when you untangle from its grip. In bringing your attention towards boredom, with curiosity in this way (Exercise 6.4 from earlier in this chapter might also help you further along with this), rather than continuously trying to avoid or run away from it, you may find that it lessens its hold over you, and that wherever you are or whatever you are doing/listening to becomes interesting once again (you never know, you may even learn something new!) and your enthusiasm is rejuvenated (for some further tips on how to break out of the boredom habit while on the job, you might like to read the blog post listed in the 'Useful resources' section at the end of this chapter).

Attention truly is an amazing and slightly bizarre thing (to see for yourself, take a look at the 'Awareness Test' video listed in the 'Useful resources' section – it's brilliant!). Mindfulness helps our development of focus *and* broad attention, but it is still up to us how and when we direct it, and for what specific purpose. As always, our first step is simply becoming aware of what our mind is up to, then we get the chance and the choice over what we may wish to do with this.

Stress monkey

Michael: No matter how many corporate training workshops I deliver (despite the excellent feedback that I get, WINK, WINK! – I know, shameless plugging!), my mind still continues to give me thoughts about how badly they will go, 'I'll muck it up!', 'They're all going to think I'm terrible!', 'They'll just get up and walk out of the room!', etc. Now the more I think these thoughts, the more stressed and anxious I feel. Then I notice that my mind throws up some further thoughts like, 'I hate feeling anxious', 'It's just not fair, I'm always so stressed, everyone else has such an easier life!', 'Why do I have to do these f***ing workshops anyway?', 'Why do I have to feel this way?', 'Surely now everyone is bound to notice just how anxious I am and then they'll definitely think I'm cr*p!' Now I'm just getting stressed about being stressed; anxious about being anxious – argh!! Will this ever end? I'm clearly my own worst enemy – STOP!! Breathe ...

Buddhism has a really great term for this thinking mind; it's been called 'monkey mind'. We can't, nor would we want to, banish the monkey or our thinking mind from existence. We admire the monkey just like our thinking mind for its amazing problem-solving abilities and creativity and sometimes it can be a real hoot! Sometimes, however, our monkey mind can be mischievous, get in the way of what we are trying to do and frankly be a bit annoying. It can make a real racket and leave us feeling petty distressed in the process, and in doing so it just stops us getting on with the job in hand. So when your own monkey mind is up to no good, you might find it useful to use mindfulness to get out of your head and back on to the job. There are specific mindfulness techniques and metaphors which can be incredibly useful for this and can be incorporated into our mindfulness practice as vehicles to enable us to tune out the chatter. So, next time your monkey mind is chattering away, you might first like to consider the following two questions:

1 Does thinking these thoughts help me to do the things that I want to do? If your answer is 'no', then ask:

2 Am I then willing to respond differently to these thoughts when they arise? If your answer is 'yes', then you might like to take a look at our top eight mindfulness techniques (to help you to respond to your thoughts differently) listed below, and consider giving them a go to help you to get out of your monkey mind and back on to the job.

Exercise 6.7: Work in progress

Manic Monkey Mind Mindfulness Metaphors (say this fast ten times)

1 No, we mean it, really! If you (silently if you prefer) repeat worrying thoughts rapidly, you'll soon notice how they become a nonsense, just a blurred sound – waking us up to the fact that that is all a thought is: a sound in our mind that we can choose to listen to or not.

2 You may also like to imagine the chatter in your mind like a radio DJ, with lots of nothing to report. Now turn down the volume and continue with your work; you may find the DJ has given up after a while, or at least switched from Radio 1 fervour to Classic FM calm – phew!

3 As we highlighted in Exercise 6.3 earlier, you might like to repeat a few mindful words before any stressful thoughts that your mind gives you; these mindful words are: 'I am having the thought that … (insert your stressful thought here).'

4 Picture your mental chatter as if it were a monkey; now chuck a banana off into the distance and watch him/her run off with glee. Now you can work in peace.

5 Imagine your thoughts as leaves on a stream; watch them race past or drift languidly by, with no need to get caught up in them.

6 With an in-breath give your thoughts vibrancy, by either using a vivid colour or increasing the volume. As you breathe out, imagine the volume or colour fading; take a few more breaths and decrease the intensity at little more each time. As the mental noise fades, you can give more attention where it is needed for your work.

7 Sometimes the mind is referred to as being like the sky; see how the weather is (cloudy, stormy, windy, etc.) in your mind and watch your thoughts like clouds, passing. You may find that the heavens clear, and along with this you also find clarity for the tasks ahead.

8 Imagine your mind like a snow globe, all shaken up with the thoughts whirling everywhere. See your thoughts like glitter or snow-flakes and watch them gradually settle, allowing you to concentrate clearly now on the day ahead.

If these techniques and metaphors either don't work for you or you simply find them difficult to practise or picture, don't worry. There is definitely no merit in setting up further mental struggles! These are simply suggestions which can work brilliantly well for some of us, some of the time and are offered as another potential, easily accessible tool when you are feeling overwhelmed by the monkey mind. They can be adapted in any way you like to suit you, or you might find other techniques within this chapter that are more helpful. The important feature here is to recognise the thoughts and mental chatter as activities of the mind and products of stress, and these activities of the mind are perfectly natural occurrences. We certainly would not want to be rid of them entirely; our brains rock! Where would we be without one? However, sometimes we do need to remind ourselves that it is important to train our mind and practise this training so that we are not at the mercy of a monkey. One aspect to this is in recognising mental chatter as an activity and not as 'who we are'; this activity (racing stressful thoughts) occurs in the context of us, and is in constant flux and ever changing. While this might seem a little disconcerting, what it actually means is that we can free ourselves from any fixed view, any contracted or restrictive way of being or any 'shoulds', 'oughts' and 'musts' that are usually a central component of our stressed-out thinking. So, 'I should get on with this proposal', 'I must work harder', 'I ought to have done this yesterday', 'I shouldn't feel this stressed' can be seen as mental chatter, a product of stress, and we can begin to recognise that their incessant repetition in our mind is actually not effective or beneficial.

Exercise 6.8: Work in progress

Everything is transient

In thinking about managing our stress at work, we invite you to recognise how everything is transient. Our thoughts, feelings, body sensations and behaviours are fleeting, they come and go. To see what we mean, try this quick exercise right now.

1 Just for a second, right now, bring your attention to a sensation in your body, wherever you are, whatever you are doing – this might be the sensation of your backside against the seat you're sitting on, or even your fingers on your keyboard or on your phone, tablet or the book you're holding.

2 Just hold that sensation at the forefront of your mind for a few seconds – got it? Good.

Now, that sensation is always there when you sit at your desk at work (tap away on your keyboard, hold your phone, tablet, this book, etc.), but until we encouraged you to focus on it just now, you probably weren't that aware of its presence. As you keep reading and your mind becomes distracted by what you read, that sensation will pass by the forefront of your mind. That sensation is just like any thoughts, other sensations or emotions that you experience, including the stressful and painful ones. You might also try to imagine yourself like a mountain, standing firm, secure and stable and these experiences are clouds that pass by the peak of the mountain. The problem is that we lose sight of the fact that our experiences are fleeting in this way, particularly when we experience stress and other unwanted thoughts, feelings and sensations. At those times we tend to want to get rid of it straight away and usually by exterminating (in true Dalek style) the cause of our stress, as we see it anyway – like our unforgiving boss, the lazy, good-for-nothing colleagues who won't pull their weight or those trillion emails in the inbox glaring at us for attention! The problem arises in that, although we tirelessly try, our experiences are simply not a problem to solve; they are a condition of life (as we mentioned in the previous chapter too), and the more we try to eradicate them the more they stick around, just like those weather clouds now hovering above the mountain top. It's interesting, as there are many other conditions in life that we tend to accept day to day, like the weather, say. Just imagine believing that you would never leave your home unless the sun was shining. We're sure that you wouldn't get much done at all, especially when you consider the weather we tend to get here in Britain.

Swatting sweat flies

Running from stress at work is not clever, not if you want to feel more composed and calm, not to mention get the job done. Instinctively we try to rid ourselves of stress, just as we might try to swat away a fly as we lie relaxing in the sun – and the more we swat, the more we sweat and, well, we're sure you get the picture. Take a look at Steve, for example.

Steve

Steve, a high-flying management consultant, had returned to his work following a period of recovery after undergoing an operation on his heart. He felt pretty overwhelmed with all the work that he had to catch up with. He was anxious not to feel stressed to ensure that he didn't aggravate his delicate heart condition and that he recovered well. He felt the need to get on top of all his work as quickly as he could so that no more would pile up and he could keep any future stress at bay. He decided to work a bit harder and longer for a while in the hope of getting everything done, so he could de-stress, as quickly as he could. Steve found that although he had good intentions to stay on later in the office and arrive earlier than everyone else in the morning, he just didn't seem to have the same energy reserves that he used to have before his operation. He became frustrated that he couldn't function in the way he wanted and he found that more work just kept coming his way. The more anxious he got the more tension he felt in his body; his chest began to feel tight and he then began to worry about his health. He became stressed about being stressed and as his bodily tension continued to increase, he became more anxious, and so on ...

We can develop our reactivity to the precision of a samurai (please see the YouTube video of a fantastic animation, listed in the 'Useful resources' section at the end of this chapter to see what we mean), slashing the flies with our razor sharp sword, only to find that, somehow, we now have two flies; with another couple of swift cuts, we have four, then eight, sixteen and so on. We work harder and harder, sweating away, with nothing to show except an increasingly large swarm of increasingly irritating flies. It is enough to drive anyone to the brink of sanity, and yet many of us live our daily working lives just like this, gasping for breath at the end of the day, left frazzled and furious. The fear, of course, is that if we stop, the flies (or fly) will just continue, get worse and/or never ever leave. So recall your skills already from this chapter, see the fly storm just as it is. Stop fighting with reality (you will never win). Turn down the volume of the monkey mind and be still for a moment.

Great! So now we've covered swamps, monkeys and flies – we hope you don't have all three at once, but even if you are up to your neck in a swamp with a monkey on your head and a fly biting your nose, we know that you have plenty of ways of seeing that these are actually not worth the added stress of reacting to with the usual defensive, demanding or distracting habits we tend to use. The techniques above have so far called for you to acknowledge, discriminate wisely, develop mindful discipline and recognise the transience of mental experience. To master the next steps, of what begins to surface once we still the mind and see the swamp, the monkey or the fly storm, we are going to look into a recent and very successful area related to mindfulness which is often referred to as 'emotional resilience' ...

Emotional resilience

The concept of psychological resilience began in the 1970s when studies were made of people who, despite experiencing extreme adversity in early life, were still found to thrive in later life. This was initially attributed, in the main, to hereditary traits in personality. More recent modern-day authors and researchers, such as Steven Southwick and Dennis Charney (2012), have studied resilience extensively to try to discover more about why people react so differently to adversity. Through their research, Southwick and Charney have identified ten psychological and social factors that they think make for stronger resilience:

1 facing your fears;
2 having a moral compass or ethical code;
3 drawing on faith or self-belief;
4 using social support and friendships;
5 having positive role models;

6 keeping physically fit;

7 making sure you are mentally challenged;

8 having 'cognitive and emotional flexibility';

9 having 'meaning, purpose and growth' in life;

10 'realistic' optimism.

Moreover, Southwick and Charney believe that it is possible to develop these ten factors, and that this can lead to a positive change for generally healthy people in their ability to cope not just with a major trauma, but also with the day-to-day stresses of life. The technique they believe to be the most helpful? Yep, that's right! Mindfulness.

Emotional resilience is important to you and your work because it gives you the ability to withstand emotional difficulties skilfully, to use mindfulness to your advantage and to further promote your well-being and quality of functioning at work. Moreover, through emotional resilience you demonstrate strength to your team, you recover well from setbacks, you build healthy relationships with colleagues and you and your business are able to thrive and succeed in competitive environments when others might buckle under the stress. According to research by Richard Davidson, a neuroscientist at the University of Wisconsin (you can watch a video of Richard Davidson and John Kabat-Zinn talking about resilience and mindfulness, listed in the 'Useful resources' section at the end of this chapter), resilient people bounce back from adversity, no matter what happens. Instead of suffering from the physical and mental symptoms of stress (such as back pain, headaches, high blood pressure, anxiety, depression, etc.), they are able to return to a state of calm composure even after the most upsetting events. One of the key techniques Davidson and other researchers have found to developing emotional resilience is the rehearsal of letting go of, or letting alone (taking our 'hands off') our thoughts and distractions and returning our attention to a chosen topic or task (the very essence of any mindfulness practice). Davidson says *the wherewithal to pause, observe how easily the mind can exaggerate the severity of a setback, note that it as an interesting mental process, and resist getting drawn into the abyss* is key to cultivating our emotional resilience and recovering well from stressful encounters. The more we become practised at doing this, like any skill, the better and more resilient to stress we can become. So why not try this next practice now (and repeat it as often as you can) to boost your emotional resilience.

Exercise 6.9: Mindful on the job 🎧

Mind training for emotional resilience

This is an adaptation of an exercise used by SIYLI (Search Inside Yourself Leadership Institute), who work with Google. Take your time with this; we suggest ten minutes at least, but any time will be beneficial.

1 Begin by taking three breaths to bring the mind to the present. Focus on the in- and out-breaths and the spaces in-between.

2 Bring the attention into the body, becoming aware of the physical body, your posture, the ground beneath you and the air and space around you.

3 Now bring to mind an experience or event in which you experienced stress. This may be a failure, a sense of letting others down, missing a goal or target or finding a situation humiliating.

4 Observe what arises in the memory of the senses, like sounds (such as a conversation), sights (the people or places), or other sensory experiences.

5 Now attend to the emotional qualities which arise (anger, shame, regret, sorrow, etc.). Let yourself feel the accompanying sensations which arise within the body. These are likely to be uncomfortable and aversive; just stay with them.

6 Stay with the emotions and sensations arising and see if you can allow yourself just to experience these as physiological experiences. Just focus on these in this moment, allowing them to come and go as they wish. Arising and passing, try to let them alone, without interfering, adding narratives or distracting away, simply 'take your hands off' and allow the experience to be. Take an attitude of kindness and gentleness towards yourself.

7 Now switch to recalling an event of success, pride or achievement at work. This might be a time of receiving praise, meeting a goal or getting a promotion or bonus.

8 Again, observe what arises in the memory of the senses, like sounds (such as a conversation), sights (the people or places), or other sensory experiences.

9 Now, once more, attend to the emotional qualities which arise (joy, pride, fulfilment, satisfaction). Let yourself feel the accompanying sensations which arise within the body. These are likely to be pleasant and desirable; just stay with them.

10 Stay with the emotion and sensations arising and see if you can also let them be, just as they are, simply an experience of physiological sensations arising and passing in the body. Try to leave them alone, without interfering, creating further stories or embellishments, letting the sensations come and go with an attitude of kindness and gentleness.

11 Now return to the present and focus again on the breath for approximately three minutes. Continue to notice what happens in the body; see how it feels right now and allow yourself to breathe freely.

Getting unhooked and swimming free

Exercises like the one above train our ability to relinquish reactive and unhelpful responses to our unwanted experiences such as uncomfortable thoughts, feelings and bodily sensations which we tend to habitually either buy into or suppress in some way. For example, we may embellish a worrisome thought and before we know it we are lost in an entire story about our impending doom and failure, or equally we may attempt to push that thought away by thinking positively and reappraising its content (i.e. 'I know deep down that I am not a failure'), which all too often is met with just another compelling counterargument ('But what if I am wrong and I am a failure?!').

So, neither of these reactive responses (buying into or suppressing) is usually a workable behaviour if our goal is to maintain our well-being and peak performance while on the job.

By recognising these habitual responses and labelling thoughts and feelings for what they are, instead we increase our *psychological flexibility*; that is we become unstuck, broaden our perspective and expand our choices, and we unhook ourselves from either becoming entirely caught up in the stress-inducing story or in energy-zapping struggles to push them away. We can then increase our willingness, choose to make room for these experiences and accept them for what they are, just as they are. Essentially, with mindfulness, we notice these experiences and our unhelpful struggle with them and instead choose to respond in a more open and flexible way. This frees up time, energy and much needed resources, which are all essential in enabling us to take actions aligned with what matters most to us in our work.

Numerous studies (some of which have been listed in this book already), from Frank Bond at Goldsmiths, University of London, Paul Flaxman at City University in London and several others, have shown that the development of this specific skill, *psychological flexibility* (arising from practising the mindfulness-based principles of Acceptance and Commitment Therapy or ACTraining) – which includes the ability to be in the current moment, mindfully aware of thoughts and emotions, and committed to valued-based workplace goals – can help workers to alleviate stress and reduce burnout and absenteeism, as well as increasing job satisfaction and job performance. As we can see, one key element to all this is clarifying and then aligning and committing our actions to our values or, in other words, a deeper sense of purpose and what matters most to us in our work.

Similarly, in her seminal paper, 'How resilience works' (which you can find a link to in the 'Useful resources' section at the end of this chapter), published in the *Harvard Business Review,* Diane Coutu also highlights a sense of purpose and meaning as a fundamental characteristic in the cultivation of emotional resilience. She outlines three crucial building blocks for emotional resilience in the face of stressful experiences within the workplace:

1 **Face down reality (acceptance of harsh realities):** Instead of trying to remain positive or live in denial (which only lasts for a while), having a deeper sense of realism and acceptance of how life is prepares us to act in ways that allow us to endure and survive extraordinary hardship. With the practice of acceptance, we train ourselves how to survive before stressful events arise. The concept of seeing reality clearly and experiencing ourselves and our lives just as they are appears also within Buddhist teachings; it is known as 'radical acceptance.'

2 **Search for meaning (finding purpose in hardship):** Instead of ranting 'why is this happening to me', create some sort of meaning and purpose and concrete goals that are aligned with this purpose: e.g. Viktor Frankl, the Austrian Psychiatrist and Auschwitz survivor, helped himself survive the concentration camp by imagining how he would give a lecture on the psychology of the camp, following the war, to help people understand what he had been through.

3 **Continually improvise (remain creative, think outside the box):** Within the boundaries of standard rules and regulations, be inventive: imagine how you could use whatever resources are available, to solve problems in novel and creative ways.

So, we already know well how regular mindfulness practice helps to develop our acceptance of life, just as it is, as well as enhance our creativity, confidence, productivity and focus, but what about this other fundamental element in cultivating our resilience: finding a sense of purpose and meaning, and what really matters to us? How can mindfulness help us with that? Well, let's take a look at that right now.

> **"Regular mindfulness practice helps to develop**
> **our acceptance of life."**

What matters most?

'Try not to become a man of success but rather try to become a man of value.'

Albert Einstein

Together with accepting our current working life, discerning when we are being reactive, and developing emotional resilience, looking at the relationship we have to our workplace can assist us to move in a direction that matters most to us, increasing our sense of fulfilment with our career and reducing the likelihood of burnout. Without a clear understanding and awareness of our values, our working life can feel as if it is at the whim of other forces (like swamps, monkeys and flies, for instance), which can leave us feeling pretty stressed out, anxious and underconfident and, like our work, lacking any meaningful substance.

Each day we are faced with making choices while on the job; work is often just a series of decisions, one after another, day after day. Some of these can be quite easy to make, and some may be based on fear, and we can act mindlessly as a result. At certain junctures we are often left paralysed, as if the road ahead looks dug up, lacking in any confidence about which way to turn, what direction to take, what decision to make or what the next step should be. 'What role should I take? Shall I leave my current job? How shall I respond/what shall I say to my teammate, my manager, or that client? How can I maintain my performance at work?' Our values can really be of great value at such times, as we take a moment to mindfully step back, check in with what our values might tell us about what matters most to us in that moment and situation and then act accordingly. They give us a much needed framework to fall back on, and the confidence to move forward with what we really care about in our work, even in the face of hardship and highly stressful moments.

Values refer to the way we want to interact with our work, our colleagues, superiors, customers, clients, competitors and ourselves. They are what we want to stand for in our work, how we want to behave, what sort of person we want to be, what sort of strengths and qualities we want to demonstrate. If we feel the assurance and conviction that we are acting in alignment with what matters most to us (and when these actions also happen to align with our team's, company's or organisation's values and action plan, it can all become doubly energising and motivating), we will benefit from feeling more centred and connected to our role. As a result, our performance in the workplace is likely to feel more authentic (i.e. not something we are 'trying to be' but something we 'are') and our work endeavours more meaningful and satisfying. We begin to experience a greater sense of well-being, and our performance and resilience are also likely to improve further.

In fact, in a very recent longitudinal study[10] carried out at Flinders University in Adelaide, Australia, it was found that having a sense of purpose in life, or, in other words, recognising what you want out of life and having a plan to achieve it, is a significant contributor to ageing well generally. The results showed that individuals (1,475 adults participated in this research over an 18-year period) with higher scores measuring their sense of purpose reported lower functional disability, better self-rated health and fewer symptoms of depression compared to individuals who scored lower on measures of purpose. The study also found that having a strong sense of purpose appeared to be linked to better performance on tests of short-term memory and mental speed. The researchers conclude *'that having a strong sense of purpose allows people to set meaningful goals in life and manage their time and effort more effectively.'*

It would seem that a sense of purpose can really boost our emotional resilience and provide a major buffer to the daily, as well as the more severe, experiences of stress that are an inevitable part of our working lives. Redundancy (although sometimes much welcomed) can often come as a huge blow and has left many of the executives that we have coached feeling pretty lost, directionless and pessimistic, with increasing feelings of depression and anxiety. However, following an effort to clarify deeper values and meaning in their work, many of these people have been able to find a new sense of optimism and forward direction. Many have turned their experience of redundancy (once they have unhooked themselves from the unworkable rumination and worry that tends to undermine their confidence and fuel their depression and anxiety, that is!) into a positive by using the time wisely to reflect on what they truly want their working life to be about. Some have retrained, or transferred their skills to another industry once they have identified the steps that they can begin to take to experience greater meaning and satisfaction from their work.

Values are not targets or goals

In further considering values, it's important to differentiate between values and goals. Often when we ask our clients what their values might be in the context of their work, they often respond by running off a list of goals, what they want to achieve, etc. We really want to clear up the fact that values (as we are presenting them here, anyway) are not goals, or something that we can attain, win or gain. That promotion, new job, more money, success, respect from colleagues or the support from a manager may matter to you BUT they are all goals. These are things we can hope to attain, and then tick off a list. Once we get them they are no longer goals. Values are more to do with the qualities that we want to bring to our actions, how we want to be and what we want to stand for as a worker, employee, colleague, service provider, employer, manager, leader, business owner, etc. Values are concerned with how we want to be and act on an ongoing basis, i.e. the quality of our actions. They are best described as the *'desired global qualities of ongoing action'* (Hayes, Bond, Barnes-Holmes and Austin, 2006, p. 16) that we want to demonstrate through our behaviour in our work. Values, unlike goals, can never be completed. For example, if you want a better job that is a goal, and once you get it you have achieved it, crossed it off the list; but if you want to be more efficient or productive at work, these are values and you can act on them in any moment, even if you don't like your job or even if you don't have one. Values are also about 'the quality of our action'. So although you can 'work' on an ongoing basis, 'work' itself is not a value as it lacks any description of the quality you may bring to your work. The question to really ask yourself is: *how* do you want to work? What personal qualities or strengths do you want to model or demonstrate while you work? How do you want to behave in your relationships with your teammates, your reports, your manager, your clients and customers? Asking yourself these types of questions may help you connect with values such as being focused, fair, kind, competitive, cooperative, skilful, supportive, etc.; these are examples of values. Remember that values are also 'global', which refers to the fact that these qualities can be brought to many different behaviours and actions. So if you valued being supportive to your colleagues at work, there are many different actions you could do to be supportive towards them – i.e. spend time listening, help out with projects, etc. Values are also freely chosen by you; there is no rule book or law about which you should have; they are yours and reflect what is important to you.

Working with values

Sometimes our clients can look rather lost, anxious or frustrated when we ask them to tell us about their values, which is not surprising at all as most of us work in highly goal-oriented environments and we easily lose touch with our core values. Of course targets and goals are an essential part of successful business, but the problem is that when we live and work by these alone (losing touch with our values) our experience of work is pretty stressful and unfulfilling. Working in a purely goal-focused fashion is all well and good, but we tend to experience a perpetual state of lacking, anxiety and frustration until we reach our next goal, and when we finally get it (if we ever do) we are then left anxious about losing it and/or lost and directionless once again until we find another goal to strive towards. We always want more, assuming that the next thing/achievement will fulfil us and/or make us happy and successful. We are constantly raising the bar, striving for the next achievement, but all the while never really experiencing any lasting sense of satisfaction or stability in our work. We are not for one second saying that you should do away with trying to move onwards and upwards in your work and career, but if you were to introduce more value-driven behaviours into the mix you might find that your sense of motivation, purpose, confidence, fulfilment, contentment and resilience were more stable and hung around for a bit longer and you were therefore better able to maintain your performance, at its peak, at work. Take the case of Jon and Edward, for example.

Jon and Edward

Both Jon and Edward were lawyers working within a large corporate law firm. They were both working towards making Partner at the same time. Both had strong aspiration and were determined to get the promotion. While Jon was preoccupied (you could say somewhat obsessive actually) about landing the promotion, Edward although still equally eager seemed rather less obsessed. We heard from Jon that in his preoccupation with achieving this goal, he had actually become pretty stressed out, anxious and was finding it difficult to sleep at night. He had also become a real pain in the arse to work with, only ever talking and worrying about the promotion and dropping all his other usual day-to-day stuff to ensure that he was doing everything he could to secure the promotion. Although Edward was also focused on this goal he didn't lose focus of his values. Edward continued with all his other work commitments, including mentoring junior members of his team, chairing the committee of the charity work his firm was involved in and supervising a couple of colleagues who were involved in some rather high-profile and complex litigations, as well as making sure that he continued to spend quality time with his kids at home. Some of Edward's values at work included being supportive, contributing and kind. Ensuring he continued to work by these, among other, values, he was able to ensure that he continued to have a more rewarding and less stressful time than Jon at work, while working towards making Partner – even with the same level of uncertainty about landing the promotion.

Irrespective of our successes or failures, and of anyone or anything else, we can always choose to act on our values at work. Unlike our goals, our values are always available to us and we can act on them whenever we want. As we know all too well by now, thoughts change endlessly and emotions change like the weather, but values can be called upon at any time, in any situation. We can never guarantee that we will get that promotion, but we can always choose to work confidently and conscientiously, for example, if that is what matters to us most.

'Your beliefs become your thoughts,'
'Your thoughts become your words',
'Your words become your actions',
'Your actions become your habits',
'Your habits become your values',
'Your values become your destiny.'

Mahatma Gandhi

The mindful route to values

So you might be thinking, 'this all sounds great but *what's all this values stuff got to do with mindfulness?'* Well, mindfulness and values go hand in hand. In order to identify our values we need to be present and pay close attention, moment by moment, to our feelings and behaviours and the sense of satisfaction and purpose that these may or may not bring. When we take time to notice our present moment experience in this way, we can begin to identify the behaviours and understand the underlying values that bring us a sense of satisfaction and meaning in our work. After we have recognised what is most important to us in our work, we may then wish to implement more values-based actions at work – which can be no mean feat. Working in ways that we really care about (although ultimately satisfying) can at times be a real challenge and a difficult thing to do. For example, if we want to contribute in the corporate world we need to be willing and prepared to experience the anxiety and sense of vulnerability that, say, creativity, innovation and/or public speaking may bring. So in acting on our values we need to continue to practise mindfulness as best we can. By practising present-moment focus on the here and now, we can do our best to ensure that we don't get caught up in the inevitable obstacles (and excuses!) that our minds give us about why we just can't do that or this right now (even though it is important to us) – at these times it is important to use your mindfulness skills and *never mind your mind* (Exercise 6.7 in this chapter can help you out with this) and carry on anyway. It is also important to recognise that although we can set goals to work towards that are aligned with our deepest values, we can also make an effort to work by our values in any given moment, right here and right now. So although you can plan value-based actions which you may want to take over the next six months, four weeks or during the week ahead, the other helpful questions to ask yourself (as often as you can) are:

▶ 'What can I do right now, in this very moment that is aligned with my values?'

▶ 'What do I want to stand for, right now, in the face of this challenging situation?'

We bet by now you are eager to get on and think about your own personal work-related values and how you might start to incorporate these into your work. OK, let's take a closer look at all that now.

Uncovering values

Why don't you try to identify some of your values right now with the following exercises? Remember, there are no right or wrong values; you are free to change your mind at any point or to sit with not fully knowing; these exercises are about exploration, curiosity and inquiry.

Exercise 6.10: Work in progress

Your retirement party

To identity your values it may be helpful to reflect on how you might like to be remembered and what you might hope to leave behind: in other words, your legacy (we know, deep, right?). So why not take a few moments now to try to imagine that you are at your very own retirement party and a few of your colleagues stand up to make a speech about you (imagine what you'd most like to hear them say about you) as you reflect on the following questions:

▶ What do they say about the sort of colleague, manager, employer, etc. you have been?

▶ What have you stood for in your work?

▶ What have you meant to them in their work?

▶ How do you feel as you hear them describe these qualities in you?

▶ Which qualities feel most important and meaningful to you?

You may like to continue your exploration into your deepest values with the following exercise now.

Exercise 6.11: Work in progress

Finding true value

1. Identifying core values

Below, some of the common values that people may hold at work have been grouped into four sets; *active values, values of the heart, personal development values* and *social values*. Although these groupings are arbitrary to an extent, they may also help you place your preference in terms of how you may choose to communicate or develop the values that you have and help you discriminate more clearly how and where your actions at work meet these, or not. Not all of the values listed may resonate with you and that is absolutely fine. Also, these are not the right or correct values to hold at work – remember there is no right and wrong when it comes to values.

Run through the lists and see which, if any, fit for you. For the ones that do seem relevant to you, why not try to rank them as 'very important' or 'quite important'. You may also find that one category is more dominant than another, or maybe you have a little bit of everything. After identifying some values from below, move on to part two of the exercise for some guidance on how to start acting by these values in the workplace, to help you feel more in tune with your work.

'Active' values: achievement, adventure, assertiveness, excitement, fun, pleasure, power, expertise, creativity, fitness, industry, order, skilfulness

Values of the heart: acceptance, authenticity, autonomy, caring, compassion, courage, forgiveness, generosity, gratitude, honesty, humility, humour, kindness, patience

Personal development values: accuracy, challenge, curiosity, encouragement, flexibility, freedom, health, mindfulness, open-mindedness, persistence, self-awareness/care/development/control, tolerance

Social values: connection, contribution, conformity, cooperation, civility, fairness, friendliness, helpfulness, independence, intimacy, respect, responsibility, safety, trust.

2. Value boost

If you found that you had values in a particular category, or even some in each, you may also reflect on how these are met by your actions while on the job. If you do feel that you could take more active steps to align yourself with your values, here are some suggestions:

Active values: Look for ways to demonstrate these values at work, either through presentations, team-building, skills development, training or other overt, concrete and definitive means. You may wish to set up new initiatives at work in order to best promote the values that are important for you to feel fulfilled at work.

Values of the heart: Show these values, even in tough-talking environments, by spending time listening to others, making space for saying 'thank you', 'sorry' or 'well done' or simply remembering to give yourself and others that well-deserved tea-break from time to time.

Personal-development values: Remind yourself that these values are important on a regular basis by listing the ways in which you are achieving goals, developing yourself as a person and rising to the challenges of your working life in alignment with what matters most to you.

Social values: Focus on networking, team-building and social events at work, but make time to consider how your values are being met through these activities. You might want to adjust the emphasis of particular meetings, or review work policies and team culture in order to enhance these values for yourself at work.

After identifying some of your values through these exercises, you may have found that you are already acting on your values at work. Maybe you already work hard and are supportive of others, for example, but you still feel unfulfilled. If so, that's probably because you are on autopilot most of the time, rushing around, from one task to the next, caught up in all your thoughts, ticking off items on your to-do list, rather than actually being present to really take in and savour any of your meaningful moments on the job. If that is the case, then it's time to get present and practise more mindfulness! In this case, maybe you could add *mindfulness* to your list of values (if it's not already there). On the other hand, if you have found that there are a number of values that you aren't bringing to your work, then maybe you are keen to start implementing them now? Try the following exercises to begin putting your values into action in more concrete ways.

What steps can you take to move towards being the worker/colleague/manager/leader/employer (delete as appropriate!) you really want to be?

Attempt the following exercises to first identify what actions and goals you can set yourself to ensure you are working by your values, and then begin to put them into actionable terms with a considered and concrete plan. You may find this a helpful tool to reflect on weekly or even daily.

Exercise 6.12: Work in progress

Identifying value-based goals

To begin to understand how your values can be connected to your actions and goals at work, try to answer the following questions (keeping your values in mind):

▶ What sort of things would you like to start doing more of at work?

▶ What would you like to stop doing?

▶ What are you currently doing that improves your work in the long run?

▶ What work-enriching goals do you want to achieve?

▶ What work-enhancing actions do you want to take?

▶ What work-improving skills would you like to develop?

Values-based goals action plan

To set specific values-based goals and ensure you implement them at work, try the following exercise (which has been adapted from Russ Harris' brilliant modification (Harris, 2012, p. 213–17) of the widely known SMART goals acronym):

1 First remind yourself of your values and make sure you keep them in mind to ensure your actions are meaningful.

2 Now, choose a value (one at a time) that you want to set some goal/s around (e.g., 'supportive').

3 Now, get SMART:

Specific (Do not set ambiguous, poorly defined goals like, 'I'll be more supportive at work'. Instead, be specific about your actions, like: 'I'll arrange a time to speak to each team member about their concerns'.)

Meaningful (Check to make sure this goal is aligned with your values, i.e. 'supportive'.)

Adaptive (Is this goal likely to improve your work in some way? – 'Yes, teamwork and group productivity will improve'.)

Realistic (Do you have the resources available to carry out this goal – such as time, money, physical health, social support, knowledge, skills? If these resources are needed but not available, it's best to change your goal to a more realistic one. The new goal might actually be about finding the missing resources: to create more time, or develop the skills, etc., i.e. 'I'll delegate some of my project so I can free up some time to talk with the team' – remember this would still be related to the core underlying value you have identified.)

Time-framed (Be specific about the day, date and time when you will act on your value-based goal – i.e. 'I will speak to a different team member for 30 minutes, each morning from 10am'.)

4 Make a commitment: Research shows that if you make a public commitment to your goal (i.e. if you let at least one other person know what you intend to do), then you are more likely to follow through with it. If you're not able or willing to do this, then try at least to make a commitment to yourself (in this case, you might find it helpful to write it down somewhere – where you'll see it as a reminder!).

Take bold action

To end this chapter, we wanted to leave you with another acronym (which we find very helpful and which is commonly cited in the ACT literature), which we hope will serve you well in your goal of maintaining your peak performance while on the job. If you are up to the eyeballs with the whole acronym thing, then just remember this one, as, along with the 'mindfulness of breathing' practice, it is simple, relevant and easily accessible. So when you find yourself confronted with difficult situations at work, when stress seems to be high, try to follow these simple steps to mindfully regulate your emotion, tap back into your source of resilience and then take productive, valued-based actions to maintain your peak performance. Remember to be **BOLD**:

Breathe: breathe in and out slowly, slow down, focus on now.

Observe: notice what you are feeling and thinking. Allow these internal experiences to flow through you, without getting hooked up in them.

Listen: listen to your values, i.e. what kind of person do you want to be in this moment?

Decide: choose actions that will reflect your values, and make a decision to act on them.

Josie:

B: Sitting here I observe my in-breath; noticing my sit bones I breathe out.

O: I am observing physical discomfort in my lower back and a slight headache. I notice tiredness and a desire to go for a walk. I notice my mind telling me what else I need to get done.

L: I listen to my inner stillness and values of self-care.

D: I choose to stand up, stretch gently and have a drink of water.

We would also like to remind you that one of your most common methods for dealing with stress is likely to look much like this:

In the interests of health and safety, if you must revert to this technique, we are obliged to recommend attaching a cushion to your head first. This 'anti-stress kit' will do nothing to solve a problem, to help you radically accept a situation or find healthy ways to build confidence and emotional resilience at work. In the face of adversity, the above technique will feel oddly familiar and just might remind you that when you are stuck in a rut, trying the same old thing over and over again and hoping for some kind of miracle, banging your head against the wall just leaves you with a headache. Stop it. Perhaps, instead you could just sit down and breathe for a bit instead?

Here are our take-away top tips from this chapter.

Mindfulness top tips to go

▶ Practise mindfulness regularly, not only in response to stress but as often as you can, even when you aren't feeling particularly stressed. That way you'll be better able to manage stressful times more easily and reduce the chances of stress escalating and leading to total burnout.

▶ Any new habit needs regular practice, so to ensure that you remember to practise mindfulness regularly (even at less stressful times when it's easy to forget), set reminders on your phone or other device; you may like to use your phone ringing itself, pausing before responding to the call. You might also like to use one of the many apps available that provide guided mindfulness instruction (more about these in Chapter 8).

▶ Use mindfulness as an alternative way to respond to the inevitable stress that you will experience on the job. Tirelessly struggling with your stress, trying to push it away, suppress or eliminate it will only lead to distraction, lower levels of productivity, exhaustion and a decline in your overall performance.

▶ Make efforts to notice your reactivity towards unwanted experiences (emails, troubling thoughts, feelings and bodily sensations), and instead practise mindfulness to accept these least desirable (yet inevitable!) experiences of your working day to ensure you stay fit and energised at work.

▶ Weave specific mindfulness techniques and metaphors into your practice to ensure that stressful thoughts don't get in the way of the tasks that you want to get done.

▶ Build your emotional resilience to reduce your chances of burnout and to increase sustainability in the face of inevitable stressors at work.

▶ Use mindfulness practice to develop acceptance, creativity and a deeper sense of purpose and meaning to stay resilient and ensure that you continue to perform at your best even in times of adversity. ➤

> ▶ Identify your work-related values and take action on specific goals that are aligned with these values to ensure that your work remains meaningful and satisfying. This will help you buffer against stress and burnout and increase your performance too.

As we draw this chapter to its conclusion, it might be helpful to remember that well-being and the ability to maintain your performance at work at an optimum are best developed through cultivating a mindful sensitivity to yourself in the moment – frequently, through simple, regular mindfulness practices. It is a skill built upon through small and, at times, seemingly irrelevant moments of contacting awareness of the breath or the body. These mindful moments, and then the further inquiry provided in many of the exercises given in this book, are to encourage deepening your understanding and reflection into mindfulness as it is applied to your working life. Practising mindfulness will hone your ability to make choices, to discern, to act from values and to notice your place and purpose in your work, your workplace and your world. With perseverance, gentleness and a stance of curiosity, gradually you will find freedom from the tyranny of habitual and unconscious thoughts and behaviours so that you are able to find a deeper sense of meaning and connection to your work and to your life. This simple process, born from the observation of one breath, one moment at a time, can flourish into a radical shift in the way you interface with your work, your colleagues and your business, bringing a refreshing and healthier glow to your performance at work and subsequently, as we will be looking at in the next chapter, to the whole ethos of the workplace.

Useful resources

> ▶ Bertin, M. (2015, July 1). *7 ways to take control of your tech habit* [article from mindful.org]. Retrieved from: http://www.mindful.org/7-ways-to-take-control-of-your-tech-habits/

> ▶ Brown, C., Killick, A. and Renaud, K. (2013, September). *To reduce e-mail, start at the top* [*Harvard Business Review* article]. Retrieved from: https://hbr.org/2013/09/to-reduce-e-mail-start-at-the-top

> ▶ Coutu, D. (2002, May). *How resilience works* [*The Harvard Business Review* article]. Retrieved from: https://hbr.org/2002/05/how-resilience-works

► Davidson, R. and Kabat-Zinn, J. [Nour Foundation]. *Can mindfulness increase our resilience to stress?* [video file]. Retrieved from: https://www.youtube.com/watch?v=ALjF1yb-VLw

► Dothetest (2008, March 10). *Test your awareness: Do the test* [video file]. Retrieved from: https://www.youtube.com/watch?v=Ahg6qcgoay4

► Figuredo, P. (2015, September 7). *Forget inbox zero: Focus on reaching inbox zen* [article from entrepreneur.com]. Retrieved from: http://www.entrepreneur.com/article/250302

► foxy10000's channel (2009, May 29). *The Fly & Samurai* [video file]. Retrieved from: https://www.youtube.com/watch?v=ragM3CI0USA

► Marr, B. (2014, February 3). *Bored at work? Here's what to do!* [LinkedIn blog post]: Retrieved from: https://www.linkedin.com/pulse/20140203092316-64875646-bored-at-work-here-s-what-to-do

► Rosen, L. and Samuel, A. (2015, June). *Conquering digital distractions* [*Harvard Business Review* article]. Retrieved from: https://hbr.org/2015/06/conquering-digital-distraction

► Tlalka, S. (2015, September). *Conquer your inbox in 3 simple steps.* [article on mindful.org]. Retrieved from: http://www.mindful.org/conquer-your-inbox-in-3-simple-steps/

Build a healthier business

This chapter will present a natural development of the mindfulness practices we have discussed and included so far, into looking at the health of you and your business as a whole. The journey into embracing mindfulness fully is one of discovering connection, well-being and insight – each of these are qualities which not only are central to good business practice but also encompass broad ethical implications and a radical paradigm shift of how businesses might operate. This shift is gradually being reflected in businesses and business practices as we write; it is occurring already in the world around us, because it actually makes good business sense. Once businesses and their employees begin to understand mindfulness, then there is an opportunity to really see that the 'snatch and grab', anxiety-fuelled working mentality is actually detrimental to the individual, to business in general and to global health. Instead, through simple, easily implemented mindfulness practices, creativity, confidence and contentment can start to grow and prosper, and business begins to boom.

> 'We need to develop and disseminate an entirely new paradigm and practice of collaboration that supersedes the traditional silos that have divided governments, philanthropies and private enterprises for decades and replace it with networks of partnerships working together to create a globally prosperous society.'
>
> **Simon Mainwaring, CEO, We First, Branding Consultant**

Perhaps your workplace *is* already one of the cutting-edge businesses catching on to the first wave of a mindful and compassionate revolution. Perhaps you, or those at the top (if that's not you, yet!), are already beginning to look at the way in which we humans, can thrive together, rather than treating people as cogs in a machine, bent towards dominion at any cost? If so, we hope this chapter will give you even further confidence and support for the fabulous work you are already doing, and if not, we hope that this chapter can inspire you to find ways, even small and ordinary ones, to develop your practice and be part of the change you want to see in your place of work, and the world.

In this chapter we will discuss and consider:

▶ How overworking and overconsumption of our internal and external resources is unsustainable.

▶ The toxic nature of the workplace based on a 'dog-eat-dog' paradigm.

▶ How a business can stop working as if it has to survive once it learns how to thrive.

▶ Business examples and research supporting the efficacy and success of this new business paradigm.

▶ How mindfulness makes good business sense for us as individuals as well as within and between businesses, and how to implement mindfulness and compassion effectively in the workplace to ensure a healthy, thriving business.

How to stop pop from eating itself

As we have seen throughout this book, mindfulness has the potential to help us cultivate a calmer and clearer mind that increases our capacity for better decisions, more effective actions and improved performance on the job. Yet, as sharper and more effective workers, we then might also begin to question: is it possible to make more mindful business decisions for the greater good of ourselves, the people we work with, our organisations and our planet? Or, will we simply become more effective capitalists and continue to destroy ourselves and each other in the process and consume our dear home faster than its capacity to replenish itself? Is growth, capitalism and the current business model really working well for us? Is there need for change? We are going to address these questions, to some extent at least, throughout this chapter, but we sincerely invite you to make your own inquiries, to become curious and interested in this debate and how you choose to position yourself within it.

Popular culture and *zeitgeist* are hugely influential in the impact they have upon our behaviours, many of which remain unexamined and therefore unconsciously habitual or accepted as 'the way things are'. In the workplace this means that we sometimes just function on autopilot, without looking closely at the way in which we and our company are operating. If we broaden the definition of consumption beyond food to consider consumption for areas such as our own energy, market growth and use of resources, we can already begin to appreciate the wider implications of bringing greater awareness to this area of our work in a whole spectrum, from the micro/personal to meta/global.

The awareness to recognise exactly what we need to do and consume and what we do not need to do and consume, in order to keep our bodies, minds, places of work and the earth healthy is a gift afforded to us via our commitment to practise mindfulness. As with all mindfulness, the initial part of the journey is simply to make contact with and become aware of what is happening in your direct experience moment to moment.

'Mindful consumption is the way to heal ourselves and to heal the world.'

Thich Nhat Hanh

Exercise 7.1: Work in progress

Conscious consuming

To help you begin to make contact and develop interest in how you, within your work setting and other contexts of your non-working life, can develop greater consciousness of consumption, spend a few moments reflecting on the areas suggested in the numbered list below. As you do this exercise:

▶ Do feel free to add your own alternatives or additions.

▶ Please let go of 'beating yourself up' over anything you feel or are told is unwholesome; rather, contact mindfully your sensory, visceral experience as you consider each area listed below.

▶ Look to the quality of your breath, the tension/ease in your body, your habitual patterns of thinking or emotional reactions, and with curiosity then inquire as to what you consume alongside each area listed below – perhaps it is relaxation that is never quite achieved to satisfaction, or perhaps it is denial of harm; maybe you find intellectual stimulation, a sense of relief or distraction from your personal concerns, inspiration ... or any number of other realisations.

▶ Consider how next time you engage in any of the following, you can track your experience to see if you can identify, in the moment, whether the experience is positive, negative or neutral ... This way you can begin to contact and explore mindful consumption and make choices informed by your own direct experience rather than externally imposed or habitual beliefs (such as 'smoking is bad for your health', or 'smoking really de-stresses me'; if you do smoke, inquire how the experience *is* directly, moment to moment).

1 **Food:** Are you aware of what you eat, when you eat it? Do you track your hunger and notice when you are full? Are you aware of the process that this food has taken to come to you? What about the energy, nutrients and quality the food has to offer you? And the impact this and the process of manufacture has on your mind, body and planet?

2 **Watching television or playing computer games (including Candy Crush on your phone!):** What do you choose to consume visually? How does what you watch/play affect your body, mind or emotions? Are you disturbed, numbed or excited by news, violence

or distress reported on television or in computer games? Is the act of watching television/gaming enhancing your well-being and quality of life?

3 **Magazines, newspapers, books and social media:** How do you choose what you read? Are you engaged and enlivened by your consumption? Do you find it hard to stop once you begin to read or use social media? What else are you consuming as you read? Global strife. political unrest, murder mysteries, trivia, gossip, knowledge? How do these things impact on you emotionally? In what ways does this activity enrich your life?

4 **Conversations:** When you converse with others, how aware are you of your body, your breath or the content of your conversation? Are you able to listen or are you already planning your next move? Who do you choose to engage with and why? Are you enjoying your verbal interactions? Do you feel fulfilled by your conversation?

5 **Physical contact:** Who do you have physical contact with? Are you caring and sensitive about how you touch and are touched physically? What emotions, thoughts and bodily sensations arise when you are touched or touch others? Are you mindfully present with those with whom you have physical contact? Are you content with the amount and quality of physical contact you give and receive?

6 **Drugs and alcohol:** What are your beliefs about your use of drugs and/or alcohol? What do you consider to be a drug? (Class As? Marijuana? Nicotine? Caffeine? Sugar?) Does consumption of drugs or alcohol add value to your life experience? If so, how? If not, what is missed or missing? Do drugs and alcohol improve your sense of happiness and well-being?

7 **Shopping:** What mental state are you in when you are shopping? How does this affect how, where and what you might choose to buy? What are you left with, besides the goods you may have purchased, after the shopping is over: relief, anger, pleasure, dissatisfaction – an overdraft? Does the experience of shopping bring you joy? How and in what ways is shopping useful to you?

8 **Work:** Consider the reasons you work other than just financial necessity – does work bring you self-esteem, status, intellectual stimulation, social contact, meaning – or anything else? What is it that you truly want back from your work? Do you get this? What areas do you feel work detracts from in your life: relationships (especially family), leisure time, health – something else? How much of the time are you at work, physically, mentally and/or emotionally? Do you really have 'days off'?

Never quite full enough

'Feeling good about what we do for a living depends more on our moment to moment experiences than it does on prestige, status or pay.'

(Salzberg, 2013)

On an individualistic level, taking more than we need doesn't seem to allay our anxieties of scarcity at all. Overconsumption (be that of work, food, noise, alcohol, sex, media, exercise, time, etc.) somehow still leaves us feeling fundamentally dissatisfied and staring into the great big fridge of life at midnight and wondering 'what next?' Socially, we tend to normalise these excessive behaviours and dress them up as temporary, macho, determined or some other form of justification – and let's face it, they sell really well, right? Work hard, eat this, listen to that, drink this, play with this, jump over that … and then you'll be happy, just like everybody else. Usually, of course, as we have explained throughout this book, everybody else is pretending just as hard as we are. So we continue to overconsume on a normalised, culturally accepted large scale, such as within businesses, and just try to work extra hard not to be the one at the bottom of the heap. This continual striving ('you should always do better, more', etc.) is something which is frequently promoted in the workplace and within many models of business, further fuelling the sense that something, somewhere or someone 'else' is better than where we are right now. This not only sets us up for a sense of perpetual dissatisfaction, but also keeps us constantly comparing ourselves with others ('are we better or worse?'), and as our well-being is then dependent on being better than others, we can feel like a failure, isolated, disconnected and threatened – in all, a great set-up for a competitive, aggressive mentality focused on 'bigger, faster, better, more', which, as we are seeing in our health, planetary resources and communities, is exhausting and simply unsustainable.

Mindfulness, however, offers us a counterbalance to the competitive, dog-eat-dog mentality that prevails across our working cultures. When we utilise the skills and insights gained through mindfulness practice, we develop a different awareness of our co-workers and learn to treat them and ourselves with greater care and compassion. Instead of our defensive stance of fending off the other 'dogs', showing how tough and indestructible we are, we learn greater tolerance of our own vulnerabilities and humanity. Through this acceptance of ourselves and others, an inevitable consequence of consistent mindfulness practice, a natural compassion seems to arise and we then develop a work ethic based upon understanding and cooperation. And the good news is that as a result of this we actually also foster higher rates of performance, staff retention and profitability, leading to a more successful and healthy business. Rather than competing for the badge of 'cut-throat of the year', we can become more present, engaged and connected to our working life and colleagues. This way we are enabled to begin to care about what we do and how this impacts on the world around us in a truly satisfying and meaningful way.

"*Change is in constant flow, resistance is futile!*"

Change is afoot

'Change shall not take place because of decisions taken by governments or the UN. Real change will take place when individuals transform themselves guided by the values that lie at the core of all human ethical systems, scientific findings and common sense.'

Dalai Lama

Although cultivating a more mindful culture at work may be starting to sound like a very sensible and attractive way forward, it will undoubtedly bring with it some anxiety, as it also presents a significant challenge to our whole economic model and way of life. It rocks the very foundations on which corporate business is built, and it contradicts the endless pursuit of growth and the prevailing capitalist mentality that most of us in the West have become indoctrinated into. However, and especially, when we unplug for a millisecond to notice, we do know that we cannot continue at the same hectic, grasping pace, that we don't have enough energy within or around us to sustain it and something has to change. Those who deny this are going to end up in A&E with a pulmonary just as we run out of the electricity needed to run the defibrillator. Nevertheless, like any such fundamental and radical change, fear will inevitably arise: fear of failure, fear of the unknown! Surely … no, should we do this? Can we?! Well, to help you along with all this and to begin to manage any such anxieties (should they arise for you too), consider again that our goal of endless growth is unsustainable and simply not even possible; change is simply inevitable. To help you utilise change, it helps to bring the very inevitability of it into conscious awareness from time to time. Change is in constant flow, resistance is futile! Being active or passive does not stop change – it may affect our intentionality, our sense of empowerment or impact on our well-being – but change will occur regardless. The universe, as the scientists say, is in constant flux, from planetary movements to the electrons in an atom. Nothing stays the same, and trying to fixate upon ideologies, structures or events in order to preserve them and keep them static is a denial of this universal truth and can lead to great suffering.

'We cling to our own point of view, as though everything depended on it. Yet our opinions have no permanence; like autumn and winter, they gradually pass away.'

Zhuangzi

When we attend to and accept change unfolding, as it inevitably will, we are then able to enter into a more fluent relationship with life and with our work, which, while not immunising us against the anxieties of the modern business world, does enable and equip us to realise them and allow them to pass on with greater ease. Any change process requires an acknowledgement, an acceptance, a letting go and an embracing of the new. This occurs all the time, mostly in unconscious ways, like with breathing or thinking. Like all mindfulness, beginning by drawing attention to these everyday processes enables us to enliven ordinary experience and presents us with opportunities to enhance our skills for using them with greater consciousness and intention. Try this simple exercise now in order to explore this mindfully.

Exercise 7.2: Mindful on the job 🎧

Times are a'changin'

▶ Begin by noticing the sensations of contact you have with the floor, chair or other surface, or where different body parts rest against one another – any of these bodily sensations will do.

▶ Now think about changing position, but know that in order to do so you will need to let go of that contact – that piece of earth, tile, foam, fabric or whatever.

▶ To move, you will need to lose. If you hold on, you will stay here.

▶ Now, for the purpose of the exercise, choose to either move or stay where you are and then follow the relevant steps below, depending upon your choice (neither is 'right' or 'wrong').

Deciding to move

1 You have decided to move in some way (this may just be lifting your hand from your lap or foot from the floor). Notice before you take

action, any thoughts or sensations arising; these thoughts and sensations will pass. All material and immaterial objects arise and pass; it is their inherent nature.

2 Now observe the muscles tensing within the body as you prepare to move. Now move and allow the actions to be in slow motion. The body requires change in order to fulfil the intention of moving. Normally this is unconscious; you are now practising making this conscious through your sustained attention.

3 Feel the tension and focus of the body on the parts that are engaged with this movement. Maybe parts of the body are held by relationship between your muscles, your will and gravity. Some of these are conditions within your control, some are not.

4 Feel yourself make the movement through air or across a surface. Recognise that time has passed, as has your action and then come to rest.

5 Is the mind at rest? Is the body absolutely without movement?

6 Notice that you left one position behind. The thoughts of this process, the sensations, movements and efforts will not arise again in the same space or time. They are gone. You have experienced this change with consciousness.

Deciding to stay

1 You have decided to remain in the same position. Notice any thoughts or sensations arising; be aware of their arising, and also how they fall, evolve or change.

2 Now observe the body staying still. Notice that even in this particular posture there is movement: breath, heartbeat, digestion, blood flow, synapses firing. The body requires movement in order to sustain this stillness, your aliveness, your posture. Normally this is unconscious; you are now practising making this conscious through your sustained attention.

3 Feel how your body is supported by the relationship between your muscles, your will and gravity. Some of these are conditions within your control, some are not.

4 Be aware that sitting, standing or lying here, time has passed, while you have remained still and resting.

5 Is the mind at rest? Is the body absolutely without movement?

6 Notice that you have remained in one position, yet change has still occurred. The thoughts of this process, the sensations, movements

and efforts will not arise again in the same space or time. They are gone. You have experienced this change with consciousness.

Whether we choose to stay put or move with the times, one thing is certain: change is inevitable. Yet by bringing consciousness and curiosity to the process of change in this way, we contact and enliven our wider sense of stability and presence. The part of us that can observe this change is certain and unchanging, and from this perspective we may find that we are at greater ease, even in the face of the inevitability of change.

Top Dog dilemma

Recognising the need to change, and understanding the anxiety which may ensue is critically important in order to find confidence and courage to even attend to your own personal struggles, let alone being part of a huge paradigm shift (but please also remind yourself that mindfully attending to your own anxieties IS being part of a very wholesome change). Nevertheless, the culture of the 1980s power-suit brute is still prevalent and worthy of further deconstruction in order to help us understand the reasons why it doesn't work well, how depleting it is, how dissatisfying to our well-being and, yet, why it has been adopted as a dominant model for so long. It might look like we are bashing the notion of competition (which we really aren't), but it is really useful to understand that, while competition has its place, there is a need for it to move on over (not a natural inclination of the highly competitive) and make room for something new. This means that there is a dilemma for the notion of 'top dog': to stop trying to eat all the other top dogs sniffing its bum and to learn a few new (mindful) tricks.

The arena of competition, so often fostered in the workplace, has aligned itself with machismo, pumped-up ego and status, but maybe these are becoming genuinely outmoded and boorish. The paradigm of 'man as machine', ironically expounded since the industrial revolution, fails to recognise our humanity and, frankly, if you've ever worked like this it feels pretty grim after a while; long term, as we have stated already, it is simply unsustainable. We see many clients in our practice who have burned out while trying to work like machines, by stuffing alcohol and white powder into their systems in order to try to stimulate their failing bodies and minds into action and to numb out the pain of trying to exist like that week after week. Somehow there is a notion that you need to be tough, hard and strong (and often rude too) to get on in business. Thankfully, this is not the case from birth or there would be no humans, as we are ridiculously weak and vulnerable as babies and take an inordinate amount of time to grow up – some of us never, ever reaching maturity. So somewhere in the development of an adolescent, say, into the next business guru, comes a toughening, hardening and (allegedly) strengthening rite of passage so you then get to go round and act like an arsehole too. Perhaps this is a moment you can recall, something shaming and finger-pointing, when after crying bitterly in the loo you thought, 'Well sod this, I'm going to be the finger-pointing bast*rd next time!', and you put a cage around that soft place inside and stormed off in your power-suit. But when we are not under threat, should we use this same strategy? What are the consequences of always feeling defensive, on edge and in the fray? Perhaps there is a difference between the strategy needed to survive and the strategy needed to thrive?

From a psychological perspective, being in a state of perpetual anxiety is very damaging to our health and our performance (please revisit Chapter 2 for a recap if you wish) and affects cognition so that many innocuous events and situations are perceived as a threat. If we consider the competitive business model (when mindfulness is absent) as reactive and anxiety-based, it makes sense that all other businesses are seen as rivals, that we treat others with suspicion and constantly seek power over anyone or anything we identify as an opponent. A competitive culture needs a threat, we need an enemy, and then, we need to 'survive' – this is how we re-enact and perpetuate the *sickness culture* at work and how we continue to buy into the notion of 'strength/weakness'. No one wants to be bottom of the heap, to be the failure, the weakness or the one who gets the shaming pointing finger telling us (possibly with regret) that 'you're fired!'.

The truth is that in buying into a culture where 'only the strong will survive' – where anxiety remains rife, work pressures and stresses increase, cutbacks are efficiently made and competition is fierce – feels like the only way to survive among the other dogs in the pit. Competition takes out the weak in a survival of the fittest culture, but what does that mean? In animal populations 'weak' means those who are not thriving at their peak (infants, ill, elderly, infirm); this doesn't make them 'wrong', but they are simply not at full capacity. However, 'weak' may also be those who do not adapt quickly enough, or evolve fast enough or who make poor choices. This 'strong/weak' dualistic paradigm is one often adopted in the archetypal workplace and it makes sense that we would want to fight to maintain the semblance of strength, rather than facing the internal or external consequences of being (perceived as) 'weak', where we are vulnerable and prone to rejection from our stronger colleagues and peers. When we adopt this paradigm, however, we are inevitably going to find ourselves, at times at least, in a weaker place, simply through the conditions of our existence – through illness, ageing and circumstance, etc. It enhances our sense of failure, disconnection and vulnerability and sets us up to perpetually fight against the reality of these conditions occurring, breeding anxiety and ironically enhancing our potential to be 'weak'. Thus we firmly establish a culture of sickness.

> Michael: I remember a time that I led in fear. Managing a team of psychologists my motto was: 'We must win the work! We must be better, more efficient and quicker than the rest!' Inevitably my competitiveness-fuelled insecurity cultivated an environment of pressure. Stress and a consequential vulnerability prevailed across the entire team. Even the most experienced practitioners felt overwhelmed, and as a result their performance declined; they couldn't keep up and clients then understandably voted with their feet. I was misguided and I misjudged the natural ebb and flow of work from a perspective of fear (fear of failure, shame and disconnection). I assumed inevitably quieter times occurred not because they 'just do', but because 'We simply were not up to scratch! Not doing well enough! Who was letting the team down? They must go, NOW!' My insecurity gave way to a competitive culture which inevitably led to fear, and fear breads more fear, even among the strongest of us. This was clearly an unworkable model for our team. The truth is that there was and there has always been, and will continue to be, enough work to go around; there is nothing to prove, nothing to fear. Bringing a mindful perspective to this anxiety-fuelled culture soon turned our ailing business around. The foundations were laid, giving rise to the vigorous and flourishing practice that it is today, where both practitioners and clients alike can continue to thrive.

Maybe for some of us, we think that if we can just 'make it' , then we can stop (perhaps that early retirement?) and finally relax. Perhaps you don't even think or care much about bloody business models and paradigms and all that; you just have very long hours, struggle with debts, poor health, unkind managers and overwhelming workloads. In essence, even if we have a pretty peachy deal at work, we are still going to have cr*ppy days, we are still going to suffer from all the things that this earth throws to all of its planetary inhabitants (illness, ageing and death). No one of us is immune – even Mr Smarmy in his swanky penthouse office, on his six-figure-salary (plus bonus) and private jets to the Cayman Islands will suffer the consequences of eating a dodgy kebab, or get a nasty mystery rash, develop a spare tyre, find his hairline receding and finally join the ancestors pushing up the daisies. Because we are unable to guarantee that there is a great big after-party in the sky after we're done with all this life stuff, and because, just like you, we spend an inordinate amount of our time working, we think that it is pretty darn crucial to make the workplace a healthy, happy and thriving environment.

The cycle of company sickness

Punitive work cultures, driven by fear, are not working intelligently. Their focus of attention, narrowed to outmoded strategies for survival (just like any individual in 'fight or flight' mode), ignores longer-term sustainability and simply resorts to reactivity; these types of work cultures are suffering from anxiety. And as we know by now, anxiety is an irrational fear based upon real or imagined (perceived) threat. Anxiety causes long-term health difficulties, loss of functioning and fatigue. Anxiety disorders are among the most prevalent mental health difficulties and are rife within the corporate sector; they directly reflect the business mentality of anxiety shown in the wider work group of many businesses (we see this every day in our clients and in our very own business practice). In models underpinning Systemic and Family Therapy, this is a well-known and well-understood concept, an understanding of how the system and individual are mirroring certain behaviours in each other, and can be really useful for conceptualising a particular work culture and also how change can occur effectively in the workplace. For instance, 'Bowen Theory' (from the systemic paradigm) suggests that change at a higher level of a hierarchical system will have more impact than change at lower levels. If we do sit at the higher echelons of power, or even have made it above 'office dogsbody', then we have a greater responsibility to wake up and get mindful, influencing the well-being of our colleagues and reducing company anxiety as well as our own. If we choose to carry on regardless, however, we enter a vicious cycle (as anyone who has ever experienced anxiety will know) which escalates until we reach breakdown.

'The discomfort generated by the intensity of anxiety or degree of instability in the group will emerge typically as a strong pressure to relieve discomfort quickly. All things being equal, the pressures for quick relief will be self-centred on the individual or the subgroup, leading to conflict and potential polarisations as the self-interest of the various groups clash, heightened by the discomfort of anxiety. The outcome can be increased discomfort, anxiety, and instability, leading to even more intense pressures for rapid solutions which relieve discomfort.'

Daniel Papero, PhD (Please see 'Useful resources' section for link to the article 'Anxiety and Organisations')

So instead of mindlessly perpetuating this vicious cycle of anxiety, surely it is time to pass on a new model to the next junior running off to the loos, to free ourselves from being caged, disconnected and brutish, and find a way of reconnecting, being compassionate and healthy? Even after fighting his/her way up to the top, that war-wounded old dog is still going to look around for his/her pedigree chum and hope for a few mates to hang out with. We do not need to react to the reactionaries, turn into neo-liberalists, or new Marxists or kick the old dogs in the teeth. We are all suffering in the same old pile of poo after all; surely it's bad enough without adding any more stress? This revolution is pretty peaceful, man. Grab yourself a poncho and sit down next to us.

Exercise 7.3: Mindful on the job

Making peace

Use this exercise as you commute to work, are sitting at your desk or dashing out for a meeting. Let your cue become that clenched feeling in your jaw, the wrinkled-up frown on your forehead and/or the shoulders up round your ears. Whenever you notice any or all of these, try this exercise and repeat it as often as you can by following the steps below.

1 Breathe in through your nose, open your mouth ever so slightly and wriggle your jaw sideways.

2 Take a long exhalation through your mouth and then close your mouth gently.

3 Repeat this or similar, 'As I release my jaw I am making space for peace'.

4 Breathing softly, let your face uncrease – a slight smile can help with this.

5 Say to yourself, 'As I soften my face I am making space for a sense of ease'.

6 Gently roll your shoulders down and away from your ears, and sit or stand up a little straighter if you can.

7 Take a few more gentle breaths, telling yourself, 'As I let go in my shoulders, I am open to greater well-being in my body'.

8 You may wish to invite ease, well-being and relaxation to other parts of your body. Don't worry if tension is still present; your intention is simply to be welcoming to the possibility of ease, and to expand even the smallest sensations of that, not to force anything.

'Peace comes from within. Do not seek it without.'

Often attributed to Gautama Buddha

Stayin' alive

So let's think about this shift in business models some more; rather than simply becoming a victim of our own success, or turning into some unsustainable Monopoly Monster, let's begin to explore further how we turn from being in a state of 'high-alert-crush-them-all-or-die' to something a little more benign, peaceful, sustainable and less likely to cause you to die of that pulmonary (just after you've finished crushing them all).

Firstly, of course is the recognition that we, or our workplace, are representing something that feels unhelpful, perhaps inauthentic or even downright damaging and unethical. This may mean recognising that you are highly stressed, angry, working with people who don't share your views and 'pretending' to fit in: this might be working for a company whose practices or products you find questionable, or you may yourself be actively part of something (e.g. a policy, practice, manufacturing process or product) you find unethical or which causes harm. This calls for a return to mindfully reviewing our values (see Chapter 6) and seeing if how we operate at work is aligning with them. Most of us, through working with mindfulness, deepen this awareness over the days, months and years we practise, and begin to see how deeply we are connected or disconnected from our peers, friends, family, our community, our environment or ecosystem. This sense of dis/connection is deeply linked with primal feelings of belonging and acceptance, which most of us, in our deepest hearts, yearn for. It is very difficult to feel the depth of this yearning at times, and can seem self-protecting to turn away from it, to shut off, shut up or shut down. Yet, of course, the ultimate cost of denying our vulnerability and the fundamental, innate need to feel deeply wanted and at peace is that we become further disconnected from our fellow human beings and the world we inhabit. As the practice of mindfulness is ultimately about cultivating more awareness, it becomes inevitable that we will simply keep bumping into ourselves (usually showing up as that pesky inner critic) habitually shutting off from connecting, and that we will learn that our knee-jerk responses are anxiety-fuelled, redundant and ineffective. As we have proposed, a large part of business culture has been based solely on models of competition and domination, typically market/economy-focused in terms of sustainability. As an anxious reaction to post-world-war depression and periods of austerity, these paradigms have appeared to provide an economic stability when fears are rife.

However, we can see from a mindful perspective that exclusively using this model of competition keeps business constantly reactive and in the 'fight or flight' arena. It's not clever nor ultimately effective for the good health and consequential success of business (more on this to come), so what are the alternative models available for us to consider?

Business is thriving

'Corporate workplaces probably aren't in sync with our evolutionary roots and may not be good for our long-term success as humans.'

**Eric Michael Johnson (Taken from Yes! Magazine; please see 'Useful resources'
section for link to the article)**

Ideas of competition and capitalism have a lot in common with the evolutionists' theories of 'survival of the fittest', which have, as we have already discussed, manifested in the workplace as the 'dog-eat-dog' mentality of 'good business'. We have considered how this is totally unsustainable, unpleasant and actually damaging as a long-term strategy. It is even a little misguided as a purist approach to survival, as Darwin himself, in fact, did make reference to the value of cooperation and sympathetic care as essential components of communities which produced *'prolific and flourishing off-spring'*, a piece of his theory which is often forgotten. Indeed, plenty of later research studying both human and animal (including bats, ravens, ground squirrels and monkeys – see the 'Useful resources' section for an astonishing video from News Hour India) behaviour has demonstrated and observed acts of inherent altruism. Humans do appear to differ from most animal species in that we can be seen to display altruism beyond our kin or close group members to include strangers. Although still debated, there is increasing psychological and neuropsychological evidence that motivation to act arising from empathy is altruistic as opposed to egotistical motivation. In fact, the same reward system in the brain becomes activated through individualistic material gain as through acts of altruism which provide these instead to others (Fehr, cited in Singer and Ricard (eds), 2015, loc 2186).

More recently, psychologists have researched this area and developed further theories on the evolutionary value and *necessity* of cooperation for humanity, as shown by collective activities such as hunting, farming and child-rearing. Indeed, promoting group acceptance, by sharing your food for instance (rather than scoffing it by yourself in a cave), would certainly have been more advantageous in hostile environmental conditions where a group offered protection and a greater diversity of expertise and skills. Scattered humans were, as a consequence of cooperative behaviours, able to form tribal communities which then evolved into more prosperous collective societies, with clear intentionality and shared cultural identities. As (Western) human societies today are resource-rich, technologically sophisticated and mobile, our social groups are becoming increasingly integrated and the opportunities and advantages of cooperation are abundant. In business this leaves us the enormous potential to trade skills and resources globally and develop global communities when measures are taken to ensure group cohesiveness and effective communication. The huge advantage of cooperation is that we are able to negotiate conflict and seek resolution skilfully; because it is mutually advantageous, we can benefit from collating skills and ideas, and sharing resources. This is the essential progression from fighting to survive to learning to thrive. Companies do need to be proactive about collaboration and not simply assume it will happen, or ignore it in favour of being overly competitive (the tools and skills we have encouraged you to develop in Chapter 5 are essential to this within working teams and organisations). Without skills in cooperation, larger teams with greater diversity and differing work ethics, cultures and backgrounds may be susceptible to fragmenting. Effective cooperation features several components:

Six key markers of a thriving, cooperative workplace

1 Supportive relationships demonstrated from top-down: senior executives and project managers model collaborative behaviours
2 A culture of praise, appreciation and care of others
3 Good listening skills and engagement in purposeful conversations
4 Productive and creative conflict resolution
5 Shared and transparent values and goals
6 Community building and time for shared social activities.

These key markers are in part very similar to those identified by the Nobel Prize winning American political economist Elinor Ostrom, who researched successful groups that she observed to function effectively and who developed a set of design principles critical for a group to thrive sustainably. Her work has recently been extended and developed by an enthusiastic development team of eminent evolutionary biologists, psychologists and therapists called Prosocial (please visit www.prosocialgroups.org), who have created a free internet platform offering an impressive programme designed to assess and help groups improve their performance, which involves a strong component of mindfulness. The very existence of organisations such as the Prosocial initiative, which are using evidence-based programmes to adopt an intelligent strategy towards the improvement of human welfare and the development of healthier business teams and other groups, shows that the mindset of group enterprises is really beginning to change. Collaborative practices unite communities, encourage group identity and loyalty and can become highly successful long-term projects.

The rise and success of cooperative businesses such as football clubs, farming groups, food retailers and community energy projects has taken collaborative work practices to the highest level and shows that when the focus is on sustainability, community and shared values, rather than on fierce competition, businesses can still succeed. Moreover, cooperative businesses represent a real growth market in which they are gaining consumer support exponentially. At the Annual Cooperatives Conference on 6 May 2015, Mike Beall (past-President and CEO of National Cooperative Business Association – NCBA CLUSA) unveiled the results of a public opinion survey on co-ops and spoke about the rising public interest and awareness of the co-op business model, and the need to harness their influence by developing cross-sector connections between co-ops (i.e. further enhancing collaboration). He stated:

> 'We know the numbers: 1 in 3 Americans are co-op members, 75 per cent of the U.S. landmass is served by electric co-ops and more than 100 million people now identify as credit union members. We've got to keep connecting the sectors. That's where we really are powerful.'
>
> Mike Beall, past-President and CEO, NCBA CLUSA (Please see 'Useful resources' section for link to the full article)

Other companies are adopting a no/low growth policy. Rather than aiming for yearly growth targets, these companies, in line with the models above, are instead exploring different approaches which include community-based models, sustainability and quality maintenance. While the number of no/low growth businesses is still relatively small, and research is still somewhat lacking, new initiatives are beginning daily and offering thought-provoking paradigms. One company – Patagonia, the Californian outdoor clothing company – is engaging in a more mindful approach to consumption while still focusing on (sustainable) growth. The company's mission is to build the best product, causing no unnecessary harm, as well as using business to inspire and implement solutions to the environmental crisis. Yvon Chouinard, the founder of Patagonia, also sees that there is a *'proper size'* for the company, and, as he says in his inspirational talk – 'The Education of a Reluctant Businessman' – *'There are no three star French restaurants with fifty tables – it's impossible.'* To read more about Patagonia and to hear how mindfulness could help to adjust ineffective business models, leading to a more sustainable future, please follow the link in the 'Useful resources' section at the end of the chapter.

Even more traditional businesses are also benefitting from making the focus on collaboration central to their operation. For instance, multinational professional services network, PricewaterhouseCoopers (PwC) have one of the strongest capabilities in productive collaboration. With responsibility for developing 140,000 employees in nearly 150 countries, PwC's in-house training includes components addressing teamwork, emotional intelligence, networking, holding difficult conversations, coaching, corporate social responsibility, and communicating the firm's strategy and shared values. PwC also teaches employees how to influence others effectively and build healthy partnerships. Other headline companies really examining the way we treat workers and also actively upholding ethical integrity, addressing sustainability, creating global communities, promoting innovative and reputable leadership and enhancing a culture of 'thriving business' include: Accenture, GE, Empresa de Desarrollo Urbano, Google Inc., Hennes & Mauritz (H&M), The Hershey Company, illycaffè spa, Kao Corporation, Marks and Spencer, Milliken & Company, National Australia Bank, Natura Cosméticos, PepsiCo, SingTel, The Rezidor Hotel Group, Voya Financial and Wipro Limited (please see the link in the 'Useful resources' section at the end of the chapter for an article about the world's most ethical companies in 2015).

Businesses such as these, that are said to enjoy good health and success, are driven by a certain energy, an energy that comes from the deepest needs and aspirations of their own workforces (read here: need and aspiration to thrive, belong, achieve, flourish and find meaning in our lives).

> *'By giving our employees choice and treating them like the capable adults they are, we've been rewarded with increased productivity, innovation and happiness in our workforce.'*
>
> **Richard Branson, Founder, Virgin Group (Taken from huffpost.com; please see 'Useful resources' section for link to full blog post)**

A healthy business provides its workers with a sense of community within which their needs and aspirations are proactively recognised, responded to authentically and ultimately satisfied. This sense of community can be established by paying great attention to:

▶ the thoughts, feelings and actions of each individual worker and the organisation as a whole;

▶ the shared development and use of helpful tools (such as mindfulness) to help employees to effectively manage thoughts and feelings that prevent the company moving toward its valued goals;

▶ identifying shared values (what is important) and establishing the means to express and act on these;

▶ managing relationships with care, kindness and respect;

▶ ensuring employees have a sense of their autonomy (while being guided in their actions);

▶ managing differences and conflict in open, honest and constructive ways.

A more collaborative model, within and between businesses, keeps alive essential components of long-term survival such as diversity rather than monopolisation, creativity and novel ideas rather than dictates and 'established' practices, and also fosters humanistic values rather than just mechanistic ones. This is not to say we must throw the baby out with the bath water; competitiveness can also be motivating and helps to establish efficient and optimal functioning. However, it clearly makes little economic sense to ignore the importance of more altruistic modes of operating in business, especially in terms of long-term sustainability, well-being and our own (and collective) happiness. The fact that there is room for diversity, from small-scale cooperatives to multinational corporations, means that business has never been so dynamic; but also there has never before been such a need to address sustainability, ethics, well-being and accountability – these are not 'nice ideas' or the dream of ideologists but fundamental to businesses thriving.

Health, wealth and happiness

'In my view, genuine cooperation is ultimately very much based on respecting others' rights and loving others.'

Dalai Lama (cited in Singer and Ricard (eds), 2015, Loc 1253)

New initiatives within business, economics, social sciences and environmental sciences are forming, which are moving towards wholeheartedly engaging with others in mutually trusting relationships which build healthier working relationships. The Dalai Lama is a big champion of this movement, and is the Patron of the UK-based initiative 'Action for Happiness', which has just recently launched its new science-based programme (consisting of an evening course) for increasing happiness and well-being across the UK (please see the 'Useful resources' section for more on this). Recent research cited on the Action for Happiness website reveals the key to a happy life is to invest in relationships and community just as much, if not more, as you invest in the markets. This is a view expounded by Richard Layard, Director of the Centre for Economic Performance at the London School of Economics, who has spent many years investigating the relationship between wealth and happiness. Layard maintains that well-being is a serious political issue, and a more relevant measure of a country's status than GDP (although they are not unrelated). Layard argues for more economic awareness in order to increase global well-being and prosperity. He points out that as one person's income increases this means that someone else's must decline. Therefore, raising income does not increase rates of happiness – this is in direct challenge to the notion of free and competitive markets so prevalent within business, which ignores relationships or community. As such, we have seen a rise in living standards and income, but no perceptible difference in happiness. This is not to say that at an individual level happiness doesn't increase with income increase (i.e. we become happier when we are richer), but this is counterbalanced by necessary adjustments elsewhere to become, at a meta-level, a zero-gains redistribution of wealth which does not affect national happiness. Also, individual gain in happiness when wealth increases is only relevant if we compare ourselves as rich relative to our peers, and even the effect of this plateaus.

Kahneman and Deaton, in their 2010 research[1] on income and well-being concluded that:

> 'Lack of money brings both emotional misery and low life evaluation; similar results were found for anger. Beyond ~$75,000* in the contemporary United States, however, higher income is neither the road to experienced happiness nor the road to the relief of unhappiness or stress.'

Money is not the only factor affecting people's happiness of course; as we have just mentioned, relationships play a key part in our well-being, as does our level of physical and mental health. A YouGov poll

---

*$75,000 was per household, and roughly equates to £49,500 (GBP) at time of writing.

commissioned by Action for Happiness in 2014, found that 87 per cent of the British public would choose happiness rather than wealth (8 per cent) for their society. The findings were largely consistent across all UK demographics. Furthermore, the top two most important factors chosen for personal happiness were:

1 Relationships with partner/family (80 per cent)
2 Health (71 per cent).

These were then followed by Money (42 per cent), Appearance (4 per cent) and Possessions (4 per cent). Dr Mark Williamson, Action for Happiness Director, commented on the results, saying: 'The economy dominates our political and social discussions, but this survey shows that happiness is more important to people'. You can find a link to an article about this poll and some related commentary listed in the 'Useful resources' section at the end of this chapter (author England, R).

Happiness is ...

Clearly, while wealth does play its part, our well-being is primarily contingent on the quality of our social relationships and our health. With most of us spending the majority of time working, happy working relationships and well-being at work really start to stand out. Work-related stress and poor interpersonal relationships in the workplace may explain not only why you get the Monday morning blues but also the chronic cases of work-related depression and anxiety and a whole host of physical stress-related symptoms that are endemic in our working culture. Interestingly, a long line of research (some of which we have cited in Chapter 5) supports findings that social relationships are in fact a good predictor in both physical and mental health. Stanford University, on their BeWell@stanford website, includes an interesting article which reports.

> 'Studies indicate that 'social capital' is one of the biggest predictors for health, happiness, and longevity. The problem: we often do not recognise the importance of social connection. Our culture values hard work, success, and wealth, so it's no surprise some of us do not set aside enough time for social ties when we think security lies in material things rather than other people.'

(Please see 'Useful resources' section for a link to the full article)

So, we can see that connectivity, cooperation and community-building are absolutely essential to a happier, healthier workforce, which in turn will be a more productive and effective workforce. Happiness is good business. A recent (Sept 2015) article in the *Telegraph* (please see the 'Useful resources' section) entitled 'Well-being at work is good for business' agrees, citing a study undertaken by VitalityHealth which found that companies rated by employees as having the most supportive cultures also had the lowest productivity losses. The healthiest companies, in terms of well-being for workers, when compared with the unhealthiest companies, were found to have a 45 per cent lower cost of lost productivity. The report supports the clear relationship between work ethos and yield: healthier, happier employees equals healthier output and greater business success.

Mindfulness in action

'[it is agreed] … it is vital to wellbeing that we decrease stress and threat in human environments, that poverty and inequality are major contributors to these conditions, and that we need to promote reinforcement and support for prosocial behaviour, including the cultivation of caring relationships.'

Anthony Biglan, Senior Scientist, Oregon Research Institute (Taken from evolution-institue.org; please see 'Useful resources' section for link to full article)

Implementing a new, happier and healthier business model must begin at the very core of any business: it must begin with its people. Only by looking inwards and changing our internal world will we be able to move forward with the changes that are truly necessary on a cultural and organisational level too. Mindfulness is the tool for doing just that.

Mindfulness can transform your business – have no qualms about it. It has the potential to pump a rosy, energetic glow back into the cheeks of any business that may be looking a bit grim, haggard, pale and anaemic. Specifically, with practice we begin to inject a greater sense of responsibility, care, attention and warmth into the company culture. Workers begin to take more responsibility for their own actions and reactions to situations as they are better able to notice the impact that they are having on those people and events around them. Mindfulness gives rise to greater awareness of the emotions that reside in both ourselves and others and improves our interpersonal dynamics. The attention given to what others have to say also improves with mindfulness practice. Workers, managers and senior leaders are better able to put aside their own rigid and fixed viewpoints, open up and listen more and then incorporate others' opinions, views and ideas into their work, as well as changes in company procedures and policies, helping the individual, team and company become happier, healthier and more efficient. People naturally become warmer towards one another with mindfulness practice. A greater and more genuine sense of interest for one another begins to evolve, and as a result workers will begin to feel safer and better cared for and eventually creativity and general effectiveness ensues. You can rest assured that your personal mindfulness practice will help to kick-start the cultivation of all of this, and you can also strengthen the natural emergence of these qualities by purposefully implementing the following steps as often as you can, alongside your regular personal practice:

► Look for ways to assist your colleagues for no other reason than to be helpful and collaborative. Along with offering support to work tasks, this may also involve making simple, small efforts such as holding the lift doors open for a colleague, offering cups of coffee to the team, asking how people are doing and smiling more often!

► Incline your minds toward warmth while interacting with others and listening to your colleagues; try your best to reserve judgement, harsh criticism and evaluation. Replace judgement with understanding, compassion and kindness (more on this to come). And here's maybe the most difficult:

► Respond to hostility and passive aggression that may be directed towards you with calmness, warmth, understanding and kindness.

We are now going to consider these and further ways of putting mindfulness into practical application at work, giving you examples and research to illustrate and back this up, as well as further exercises for you to try. This will help you to continue to integrate the conceptual with the practical and make mindfulness an action in your place of work.

We are going to briefly focus on four main areas of concern which are frequently presented to us in our London clinic, affecting the health and well-being of employees and which we also consider as 'symptomatic' of the sickness culture we have described above. These symptoms are:

1 Feeling overstretched and time-poor
2 Lacking in energy reserves
3 Bullying (being the victim or the perpetrator)
4 Lack of compassion and kindness (feeling neglected and uncared for).

Remember that change begins with a single and often simple (mindful) step, and any capacity you have to engage with the action points and practices that follow will bring benefits.

Working 9 to 5 – what a way to make a livin'

We have seen and discussed in some detail the unsustainability of the 'work harder, longer, faster' mentality. Striving for more (and more!) breeds an anxiety of scarcity (we never feel we have enough), disrupts our sense of ease and peace and gives rise to the competitive, dog-eat-dog mentality that so many of us are used to (and tiring of) in our workplaces. Destructive norms are established (some unspoken but they are there, i.e. staying on at the office way past clocking-off time) that grow like a cancer slowly but surely, eating away at the healthy organs of any organisation. This isn't clever and is bad for business. In fact, research shows us that working long hours simply does not work and tends to backfire horribly for both companies and the very people that work there, in many different ways. According to one study[2] examining how employees at a large consulting firm navigated work pressures to uphold a professional identity of the 'ideal worker', working longer hours was not considered to produce superior output compared to working fewer hours, as perceived by mangers in that company. This study found no evidence that those employees working fewer hours actually accomplished less, or any sign that the overworking employees accomplished more. So despite what most of us have been led to believe, it would seem that working long hours is not actually necessary for the production of high-quality work.

Working long hours may actually be costly to both the individual employee and the company they work for in many ways. In fact, overworking has been associated with an array of health-related problems, including increased alcohol consumption[3], sleeping difficulties[4] and depression[5], as well as type 2 diabetes[6] and coronary heart disease[7], and a decline in cognitive functioning[8]. In a very recent study[9] (one of the largest research projects of its kind, involving more than 600,000 men and women from across Europe, the USA and Australia), researchers at University College London in the UK found that people who put in 55 hours or more of work per week had a 33 per cent greater risk of stroke than those working a more balanced 35–40-hour week. It goes without saying really, but all this just adds to the bottom-line cost for any organisation, as an overstretched workforce soon translates into increased rates of presenteeism, absenteeism, staff turnover and rising health insurance costs. Further research highlights how when we are exhausted, say, from putting in overtime at work, our ability to 'read the emotional states of others' (colleagues, clients, etc.) who we're dealing with at work[10], as well as our ability to refrain from aggressive knee-jerk responses in our heated communications[11], become severely impaired. Along with this, when we are exhausted, our ability to make clear rational decisions[12] is negatively impacted upon also. Another study[13] found that employees that were overworked were less invested in their job a year later, and were more likely to report emotional exhaustion and physical symptoms, like headaches and discomfort and pain in their stomachs. So it's pretty clear that the prevailing work ethic favouring and promoting an excessive working routine is problematic, more trouble than it's worth, simply not healthy and ultimately detrimental for business. So where does this leave us? What else is there to do if we're not working ourselves into the ground?

> *'It is high time to rid ourselves of the notion that leisure for workmen is either 'lost time' or a class privilege.'*

Henry Ford

You may be interested to know that the five-day, 40-hour working week interceded by weekends (and you may even be one of the lucky few that can remember such a time) was not just a fanciful notion that one day fell from the sky somewhere but instead a well thought-through formula for increased workplace productivity. On 1st May 1926 Henry Ford first proposed this model for all employees working at his Detroit-based automobile company. He realised that you could get more output from workers having them work fewer days and fewer hours. His model seemed to bring the expected results, and manufacturers all over the country, and then the world, soon followed suit, and the Monday-to-Friday working week became common practice. It seems that there is an optimal amount of working hours to ensure good health, performance and profitability, and if that threshold is overstepped the performance, output and health of both the individual worker and the company rapidly decline.

There are a growing number of companies that are in fact aware of the costs of employees working too many hours and have begun to address this by reducing the working week even further. For example, Uniqlo, the Japanese clothing company, has just recently joined in on the trend. The company is now paying more attention to its workers' well-being and has very recently offered the option of working a four-day week to its full-time staff working across its stores in Japan. The company is hopeful that this change will free up time and allow workers to attend to pressing demands in their personal lives, and as a result it will increase staff retention and prevent staff scaling back hours – win, win for all! The company has expressed how it is willing to accommodate the challenges that this change might bring, and if it all works well it hopes to begin to roll out the four-day working week offer to corporate staff at its headquarters too (it will be interesting to see how this all pans out). Costco and Walmart are other US-based companies that are also listening more to their employees' needs and offering flexible working hours and a variety of other options that might work for different people.

It would seem that more and more businesses are now considering the benefits of reducing the working week. In fact a number of companies are now moving towards a standard six-hour working day in Sweden, where over recent years there has been a lot of political interest, including publicly funded experiments, exploring a reduction in working hours as a means to redress work–life balance. Some of the companies that have already implemented this change include the Stockholm-based app developer Filimundus, as well as Toyota (service centres) in Gothenburg. Among the many benefits of working fewer hours that have been reported by CEOs and managers across different industries in Sweden are less stressed, happier and more energised staff, less conflict amongst staff, higher staff retention, improved focus, efficiency and productivity, and an overall increase in profits (you can find an interesting article from the *Guardian* listed in the 'Useful resources' section at the end of this chapter if you want to read more on the changes afoot in Sweden).

You may not be one of the lucky ones that are currently enjoying a reduction in your working hours – or maybe you are, but you're still feeling overstretched. Either way, why not try this next exercise right now and repeat it as often as you like throughout your working day, to take a bit of time back for yourself. This way, you might start to feel more replenished and refreshed. You might even start to notice how you actually have more 'time on your side' than you first considered and how simply taking a moment or two back for yourself has huge benefits.

Exercise 7.4: Mindful on the job

The time is now

Just to give yourself a little insight into where you are right now with the time and some of the pressures or stresses zooming about (or not) in your mind, why not try this quick – yes, just one minute – practice. Try repeating this throughout the day to remind yourself that you are actually here on planet Earth with the rest of us and not trapped inside your thoughts.

Time yourself for one minute. You might like to use the hand of an analogue clock, as this is particularly effective for this exercise. Or guess approximately one minute if you must. Let yourself have this moment; one minute can be spared even on your busy, important and hectic schedule!

1 Find your feet, your contact with the floor.
2 Take just one breath and follow this in and out.
3 Be aware of any thoughts swirling around.
4 Notice any impatience or urges 'to do' something.
5 Tell yourself 'I have time for this breath/stillness/moment/irritation/ or whatever'.
6 Breathe and repeat steps 1–5 until one minute or so has passed.

With the above exercise try to encourage yourself to allow this tiny space for the voice that might say 'I haven't got time!!!' In this exercise you do not need to shut this nagging voice up, or to act on it: simply be aware that it is there. Notice that it perhaps breeds frustration and dissatisfaction and that you, just like the workers reported in the studies above, will actually be happier, healthier and more productive, and just as effective, without paying such heed to this inner nag.

We know that there is a long road ahead before most of us have a deeper feeling that our well-being is taken seriously by our work and that we are not at risk of losing our job, promotion opportunities or respect from our employees if we put our well-being, or that of our families, into the spotlight. However, unhappiness and unhappy relationships do not work well for business and even some of the biggest corporations are finally catching on: for example, Accenture (please see the Huffington Post article which you can find in the 'Useful resources' section at the end of the chapter) are trying to make a difference by finally(!) acknowledging the benefits to themselves and their employees by better supporting new parents. Similarly, at Richard Branson's Virgin Group, workers have been given options for flexible working hours and working from home. They have also been granted unlimited leave (it's up to members of staff to decide for themselves how much leave to take and when to take it) and paid parental leave. The management at Virgin believes that their employees are their best assets and hopes that these initiatives will encourage their staff to focus on their well-being and improve their health and satisfaction – all for the greater good of the company too. Other companies are following suit as they too realise that continuing to push their already overstretched employees to work longer and harder is destroying the personal health and lives of those workers. It seems it really is the time to wise up and take action if you want a healthy business, as ignorantly continuing to work in such ineffective ways is doing a disservice to all involved.

The notion of putting in fewer hours on the job is bound to bring with it fear, even for those of us that moan about how much we have to do, and long for a time when we can work fewer hours: 'How will get I everything done?', 'There's no way I can do fewer hours. I'll only have more to do later if I work less now!' Well, if this sounds like you, then you'll be pleased to know that spending less time on your work really doesn't have to mean that you will achieve less or become less productive or effective on the job. Don't believe us? Well, here are our five top tips to ensure you remain productive while putting in less time. Try them and see how you get on for yourself.

Five top tips for how to work less (without achieving less)

1 Stop trying to multitask, and revisit Chapter 2 to enhance your focus and efficiency. Focus on doing just *one* thing at a time.

2 Take frequent short breaks to keep mentally fresh (yes!!). This means getting up, stretching, walking, having a tea – not sitting and checking your emails!

3 Learn to say 'no' (nicely, though). Stick to assigned tasks and don't take on more than your share or more than you realistically have the capacity to do within your working hours.

4 As much as possible, leave and start work at the same times each day – colleagues will soon know that they can't ask you to just do 'this or that' before you clock off.

5 Work to your strengths and get training for your weaknesses. Work to show off your skills, don't waste time and energy on what you may be less qualified or capable at doing; instead ask for support and training to strengthen these areas. This makes good practice and is a great point for annual reviews too.

Finally, but perhaps most radically, you can try (approximately ten minutes a day minimum) actually giving more time to others. Yes! Totally counter-intuitive, we know! However, research[14] by Cassie Mogilner (Assistant Professor of Marketing at the University of Pennsylvania's Wharton School) found that people who gave time to help others felt more confident, capable and useful. Furthermore, they also felt a high sense of accomplishment, leading to greater productivity and a sense of time being expansive. She also found through her research that focusing on the present moment decreases the sense of being rushed or harried by slowing the perception of time passing (so do remember to repeat Exercise 7.4 above, often). Yes, it really would seem that slowing down to feed the dog, help an old lady across the road and take a few well-deserved mindful breaths on the way to work may just be the ticket to a greater sense of spaciousness, productivity and efficiency in your working day.

Energy is abundant whereas time is finite

'When fashioned in a way that accommodates human needs and realises human potential, organisations are more productive and experience better growth. We call this being 100% Human at Work.'

**Richard Branson, Founder, Virgin Group (Taken from huffpost.com; please see
'Useful resources' section for link to full blog post)**

It really is great to hear how businesses are recognising the detrimental effects of excessive working hours and how many are taking active steps to reduce these. However, is a reduction in the hours we clock up per week the only necessary adjustment to the increasingly varied and modern work contexts that we find ourselves operating in today?

A focus on time and working hours alone may have been effective a century ago when trying to run factories efficiently. But maybe it's time to have a complete rethink and recognise how tweaking the number of hours we work isn't the only way to increase the effectiveness and productivity of a workforce. What most of us easily forget is that, as humans, we are distinctly different from machines. Therefore, maybe it is time to implement a new working culture altogether that truly appreciates and reflects our human nature. The truth is that excessive working hours, while simply churning out more and more, day in and day out, on an endless production line, take their toll and actually deplete our energy reserves – for most of us, anyway. Unlike machines, our source of energy may be a more complex affair, and understandably a crucial driving force behind our productivity at work. In their seminal paper entitled, 'Manage your energy, not your time' published in the *Harvard Business Review* (please see the 'Useful resources' section at the end of this chapter), Tony Schwartz and Catherine McCarthy highlight how responding to increasing demands by simply putting in longer hours is not the answer – instead it is better to focus on our *energy*.

Yes, instead of working ourselves into the ground by working longer and harder, Schwartz and McCarthy helpfully outline four different types of energies that need our attention to improve our effectiveness and performance at work.

Take a look at the following exercise to reflect on how you/your company can begin to prioritise *energy*, instead of continuing to ineffectively put in excessive working hours to meet increased demands:

Exercise 7.5: Work in progress

Energy is of the essence

▶ **Physical energy:** How healthy are you/your employees? Do you/they eat nutritious food, exercise well and get enough sleep and rest? Does your company actively promote and encourage good physical energy?

▶ **Emotional energy:** How happy are you/your employees? Are you/your employees good at recognising when emotions (i.e. fight or flight response) are getting in the way of efficiency? Do you/your employees actively enhance a culture of positive emotions by expressing appreciation to each other/themselves, checking in with one another about how they are feeling, and listening and attending to each other's needs? Can you/your employees effectively manage emotions, say, with mindfulness?

▶ **Mental energy:** How well can you/your employees focus on tasks? Do you/your employees deplete energy by multitasking or save energy by focusing on one task at a time? Do you/your employees take regular and deliberate breaks between tasks? Does the working culture of your company allow for breaks/staff leaving on time/promote a healthy work–life balance, etc.?

▶ **Spiritual energy:** Why are you/your employees doing all of this work? What is the purpose? Are your/your employees' everyday work activities consistent with what you/they value most and with what gives you/them a sense of meaning and purpose (prosocial or altruistic action maybe)? Is there a culture at work which encourages you/your employees to uncover your/their deeper values and align their work to these?

Make no mistake about it; a company that only focuses on working longer and harder in response to the increasing demands it faces is going to find itself *sick* in no time. If this sounds like you and/or your business, then it's time to wise up. Every business needs to recognise the humanity at its core and, instead of working its employees' fingers to the bone, find effective ways to meet the needs and promote the energy of its workforce.

Bulldozing and browbeating

'All war is a symptom of man's failure as a thinking animal.'

John Steinbeck

Bullying at work is another common symptom of the sickness culture that prevails in many businesses. Numerous articles and studies show that the impact of bullying – showing up as mocking, taunting, discrediting, intimidating or blaming others – causes serious stress and health problems (please see the 'Useful resources' section for an article if you want to read more on this). Most of us, even those saints out there, know that we can be the aggressor as well as the victim at times. But bullying the bully is rarely a productive tactic in the long term either. When you feel attacked (by yourself or others), it is instinctive to defend yourself; our fight or flight response is kick-started and the most common form of this is to attack back. This is a base response. To attack is instinctual. Remember, however, that whether you lunge forward with your razor-sharp tongue or roll over in self-preserving defence, anxiety is rife in both positions, and we know all too well by now how a culture of excessive anxiety leads to ineffectual performance and is just not good for our or our company's overall health. So instead, perhaps consider how being the bully, or even the victim, is not sophisticated or ultimately helpful. Try taking some of the following steps to diffuse the culture of *meanness* at work instead.

Exercise 7.6: Work in progress

De-meaning

Next time you're about to bulldoze over a colleague (or yourself!) or you find yourself being browbeaten by someone else (or yourself!) at work, try:

▶ Generosity – Because … it feels great to give (to ourselves too!)

▶ Forgiveness – Because … it is healing to forgive and be forgiven

▶ Compassion – Because … we connect through our shared humanity

▶ Kindness – Because … life and work is hard enough!

Sometimes this can be easily and directly done towards the person or people with whom you are struggling, or yourself. For instance you can simply:

▶ Say 'sorry', 'please', 'thank you', 'well done' or just 'hello'

▶ Offer your time and help to someone

▶ Give yourself/others a break.

If it is too hard in a particular moment to be direct or act in any of these ways with others/yourself, then:

▶ Water the plants

▶ Give to charity

▶ Wash up the mugs in the office kitchen

▶ Leave a nice note somewhere to no one in particular.

Do try one of the above today (and as frequently as you can), or invent something of your own. Start as small or big as you like.

Josie: I decided to practise some random acts of kindness as part of an experiment to see if they had a beneficial impact on my own mood and sense of well-being. One day while driving to Wales, I was ranting at the kids, who were fighting in the back of the car, driving too fast and generally being unpleasant and grumpy. I reached the toll booth for the Severn Bridge and joined the queue. I recalled a mindfulness teacher I once had who said she often paid for the driver behind when she drove into South Wales as her kindness practice. I took a deep breath–£7 something or other was quite a lot of cash for me, but to pay for the car behind too? Well, I decided to go for it – in for a penny in for 7-odd quid, so to speak. My kids were suddenly very excited and giggling, turning round to see who the lucky driver was. I felt a bit shy, but explained to the guy in the booth what I was doing and then drove on feeling actually pretty good. I was driving more slowly, the atmosphere in the car was light and quite pleasant. Yep, that worked! Then the car which I'd paid for overtook. My kids were bouncing about in their seats with happiness now as the passenger of the other car beamed at us through the window with the biggest smile I've ever seen. That smile was worth a lot more than £7, and I still feel good thinking about it years later.

Compassionate work

'In Asian languages, the word for 'mind' and the word for 'heart' are same. So if you're not hearing mindfulness in some deep way as heartfulness, you're not really understanding it. Compassion and kindness towards oneself are intrinsically woven into it. You could think of mindfulness as wise and affectionate attention.'

Jon Kabat-Zinn

Being compassionate, certainly in the world of business, can often be misconstrued and considered a display of the softer and/or weaker side of someone's nature. The truth is that there is nothing weak or even effete about compassionate behaviour; actually it's really much more about being strong, confident and courageous and it takes great effort. Think about it: would you have the strength to remain calm and composed so you could offer a kind and warm response to a stressed colleague who failed to meet the really important deadline you'd set them? Would you even be willing to be seen responding in this way? Or how about spending your time at work listening and offering support to another distressed colleague, when there are other much more pressing tasks to be getting on with? To be compassionate, we need to face our fears. We need to find the strength to accept and own how we feel, rather than trying to avoid, eliminate or ignore unwanted and painful experiences with habitual knee-jerk responses. Further, we need the willingness to behave in less comfortable (but ultimately more helpful) ways in face of the inevitable suffering that is bound to show up at work. The good news is that there are many benefits to introducing more compassion into our working cultures, and the efforts that you make to be more compassionate will pay great dividends. Staff retention is certainly something that can improve. Have a think about it: would you want to work for a manager who shouts at you if you have to call in sick? Or would you prefer to work for someone that acknowledges and empathises with the difficulties and stresses that you may encounter in your personal life? You may be interested to know that one study[15] found how compassionate people are rated more highly as strong, intelligent leaders than their less compassionate peers. People warm towards compassionate people as they generally feel better about themselves and less stressed when they are treated with compassion. They then want to extend those feelings to others; compassion becomes kind of contagious. When people are feeling supported by one another, they are more likely to work well together and productivity is then increased, which inevitably has a positive impact on a business's bottom line.

Compassion is a basic human quality which seems mostly absent from our working lives and places of work (for the majority of us, anyway) these days. This is hugely unfortunate as it may in fact be the very missing link that can lead to a healthier and more prosperous business and to each of us experiencing a greater sense of satisfaction in our work. It is a universal language that has the potential to change our working lives for the better. One major and frequent obstacle when it comes to compassion in the workplace is that people don't really know how they can, or if they even should, be compassionate at work. They may feel awkward in giving or being on the receiving end of compassion and are frequently left unsure about what is actually acceptable and appropriate to express in the context of their work. Many assume that they are expected to check their personal problems and feelings at the door before they walk into the office each day and to keep any 'soft' or overly kind or friendly qualities for their personal lives at home with friends and loved ones. The truth is that a workplace that ignores or tries to suppress human suffering and inevitable painful emotions and that doesn't recognise the most important aspect of its day-to-day functioning – its people, (and the humanness that resides in each and every one of us – warts and all) is likely to suffer great costs. It's nonsensical to assume that the psychological well-being of workers is not directly related to job performance. Companies that are able and, more so, willing to establish behavioural standards that cultivate a psychologically well workforce and work environment (such as with a culture of compassion) are at a distinct competitive advantage. The initiation of these standards can begin with small steps; even the slightest changes in behaviour have the potential to set off a ripple effect that can sweep across a whole team and eventually an organisation. Take the case of Robert, for example:

Robert

Robert had just landed a new role as an analyst in corporate finance after a number of years working in a small, local accountancy firm. He was used to a close-knit team who tended to have a genuine laugh with one another and support each other through difficult times, whether personal or work-related. He was immediately struck by the lack of any apparent warmth, closeness and unity at the bank and noticed how people in his team just tended to get on with their work without much camaraderie; his colleagues did chat but these interactions seemed more like insincere small talk without any real meaningfulness or sharing of personal experience going on. Robert was starting to feel a little uncomfortable with this air of aloofness, but he decided to simply get on with his work and suppress his natural friendliness for fear of stepping out of line and making others feel uncomfortable. However, things came to a head when one day his manager announced that one of the team had been involved in a severe road traffic accident and would not be coming in to work for the foreseeable future. The team was informed that they needed to step up efforts to share responsibilities while HR looked for a temp to fill the role. Robert was amazed by the lack of warmth with which this news was delivered to the team. He hadn't known the injured colleague for too long but was still upset to hear the news and he wondered how others who knew him longer and better might be feeling. Robert bit the bullet and sent a group email around to the team, saying that he was saddened by the news and would be really keen to chat with anyone else who might want to talk about what had happened. To his surprise the majority of his team responded, and this led to a group of them meeting after work to discuss how they felt and support each other through this hardship, including how they would manage the extra workload that they now all faced. They also decided to reach out to their colleague's wife to offer their support to her and the family. The team had found that sharing how they felt with one another was tremendously helpful, and this led to the establishment of a weekly team meeting which was reserved for them to share how they were feeling and support each other with various work and personal matters. Many of them spoke about how they had felt that work had been a heartless place, where they had previously felt emotionally unsupported, which had been taking its toll, leaving some to seriously consider whether they wanted to move on from the bank.

Cultivating a compassionate workplace

'Compassion reduces our fear, boosts our confidence, and opens us to inner strength. By reducing distrust, it opens us to others and brings us a sense of connections with them and a sense of purpose and meaning in life.'

Dalai Lama

Compassion is an emotional response to someone else's suffering that is characterised by qualities of kindness, care and concern. Embedded in this is the actual desire to behave in ways that can help to alleviate another person's hardship. This is not always a natural response or something that is commonly experienced in the competitive culture of our work. We have spoken to many executives who have had a variety of responses to others' suffering at work, such as anger, blame, avoidance, fear, discomfort and sometimes even enjoyment. We have lost count of the number of times that clients have presented to us in dismay, feeling aggrieved and neglected as they explain how they do not feel that their personal or work-related distress is acknowledged or supported by their places of work. They instead feel as if they are being penalised and treated unfairly in the context of their manager's or wider team's frustration with them. This is highly unfortunate as this seems to only escalate their levels of distress, which inevitably leads to a decline in their loyalty and productivity on the job.

"Can we be motivated by compassion at work?"

Interestingly, a number of studies[16, 17, 18] show us that as infants we actually start out in this world with a natural preference towards compassion and kindness, but as we go on to enter school we begin to display the more selfish side to our nature. It would seem that as our socialisation broadens and we move into the big wide world, our environment begins to shape our innate tendencies more and more. Then by the time we get to immerse ourselves into the cut-throat, combative and competitive culture of work, it's pretty safe to say that our tendency towards self-interest is favoured and therefore more likely to be reinforced as the more helpful tool for survival, over and above any natural kindness that we may have once been more inclined to express. However, the fact that we are naturally wired as compassionate beings brings into question whether it is self-interest alone which has to motivate us through our working life. Can we be motivated by compassion at work? Is there actually a place for compassion in our working lives?

By cultivating and harnessing more compassion, can we actually help our business to not only survive but also thrive? Now if the answers to these questions is 'yes', then bringing compassion into work may sound like an extremely effortful or even impossible task when we consider the common lack of compassion in most working cultures today. However, a number of social scientists and neuroscientists armed with a growing body of research into mindfulness and compassion are showing us that we can actually train and strengthen this compassionate side to our nature (via mindfulness practice), and in doing so we can begin to positively affect the environments and cultures around us too, as well as our own job performance, physical health and psychological well-being.

Proven in science, smart for business

Compassion at work improves overall job performance

In one study[19], researchers investigated the impact that a compassionate working culture has on the overall performance of employees working in a long-term care setting. They found that a culture of compassion positively related to employee satisfaction and teamwork and negatively related to employee absenteeism and emotional exhaustion. The researchers were keen to discover if these same results could be found in other working cultures outside of the health-care industry. So they went on to survey a total of 3,201 employees across a range of other industries, including financial services, engineering and higher education among others, and they found that these findings held true. Employees who worked in a culture where they felt free to express affection, tenderness, caring and compassion for one another were more satisfied with their jobs, more committed to the organisation and felt more accountable for their performance.

Compassion-focused mindfulness practice leads to more altruistic behaviour

In another study[20], researchers at the University of Wisconsin–Madison, found that practicing just 30 minutes of compassion-focused mindfulness (much like the loving kindness practice outlined in Chapter 5) a day for two weeks led to more altruistic behaviour towards a stranger who had been treated unfairly compared to a control group. In this study the researchers were also interested to see what changed inside the brains of the participants who gave more to someone who

➤

---

needed help. They measured how much brain activity had changed from the beginning to the end of the training, and found that the participants who were the most altruistic after compassion training were the ones who showed the most brain changes when all the participants were shown images of human suffering. They found that activity was increased in brain regions involved in empathy and understanding others as well as emotion regulation and positive emotions. This study highlights that compassion is actually a trainable skill. Furthermore, in making efforts to train our minds internally (via compassion practice), we can actually begin to alter the way our brains see suffering, which then impacts on our behaviour and this in turn influences the lives of others and the world outside of us too.

Being compassionate feels good and is good for our health

Researchers[21] at the University of North Carolina and the University of Michigan recruited 139 working adults into a randomised control trial and found that those who were taught and practised a loving-kindness (compassion) meditation experienced increased positive emotions as well as feeling a greater sense of purpose and satisfaction in life, more social support, reduced depressive symptoms and improved health. Some of the findings of this study are corroborated by a further study[22] which found that more altruistic, prosocial individuals were less prone to cardiovascular, neurodegenerative and neoplastic diseases.

'If you want others to be happy practice compassion. If you want to be happy practice compassion.'

Dalai Lama

So, when you are next around other people (if that isn't right now), take the opportunity to try this next quick exercise. In doing so, not only are you training your mind to be more compassionate (each and every time you do it) for the greater benefit of your colleagues and the greater health of your company, but, as the research suggests, you will also be taking good care of your physical health. You may also notice how you can feel a whole lot better for doing it. A purposeful effort to repeat and direct the following few kind words towards others in a meaningful and genuine way can have a profound effect on your mood; you may notice that a dull, flat or even neutral mood can shift to one of contentment, pleasure or joy.

Exercise 7.7: Mindful on the job

Spreading the love and feeling good too

Wherever you are, be that sat at your desk, in a meeting, on the train, walking along the street or through the office building or sat at a café over lunch, make a purposeful effort to look upon different colleagues/ people one at a time (don't stare, it's rude!), either strangers or people you may know and, as you do so, begin by reminding yourself that:

▶ s/he suffers just like you;

▶ s/he struggles with the same types of thoughts and feelings;

▶ s/he gets ill, will age and die;

▶ all of those s/he loves will age and die;

▶ s/he is human, just like you.

Then silently repeat these five sentences, as you genuinely direct warmth and compassion to each person, one at a time (no one will know what you are doing):

1 May you be safe.

2 May you be happy.

3 May you be free from suffering.

4 May you know well-being.

5 May you be well.

This exercise may feel a little odd at first and, if so, do try it anyway and practise it as much as you can. You'll soon notice the effects that we've listed above and how, with a little more compassion, your experience at work will be transformed in a way that makes better sense for you, your colleagues and your business. Recognising that we are fundamentally similar, fundamentally connected and fundamentally prone to the same forms of suffering, like in the exercise above, is a simple way of increasing compassion. We can then demonstrate this naturally arising quality of our humanity by being more considerate towards others. Tara Brach, a renowned teacher in the Insight Meditation tradition and a clinical psychologist, writes:

> 'To cultivate the tenderness of compassion, we not only stop running from suffering, we deliberately bring our attention to it ... as we feel suffering

and relate to it with care rather than resistance, we awaken the heart of compassion.'

(Brach, 2003, p. 200–201)

By injecting more compassion into our places of work, we can begin to build more prosocial, supportive, ethical and just environments that bring out the best in us all in terms of our health and well-being. Now, make no mistake about it, this takes commitment and courage. You can start this process right now by training your own mind to be more compassionate both towards yourself and others (please see the Breines article in the 'Useful resources' section for more ideas and strategies about how you can bring more compassion and happiness into your life and the life of others).

As we have highlighted, a work environment that cultivates a culture of compassion creates a much more positive and productive place to work. Hopefully you are with us on this by now and, if so, also eager to begin to introduce some more compassion where you work. So here are our top five tips for injecting compassion into your place of work.

Top five tips for getting more compassionate at work

1 **Start with yourself:** First off, remember to start with yourself. Sometimes the hardest person to feel caring towards is the one reading this right now. If you begin gently to be more kind to yourself, it will naturally follow that you are more compassionate to others (please revisit Chapter 3 to remind yourself of the exercises you can do to enhance your own self-compassion).

2 **Proactively notice and take care of the well-being of colleagues:** Colleagues who may have experienced some personal or work-related distress (family illness, loss or divorce, feeling overwhelmed with work, etc.) may need time and space to adjust. Look out for signs of distress among your colleagues and offer them genuine support. This doesn't have to be anything grand, maybe just lending them a listening ear. Any support you can offer them can make a fundamental difference to how they feel (please revisit Chapter 5 to refresh yourself on how you can effectively interact with a colleague in distress).

3 **Encourage open and honest communication:** Try to cultivate a 'no blame' culture. This is best created via mindful listening and speech (please revisit Chapter 5), kindness and compassion. This way, trust

will be improved and effective communication will provide a safe environment for managing any difficult and/or distressing issues which may arise.

4 **Step into someone else's shoes** (put the high-heels down, we mean metaphorically!): Try to imagine the other person's viewpoint, emotions and perspective (revisit the acronym WARM in Chapter 5). Encourage your own, and others', empathy, by seeing or hearing a situation from different angles than your own. This can free up 'stalemate' situations, help people feel less defensive and also motivate others to do the same for you.

5 **Create positive social contact between employees:** Use meeting spaces for informal groups and socialising. When there are stronger, supportive and nurturing interpersonal relationships, people are more likely to notice and share concerns and to feel inclined to offer support, as well as offer their best efforts on the job.

As we come to the end of this chapter, we do hope that it has helped you to consider how healthy (or not) your place of work is. By reflecting on the insights and implementing the action points and practices included here, we are confident that you will have the foundations to build a healthier business. Mindfulness makes good business sense. It is the antidote to the sickness culture that prevails across many of our places of work these days and that frankly so many of us are fed up of. It has the potential to help any company thrive by supporting the structure needed for a healthier working culture both within and between businesses.

Here are our top take-away tips from this chapter:

Mindfulness top tips to go

▶ Bring mindfulness to your anxiety-fuelled consumption of work and other activities and areas of your life. This way, you can begin to notice how you take care (or not) of yourself, others and the world around you, to promote good, improved and sustainable health for all.

▶ Practise mindfulness around the inevitability of change. Your willingness to accept what is new and unfamiliar will help you to retain a deeper sense of security in the face of the unknown.

▶ Try to recognise how you/your company may become caught up in the pursuit of endless growth and the anxiety-fuelled competitiveness of ➤

---

work that only perpetuates a working culture of sickness. Practise mindfulness to notice your excessive competitive edge and to instead ease up and offer some peace to yourself and to others at work.

▶ Consider the alternative, less competitive, no/low growth business models available to us and how businesses that are less target-driven but instead focused on different principles of shared values, cooperation, community-building and being prosocial are still successful and actually thriving. These business models promote humanistic values and healthy working relationships over competitiveness, keeping in mind the sustainability, well-being and happiness of their workforces.

▶ Promote the good health of your company by practising mindfulness to address issues of feeling overstretched and time-poor, lacking in energy, bullying in the workplace and feeling uncared for and neglected. Whether you take small steps on an individual level or implement larger-scale interventions on a team or organisational level, be assured that your efforts will make a positive difference.

▶ Practise compassion at work as much as you can. The more compassionate you are towards yourself and your colleagues, the healthier, happier and more productive you, your colleagues and your business will be.

In the next and final chapter we are going to pull together and summarise some of the key insights and learning points that we have covered throughout the book so far. We are keen to provide you with a summary of the mindfulness practices that we have introduced to you and when best to use them. We also want to provide you with some further information on some of the latest debates and happenings around the secular mindfulness movement and where you might go from here to further your journey and deepen your practice should you wish to.

Useful resources

▶ Action for Happiness. (2015, September 20). *Dalai Lama launches new course for a happier and more caring world* [actionforhappiness.org]. Retrieved from: http://www.actionforhappiness.org/news/dalai-lama-launches-new-course-for-a-happier-and-more-caring-world

► BeWell@stanford. (date unknown). *Social ties are good for your health* [from bewell.stanford.edu]. Retrieved from: https://bewell.stanford. edu/features/social-ties-good-health

► Biglan, A. (2015, May 20). *Evolving a more nurturing capitalism: A new Powell memo* [from evolution-institute.org]. Retrieved from: https:// evolution-institute.org/article/evolving-a-more-nurturing-capitalism-a-new-powell-memo/?source=tvol

► Branson, R. (2015, September 11). *It's time to reinvent work* [The Huffington Post Blog]. Retrieved from: http://www.huffington-post.com/richard-branson/its-time-to-reinvent-work_b_8123768. html?1441991776

► Breines, J. (2015, September 16). *Three strategies for bringing more kindness into your life* [from greatergood.berkeley.edu]. Retrieved from: http://greatergood.berkeley.edu/article/item/ three_strategies_for_bringing_more_kindness_into_your_life

► Co-Operatives of the Americas (2015, May 20). *Survey results reveal untapped co-op potential in the U.S.* [from www.aciamericas.coop]. Retrieved from: http://www.aciamericas.coop/ Survey-results-reveal-untapped-co-op-potential-in-the-U-S

► Crouch, D. (2015, September 17). *Efficiency up, turnover down: Sweden experiments with six-hour working day* [*The Guardian*]. Retrieved from: http://www.theguardian.com/world/2015/sep/17/efficiency-up-turn-over-down-sweden-experiments-with-six-hour-working-day

► England, R. (2014, March 20). *Brits choose happiness over wealth* [from positivenews.org.uk]. Retrieved from: http://positivenews.org .uk/2014/wellbeing/14997/brits-choose-happiness-wealth/

► Ethisphere. (2015, March 9). *Ethisphere announces the 2015 world's most ethical companies* [from ethisphere.com]. Retrieved from: http://ethisphere .com/ethisphere-announces-the-2015-worlds-most-ethical-companies/

► Johnson, E. M. (2013, May 3). *Survival of the nicest? Check out the other theory of evolution* [yesmagazine.com]. Retrieved from: http://www.yes-magazine.org/issues/how-cooperatives-are-driving-the-new-economy/ survival-of-the-nicest-the-other-theory-of-evolution

► News Hour India. (2014, December 22). *Monkey saves dying friend at India's Kanpur railway station* [video file]. Retrieved from: https://www .youtube.com/watch?v=ulg1Imcavew

► Papero, D. (date unknown). *Anxiety and organisations* [www .bowentheory.com]. Retrieved from: http://www.bowentheory.com/ anxietyandorganizationspapero.htm

▶ Peck, E. (2015, August 26). *Accenture just upped the ante on benefits for new moms and dads* [The Huffington Post Blog]. Retrieved from: http://www.huffingtonpost.com/entry/accenture-parental-benefits_5 5dc8595e4b08cd3359d504c

▶ Phillips, S. (2015, August 27). *Mindfulness: an unexpected antidote to workplace stress* [article from psychcentral.com]. Retrieved from: http://blogs.psychcentral.com/healing-together/2015/08/ mindfulness-an-unexpected-antidote-to-workplace-stress/

▶ Schwartz, T. and McCarthy, C. (2007, October). *Manage your energy, not your time* [article from the *Harvard Business Review*]. Retrieved from: https://hbr.org/2007/10/manage-your-energy-not-your-time

▶ The Telegraph. (2015, September 8). *Well-being at work is good for business*. Retrieved from: http://www.telegraph.co.uk/sponsored/ business/britains-healthiest-company/11848801/wellbeing-good-for-business.html

▶ Townsend, M. (2013, April 23). *Could mindfulness hold the key to unlock a sustainable future?* [The sustainable business strategy series]. Retrieved from: https://www.2degreesnetwork.com/ groups/2degrees-community/resources/could-mindfulness-hold-key-unlock-sustainable-future/

Mindfulness here and now

This last chapter is a going to focus on bringing mindfulness into your working life in practical ways, which will summarise the work in the rest of the book and provide you with a quick reference to practices and some further tips to help you along the way. Before we offer you an overview and summary, however, we will drop in a few more areas of debate which are currently present in the world of secular mindfulness and offer you some points you might want to consider about this interesting topic. We are then going to give you some summary points and quick reference guides, including a 'Mindful on the job' reference chart outlining which particular practices in this book can be applied to certain situations you may find yourself in at work. We know that, like us, you probably also feel pretty time-poor most of the time, so we hope that this chart will be something that you can easily refer to and will help you to quickly identify the best mindful course of action, while you're on the job and already pressed for time.

In this final chapter of the book we are going to:

▶ Take an overview of how mindfulness is being disseminated in Western society and work today.

▶ Offer a few thoughts and points of inquiry regarding a recent UK government report.

▶ Offer a quick reference guide for everyday work issues and dilemmas using the exercises in this book.

▶ Suggest ways that you can keep your mindfulness practice alive while on the job, including how you can troubleshoot common obstacles, as well as how you can begin to effectively introduce and enhance mindfulness in your place of work.

How to understand the difference between McMindfulness (a fad) and the real McCoy (Mcthankfully)

As we discussed briefly at the end of Chapter 1, we, as authors and psychologists, take a position that the dissemination of mindfulness is beneficial to the alleviation of suffering. Mindfulness is a marvellous means of developing contentment, peace and well-being – who wouldn't want to share that?! Experience offers a depth and breadth to practice and to teaching and this is only something that comes with time and commitment. However, mindfulness itself is ever present, instantly accessible and abundant. It requires no special tools or privileges, no need to be intellectual, super-spiritual or 'special' in any way, because if you just bring your attention into now, you are mindful – simple!

'Unease, anxiety, tension, stress, worry – all forms of fear – are caused by too much future, and not enough presence. Guilt, regret, resentment, grievances, sadness, bitterness, and all forms of non-forgiveness are caused by too much past, and not enough presence.'

Eckhart Tolle

We do not suggest a 'one size fits all' approach, meaning you must practise 'like this', for 'this long' – many of us already struggle to 'get it right' and constantly make 'extra time' – bah! As you already know from us, the practice of mindfulness is a constant and careful attunement to life's flow and unfolding – sometimes requiring measure and discipline and sometimes requiring an ease and softening. We cannot say for you which you need at any particular moment: we only hope to provide you with beneficial tools from which you can learn to discriminate and discern for yourself. Likewise, neither do we intend to position one mindfulness experience as superior to another: instead, the reflections we have offered you are simply another point of inquiry and deepening of awareness open to you through your own practice. Deifying one particular practice, mind-state or set of conditions necessary for 'good' mindfulness is simply another form of attachment, which only leads to greater suffering. Nevertheless, mindfulness is in a period of booming (mindful colouring book anyone?), and rapid change brings the inevitable anxieties and concerns along with it.

The community around mindfulness, of both secular and traditional Buddhist practitioners, is currently questioning and exploring how mindfulness practice sits alongside traditional competitive business models. We have discussed some of these issues in Chapters 1 and 7 but it is worth pointing out that some practitioners worry that the ethics central to traditional mindfulness practices are lost in the process of secularisation and that therefore mindfulness becomes little more than a passing trend and is even perhaps somewhat demeaning to an ancient tradition and its lineages. Businesses appear to have been very receptive; however, questions arise regarding how to continue to grow wealth, increase productivity and maintain economic viability alongside the development of compassion, acceptance, simplicity and generosity. In order to fit more with an 'acceptable', westernised perception – perhaps to be more palatable, manageable and marketable – some secular mindfulness schools have veered more towards creating a mindfulness 'product', with a set programme, set practices and accredited teaching routes. These are positive in perpetuating research (which can be standardised easily), trying to create quality control and offering the public a recognisable 'brand'. Mindfulness or 'McMindfulness' (as it is sometimes referred to) can be neatly presented as a replicable package, sold at cost, to a (currently) hungry audience. On a superficial level, mindfulness 'teachers' can be trained within weeks to reproduce this product, with its standardised, replicable format and sell it onwards and upwards. Skills and experience are inevitably diluted in this process, and thus onto the 'McMindfulness' bandwagon jump a plethora of cheap imitations and counterfeits. No one has a clue what is really good quality; is it all a sham? Who do we believe? Can I get fries with that? Perhaps one way will be hailed as 'the real one', but it will also begin to smack of superiority, privilege and self-interest; it will begin to monopolise, the entrepreneurial interest will wither and creativity will die, the cool kids will move on to seek newer thrills. Pop will eat itself. Mindfulness – 'oh yeah, that's so last year' (and so is that comment).

> '*If you consider mindfulness as a means to having a lot of money then you have not touched its true purpose … It may look like the practice of mindfulness but inside there's no peace, no joy, no happiness produced. It's just an imitation. If you don't feel the energy of brotherhood, of sisterhood radiating from your work, that is not mindfulness.*'

> Thich Nhat Hanh (cited in Gelles, 2015, p. 227)

A similar journey has happened with other traditionally Eastern practices that have caught the West's imaginations, most notably Yoga which has become almost totally secularised, often representing some form of convoluted gymnastics (asanas) rather than just (a relatively small) part of a complete spiritual system.

> '*To be a miner of diamonds, take care of your picks and shovels. To be a miner of your spiritual Self, take care of your body, breath, and mind. But don't confuse the tools and the goals.*'
> '*The goal of Yoga (union) is Yoga (union), period.*'

> Swami Jnaneshvara Bharati (Please find the link to the full article in the 'Useful resources' section)

Ultimately, each individual will make of their journey into mindfulness what they will. Even in the monasteries of distant lands there will be plenty of students sitting at the back picking their noses. We would, however, like you to be aware that there may well be more to your mindfulness than meets the eye; if you wish to turn that eye away and go 'lalalalala' with your fingers in your ears, I'm afraid we are just going to leave that up to you – we simply are not that powerful, and we don't get to decide what you want. If you are interested, please do look through the recommended reading lists, join a group and listen to the voices in the debate (you might find the article by Jenny Wilks listed in the 'Useful resources' section a good place to start). It is also important to acknowledge the components of mindfulness within this debate too: nothing is fixed or permanent, and clinging creates suffering; habitual, critical responses tend to come from a place of disconnection and distress; mindfulness helps us tune into and/or broaden our experience of each moment; with practice we can learn to discern and discriminate with skillfulness. Using mindfulness will also free us up from dogma of mindfulness:

'Impermanent are all created things; strive on with awareness.'

Buddha

Of course, we want you to buy this book and tell all your friends to buy it and hopefully we'll make a few quid (we've gotta eat too), but actually this isn't our main motive. We just want to share … and we're really lucky that we get to do that by writing to you … ah, thanks … group hug? Seriously, we love our work and are very motivated to promote mindfulness. Motivation, passion and enthusiasm are surely the three most overused words on a CV, but also the most fabulous qualities. Mindfulness keeps these qualities invigorated and alive and encourages us to keep seeing things anew. Even McMindfulness can benefit from mindfulness, and it is its very own path towards thriving. Let's remind ourselves to keep it fresh and the next exercise may help you along with that.

Exercise 8.1: Mindful on the job

A breath of fresh air

Returning to a practice regularly gives you the chance to consider that voice which says, 'Oh, I already know this' or 'bo-ooring'; this is the killer to your enthusiasm, your verve and the delight in the amazingness of little things. Likewise, being too restrictive and prescriptive kills off creativity and openness – we don't need a manual to know how to breathe (thank heavens), we don't need special qualifications or lots of money, just willingness. Mindfulness is simply the gentle discipline of drawing attention to our natural state of abiding. So, take a seat or find a place to stand or walk with ease as you return anew to a practice with the breath. Follow these steps:

1 Find your ground, feel the physical solidity of the contact with the surface upon which you sit, stand or walk. Feel into the feet, the legs, the hips. You are present.

2 Feel your uprightness, your openness and your receptivity in your body, in very small or not-so-small ways. Feel into the spine, the chest and the shoulders. You are engaged.

3 Allow ease to be present in the body, with a soft belly, relaxed gaze and ease in the facial muscles. You are kind.

4 Bring the attention to the breath, just as it is, allowing the moment just to be this simple. Just this body breathing.

5 Follow the in-breath, notice the newness of each in-breath, the receiving, the energising, these qualities that are present right now.

6 Follow the out-breath, notice the body easing, naturally relaxing and letting go, these qualities that are present right now.

7 Following each breath, the taking in and letting go, rising and falling, each moment simply unfolding ... just ... like ... this.

8 This very body, this very breath, nothing more, nothing less.

9 The Buddha once said: 'The whole universe is available in the very body'.

10 Feeling each breath afresh. Continuing to breathe with the body, the breath, the universe.

> **"Mindfulness is simply the gentle discipline of drawing attention to our natural state of abiding."**

Sometimes it is the case that in our own arguments for or against this or that, particularly with our delight in gossip and overcritical thinking, we can recognise, quite independently of what might be 'true' or not, our own mind's habitual tendencies. Many of us are plagued by cynicism and doubt. These can be corrosive to building up a sense of goodness and joy and to making yourself wise to skilfully discriminating how best to get the most juice from whatever it is we are doing. Mindfulness has certainly had all the trappings of a modern-day fad – but it is after all an ancient tradition found across many cultures and not really new at all. No monks with meditative or contemplative practices in times of yore, as far as we know, ever had to have their practice validated by a constant stream of empirical research in order to feel it was acceptable, but there was often lively and heated debate even hundreds of years ago, usually also over issues of philosophy, ethics and morality. Take this well-known Zen story, for instance.

Two Zen monks were walking together and came to a river. By the side of the river was a beautiful young girl who was unable to cross by herself. The younger monk picked her up and carried her over the river. The two then proceeded on their journey, but under stony silence. The older could not contain himself any longer and proclaimed 'How could you break your monastic vows by touching that woman and carrying her across the river?', to which the younger replied 'but brother I put her down on the other side of the river, whilst you, you are still carrying her!.'

The practice of mindfulness, as we have discussed throughout this book is one of adaptive, fluent and creative attention, which responds skilfully to what is present in any given moment. This is not prescriptive; there are no absolute or fixed rules, as these, as in the story above, can cause us to become rigid and overattached to ideologies rather than keeping our responses alive and bright and open to renewal. Through this very practice we can then release what is no longer helpful and have our (metaphorical) arms open to embrace and retain what is. The same is true of creeping cynicism, overzealousness, doubt or any other behaviour or thought which produces a sense of contraction or fixation; such intensity requires the skilful use of mindfulness to free us back up and to see again with clarity. With its popularisation, mindfulness will attract criticism and debate, there's no doubt about that, but when we use our practice to notice and stand back we again recognise how things actually are, just as they are.

'Mindfulness has been hyped and overpromoted. And that naturally draws criticism, which should be carefully considered. But under all the hooplah, people are getting the help they need.'

Barry Boyce, Editor-in-Chief, mindful.org (Taken from mindful.org; please find the link to the full article in the 'Useful resources' section)

We, as authors, hope that we have inspired you to consider, for the price of this book, that you can undertake your own journey and learn through your own experience the benefits of mindfulness for your work. While this may indeed be with an intention of simply becoming more focused and productive, feeling a little less stressed or because it might just give you an edge at work, you will find, if you continue to practise and inquire, that much more will unfold, which will ultimately increase your deeper well-being, your connection to others and change the way you do business altogether.

These are mindful times

> *'You who are journalists, writers, citizens, you have the right and duty to say to those you have elected that they must practice mindfulness, calm and deep listening, and loving speech. This is universal thing, taught by all religions.'*

Thich Nhat Hanh

Wouldn't it be great to see our politicians and leaders adopting this approach? Well, just maybe, they will begin to practise what they are apparently beginning to preach. At the time of writing and hot off the press, is the recent release of the (October 2015) Mindfulness All-Party Parliamentary Group (MAPPG) report, entitled 'Mindful Nation UK' (please follow the link in the 'Useful resources' section at the end of this chapter to read the full report). Chapter 4 of this report focuses exclusively on the role of mindfulness in the workplace and offers some interesting commentary which really is worth looking at if you have time and interest. In case this falls off the bottom of your 'to do' list, here are the main recommendations stemming from the paper in relation to workplace mindfulness:

1 The Department for Business, Innovation and Skills (BIS) should demonstrate leadership in working with employers to promote the use of mindfulness and develop an understanding of good practice.

2 We welcome the government's What Works Centre for Wellbeing, and urge it to commission, as a priority, pilot research studies on the role of mindfulness in the workplace, and to work with employers and university research centres to collaborate on high-quality studies to close the research gap.

3 Government departments should encourage the development of mindfulness programmes for staff in the public sector – in particular in health, education and criminal justice – to combat stress and improve organisational effectiveness. One initiative could be seed-funding for a pilot project in policing where we have encountered considerable interest.

4 The National Institute of Health Research should invite bids to research:

   ▶ the use of mindfulness as an occupational health intervention, using both face-to-face and online programmes across different sizes of organisations and businesses;

▶ the effectiveness of mindfulness, including its different components, in addressing occupational mental health issues such as stress, work related rumination, fatigue and disrupted sleep.

(MAPPG, 2015 pp. 45–46)

In essence, a lot more (quality) research is wanted. This is absolutely welcome *and* since there is little harm to be found simply watching your own breath (if you do need help: in, out, repeat), we invite you to vote with your feet (or lungs perhaps). The final part of the paper, called 'The Implementation Challenge' makes an excellent summary of the McMindfulness issues discussed earlier in this chapter (please see below). Consider where you find yourself with this debate; consider how this book (cheaper than a course, for sure) may or may not be of value to you on your way towards working more mindfully and compassionately.

'In order for shorter courses, books and digital resources to be called 'mindfulness-based', they must also differentiate themselves from simple attention training, by fostering the attitudinal foundations such as compassion, non-judging and non-striving. These qualities form an integral part of the approach, and progressively bring greater awareness to thoughts, feelings and emotions in order to cultivate insight into the workings of one's mind. Without direct teacher contact to model the approach, books and digital resources must find a way of making these key aspects an explicit part of the training. Otherwise participants may not experience the benefits associated with mindfulness cited in the scientific literature.'

(MAPPG, 2015 p. 63)

We hope we have fulfilled these criteria, but ultimately you need to find out for yourself what works best for you. There are many courses available, and a list of resources, such as retreat centres and other books, is to follow at the end of this chapter. Just watch out for the potential trap here though – of judging yourself as a failure if (as may be promised by some 'scientifically proven' forms of mindfulness training and endorsed by all their own internally funded supporting research studies) you do not instantly find yourself levitating across the office in a state of non-judging, acceptance and compassion after completing an introductory course. You are not failing! You are becoming aware of, and meeting, the human condition of the judging mind, the attachment to perfection and the very causes of your own stress. Notice your critic attacks ('I'm no good at this!', 'the course promised me I would feel less stressed and look at me now!!', 'mindfulness stinks!') and do not let these thoughts sabotage your good work. There is no 'set' way to do mindfulness. After all, the Buddha and his buddies didn't do an eight-week course, and they didn't do too badly (no confirmation of levitating, though). Mindfulness is for life, not just for Christmas; and practice, in order to gain the merits, does require patience, effort and persistence. The benefits from mindfulness will arise from its practice and constant deepening and broadening of balanced effort, insight and skilful discrimination. A famous discourse of the Buddha, regarding mindfulness practice and effort, involves a monk named Sona, who is exploring 'right effort' (part of what is known as 'the Noble Eightfold Path' in Buddhism). The Buddha instructs him, referring to his previous non-monastic life when he played the vina (an Indian stringed musical instrument) and their discourse went something like this:

'Sona, when you were a house-dweller, were you skilled at playing the vina?'

'Yes, venerable one.'

'Tell me what you think: when the strings of your vina were too taut, was it in tune and playable?'

'No, Lord.'

'And when the vina strings were too loose, was it in tune and playable?'

'No, it was not, Lord Buddha.'

'And what do you think: when the strings of your vina were neither too taut nor too loose, but tuned to be made right on pitch, was your vina in tune and playable?'

'Yes, Lord.'

'In the same way, Sona, overaroused persistence leads to restlessness, overly slack persistence leads to laziness. Thus you should determine the right pitch for your persistence, attune to the pitch of the five senses and there pick up your theme.'

(Translation from: www.accesstoinsight.org, please see 'Useful resources')

Take your time, with compassion and a little humour too if possible, allowing your journey to unfold and your skill of fine-tuning to develop. While we have shown you the abundance and ease of accessing mindfulness practice, even in the seemingly incompatible areas of business and your working life, mindfulness isn't about making an instant one-hit wonder; it is about continually revisiting the present, refreshing yourself, being open to what life throws at you and making space to see deeply into how you operate, what makes you content, glad and connected and taking good care of yourself and others in the process. Who wouldn't want to stroll along this path, rather than race to a never-arriving finish line (there really isn't one)? Please enjoy your practice, stop to smell the roses and watch the clouds passing by. Perhaps you really can revive your hard-working soul with a few breaths, mindfully observed each day, and just possibly we will see some radical changes occurring as you join the many interested others in your workplace, city and society as a whole. Jon Kabat-Zinn, writing in the *Guardian* very recently in response to the Mindful Nation UK report, stated:

> *'If the unique genesis of the Mindful Nation UK report as a cross-party collaborative effort is recognised, and its forward-looking recommendations for further research and implementation acted on by government and other agencies, there is no question in my mind that the repercussions and ramifications of this report in the UK will be profoundly beneficial. Indeed, they will be addressing some of the most pressing problems of society at their very root – at the level of the human mind and heart.'*
>
> **Jon Kabat-Zinn (Taken from theguardian.com; please find the link to the full article in the 'Useful resources' section)**

“Mindfulness is very much alive and kicking in the workplace.”

As we have stated, and as you may already be experiencing for yourself, mindfulness is very much alive and kicking in the workplace. A study conducted towards the end of 2014 commissioned by the American Management Association, in association with the Business Research Consortium (please see the 'Useful resources' section for a link to the executive summary) surveyed 991 individuals working in the corporate sector (mostly across the USA), asking them about mindfulness in the workplace, exploring themes of stress, leadership, emotional intelligence and decision-making. This study highlighted three key findings:

1 **Mindfulness is needed:** Workplace stress is a major problem in corporate organisations, ranking as the highest problematic issue reported by workers. Over 50 per cent of respondents reported significant stress levels, with only 8 per cent reporting low levels of stress at work.

2 **Mindfulness is happening:** About half of the firms included in the study were already implementing some form of mindfulness training or management practice, three quarters of these to a prominent degree.

3 **Mindfulness really works:** Where mindfulness was implemented in an organisation, it was rated by 85 per cent of respondents to be beneficial; while 40 per cent reported mindfulness to be 'very beneficial.'

With all this in mind and assuming that you are just raring to go and get practising yourself some more, we thought that this might be a good time to share a few quick reference summaries with you. Firstly we want to summarise some of the main points to keep in mind as you continue on your mindfulness journey and in your practice. Here are our top ten reminders that you can keep to hand to help you along the way.

Top ten reminders about mindfulness

1 Practise, practise and (guess what) practise!

2 You do not need to feel relaxed, clear-headed, calm, spiritual, patient or inspired – just do it!

3 Be kind and compassionate to yourself.

4 Forget about trying to 'clear your mind of thoughts' (AKA 'no brain activity = dead'). Thoughts will arise: trying to stop or suppress them causes stress; leave them be.

5 Frequent short practices (ten minutes a day) have been shown to give a plethora of physical, emotional and mental health benefits.

6 Your body and your breath always connect you to the present moment, so tune in to them and be here, now.

7 All feelings, thoughts and mental states are welcome, none are excluded, not allowed or not OK; meet them kindly.

8 There is no perfect state or condition to achieve, sustain or strive for.

9 You do not need to have perfect conditions around you in order to practise (i.e. silence, calm, nice people, a tidy desk, etc.); just do it!

10 Practise, practise and (yep, that again) practise.

Along with your regular mindfulness practice, you might want to consider some of the other mindful actions that you can continue to implement in among the daily grind of work. Try the practical exercises listed below to enhance a deeper sense of compassion and connection, as often and as frequently as you like.

Exercise 8.2: Work in progress

Daily boost

When you're in a pinch, just wanting a morale boost or feeling inspired to supplement your mindfulness practices further, try these quick exercises:

1 **Make a list of what you are grateful for today.** This could include things you have accomplished, comforts you have enjoyed or observations about the people and world around you – if your mind turns towards what is lacking (not good enough), refocus it onto gratitude.

2 **Do something kind for yourself (and others too if you wish!).** For example: take a short walk, make a lovely cup of tea, stand up and stretch, wish yourself well, or anything else you like. Be mindful of the caring intention and loving quality of these gestures.

3 **Organise something that will bring you into closer contact with friends or loved ones.** For instance: go out with colleagues for lunch or a drink after work, plan to cook yourself, your partner or family a nice meal, phone a friend just to say 'hi', take or send flowers to your Mum (oh, go on!). Do anything, great or small, to remind yourself and others of the preciousness of connection. Recall how healthy relationships are a key factor in happiness and well-being; it pays to attend to these.

4 **Quit the comparisons.** If you find yourself thinking 'I am better than them' or 'they are better than me' – drop it. Focus on how well you are doing, notice and allow yourself to bathe in any feelings of self-worth and contentment and practise gladness for the well-being of others.

5 **Write yourself a little love letter.** Write a note for when you are having a hard time: remind yourself of ways in which you are loved and lovable; you might want to note your talents, skills, personal qualities and how your heart's intention is to take care of yourself and others. Put the note aside on your tablet, phone or piece of paper for that 'rainy day.'

As you commit to your own personal practice it is likely that your eagerness to implement and disseminate mindfulness across your place of work will also grow (if it hasn't already). With this in mind, here are our top tips for introducing and enhancing mindfulness in your workplace.

Top tips for enhancing mindfulness in the workplace

▶ Practise, practise, practise (did we mention that one before?). Even with just ten minutes a day you will reap the rewards and others will simply see how you are benefiting.

► Talk about your experiences with your colleagues; name the benefits, the research findings and how mindfulness can have a positive impact on the workplace, and real-world everyday work problems (and the bottom line!) and share the exercises in this book. Encourage colleagues to practise too (don't be pushy, though!) and invite them to share their experience with you. Get talking about mindfulness.

► If there is an appetite among your colleagues try practising together: suggest a practice (you might like to use the audio recordings that accompany some of the practices in this book to help you all get started), agree a time and place and go for it. It might feel odd at first, but it can really enhance your experience and encourage your commitment to practise with others.

► Spread the word as much as you can and have faith that your colleagues will 'get it' through their own direct experience, and finding their own way. Try to get mindfulness in front of managers and senior people in your company; take it to HR and occupational health departments, so they can experience it for themselves too.

► If you have, or are, a willing boss, create a tranquil space at work where you can take a break to breathe, watch the greenery or sky and refresh yourself during the day, your lunch breaks or before and after work hours.

► Remember that even without supportive colleagues or managers, and with no special spaces or materials, you can still practise – no one else even needs to know (there are no excuses!).

► If you are in a position to implement training, then get a mindfulness consultant in to deliver a quality training session or get them to help to devise a mindfulness programme and strategic intervention across the organisation, or even a simple talk to begin with (we and many others listed in the 'Further contacts' section at the end of this book are available to deliver a range of mindfulness services to your organisation, so do get in touch!).

Next, as promised, is a chart that we hope will serve you well as a summary and quick reference guide to the mindfulness practices contained within this book. We have organised these in relation to common everyday problems that you may encounter at work and while you're on the job. We've also highlighted the benefits that using these practices are likely to bring (but remember not to get too hung up on achieving those, as that's only likely to get in the way of any relief that you may be after). We hope that this chart is useful to you.

Quick reference guide for keeping mindful on the job

Work dilemma	Mindfulness practice	Benefits
I only have five minutes	Ex 1.1 Your starter for ten (p.3) 🎧 Ex 1.3 Mindfulness of breathing (p.15) 🎧 Ex 2.1 Take a chill pill (p.38) Ex 3.1 Holding your nerve (p.78) Ex 6.1 Take a moment (or two) (p.201) Ex 7.4 The time is now (p.271)	Five minutes is a great amount of time just to tune in. The breath, five senses and body are an ever-present anchor to this moment. These practices will provide you with a quick sense of peace, space and much needed stability in your busy and stressful day.
I want to practise while I am commuting	Ex 1.1 Your starter for ten (p.3) 🎧 Ex 1.3 Mindfulness of breathing (p.15) 🎧 Ex 2.6 Body-focused attention training (p.65) 🎧 Ex 7.4 The time is now (p.271)	Excellent time to use mindfulness! You might like to pay particular attention to your body, breath or the sights, sounds and smells around you; this will be especially easy to do if you go by public transport.
I am grabbing a quick lunch	Ex 1.1 Your starter for ten (p. 3) 🎧 Ex 1.3 Mindfulness of breathing (p.15) 🎧 Ex 2.4 Working lunch (p.53) Ex 2.5 Getting smart with your smartphone (p.55) 🎧 Ex 4.5 A refreshing stroll (p.137) Ex 4.6 Here-ing sounds (p.142) 🎧 Ex 7.4 The time is now (p.271)	Try just eating your lunch. Then, as you will no doubt get out your phone for a fiddle, do a quick mindfulness practice with that too. You can always practise mindfulness of your breath on your lunch break also. These practices will help you to enjoy your lunch and really have the break that you need and deserve; you'll likely improve your focus and attention at the same time.

Quick reference guide for keeping mindful on the job

Work dilemma	Mindfulness practice	Benefits
I am feeling unfocused and distracted and I want to be more efficient and productive	Ex 2.1 Take a chill pill (p.38) Ex 2.4 Working lunch (p.53) Ex 2.5 Getting smart with your smartphone (p.55) Ex 2.6 Body-focused attention training (p.65) Ex 2.7 Pencilled in (p.71) Ex 6.1 Take a moment (or two) (p.201)	Use mindfulness to harness your attention and train it to focus effectively and with a quality of ease. These practices will help you refocus on the here and now, keep your mind clear and refreshed for action. They will train your mind in doing just one thing at a time, which will likely improve your productivity and your increased awareness of the right amount of effort required to get the job done.
I am bored and fed up	Ex 1.1 Your starter for ten (p.3) Ex 2.5 Getting smart with your smartphone (p.55) Ex 4.5 A refreshing stroll (p.137) Ex 4.6 Here-ing sounds (p.142) Ex 6.4 Discernment over reactivity (p.210) Ex 8.1 A breath of fresh air (p.295)	Look at life with renewed interest, but also remember it's okay to be bored too; maybe you can rest in a state of unstimulated experience. If you need to develop creativity, look at the next 'problem'. With these practices you'll be able to unhook from repetitive thoughts and urges, likely feel re-energised, refreshed, more curious and stimulated, even with the usually mundane and 'little' things in life.

Quick reference guide for keeping mindful on the job

Work dilemma	Mindfulness practice	Benefits
I have behaved badly to a colleague(s)	Ex 3.5 Paper pusher – origami (p.97) Ex 3.10 Enough is enough (p.112) Ex 5.5 Loving kindness for conflict (p.185) Ex 6.9 Mind training for emotional resilience (p.227) Ex 7.7 Spreading the love and feeling good too (p.284)	Allow yourself to fully feel your emotions, see your thoughts and behavioural urges. Make space to be kind to yourself and repair any damage you may have caused: a simple 'sorry' could well suffice. These practices will help you to not exacerbate your own upset and free up the confidence, time and energy to enhance compassion towards others.
I am overwhelmed with work and have lost all motivation	Ex 1.3 Mindfulness of breathing (p.15) Ex 2.4 Working lunch (p.53) Ex 2.7 Pencilled in (p.71) Ex 3.7 Developing a reservoir of profound inner peace (p.103) Ex 4.4 Sparking the inner fire (p.133) Ex 6.3 Phew! (p.207) Ex 7.4 The time is now (p.271)	Try to harness your focus to get the job done. Also prioritise and delegate where you can. Failing that, be kind and compassionate to yourself right now. These practices will help you to drop the multitasking, train your mind to do one thing at a time, feel less stressed, increase confidence, efficiency and provide you with a greater sense of time.

Quick reference guide for keeping mindful on the job

Work dilemma	Mindfulness practice	Benefits
I feel low, lacking in confidence and worthless	Ex 3.5 Paper pusher–origami (p.97) Ex 3.7 Developing a reservoir of profound inner peace (p.103) Ex 3.10 Enough is enough (p.112) 🎧 Ex 5.4 Taming the mind (p.175) 🎧	Try to 'unhook' from the inner critic, beating yourself up over feeling bad, or telling yourself 'not to': it won't create less tension. Instead find ease where you can. These practices will help you to notice the inner critic that undermines your confidence, and to boost your confidence by offering more compassion and kindness towards yourself.
I can't stop worrying and I'm so worked up that I can't work	Ex 1.3 Mindfulness of breathing (p.15) 🎧 Ex 3.10 Enough is enough (p.112) 🎧 Ex 5.4 Taming the mind (p.175) 🎧 Ex 6.3 Phew! (p.207) 🎧 Ex 7.3 Making peace (p.258) Ex 7.4 The time is now (p.271)	OK, so take a little break and come back to things when you've given yourself the chance to release some tension here. Keep compassionate and forgiving towards yourself. These practices will help you to feel grounded and present, and are a great way to reconnect to now rather than being caught up in distracting thoughts. You'll likely enhance a sense of relaxation too.
I need to get creative and be inspired	Ex 2.5 Getting smart with your smartphone (p.55) 🎧 Ex 4.4 Sparking the inner fire (p.133) Ex 4.5 A refreshing stroll (p.137) Ex 4.6 Here-ing sounds (p.142) 🎧 Ex 8.1 A breath of fresh air (p.295)	Remember that simply going for a walk, being in the 'green' or having a break can really help to reinvigorate creativity and see things afresh. Try these practices to unhook from creativity-bashing thoughts and reconnect with your curiosity and inspiration.

Quick reference guide for keeping mindful on the job

Work dilemma	Mindfulness practice	Benefits
I am struggling with difficult team dynamics	Ex 5.2 Hello and how are you? (p.160) Ex 5.5 Loving kindness for conflict (p. 185) Ex 6.4 Discernment over reactivity (p. 210) Ex 7.3 Making peace (p.258) Ex 7.7 Spreading the love and feeling good too (p.284)	Try to develop your speech and listening skills and develop compassion for yourself and others. This doesn't mean not saying 'no', or standing your ground where appropriate. These practices will help you to effectively manage thoughts and feelings that are maintaining interpersonal difficulties.
I am anxious about a presentation or meeting	Ex 3.1 Holding your nerve (p.78) Ex 3.2 Finding confident ground (p.83) Ex 3.7 Developing a reservoir of profound inner well-being (p. 103) Ex 5.4 Taming the mind (p.175) Ex 6.3 Phew! (p.207)	Nervousness is normal. Take your time, keep focused and breathe. These practices will help you to find a sense of stability and security and to feel more 'anchored' and self-assured when you feel underconfident and anxious.
I am worn out and tired	Ex 2.6 Body-focused attention training (p.65) Ex 3.7 Developing a reservoir of profound inner well-being (p. 103) Ex 6.3 Phew! (p.207) Ex 8.1 A breath of fresh air (p.295)	You might well be exhausted. Use your mindfulness to acknowledge how tough things are, to keep refreshed and above all practise some kindness and self-compassion. These practices will help you feel rejuvenated, re-energised and more relaxed in your body.

Quick reference guide for keeping mindful on the job

Work dilemma	Mindfulness practice	Benefits
I have made a mistake	Ex 2.1 Take a chill pill (p.38) Ex 2.7 Pencilled in (p.71) Ex 3.10 Enough is enough (p.112) Ex 5.4 Taming the mind (p.175) Ex 6.9 Mind training for emotional resilience (p.227)	You are human, this happens. Have a breather; take stock and practise freeing yourself up from harsh, self-directed criticism. These practices will help you to 'never mind your self-critical mind' and motivate you to redress any regrets with self-confidence.
I want to feel more connected to colleagues and get my team working well together	Ex 5.1 Here I am, connected (p.152) Ex 5.2 Hello and how are you? (mindful speech and listening) (p.160) Ex 7.7 Spreading the love and feeling good too (p.284)	Good for you. Take time to centre on this wholesome desire to connect. You might like to suggest a get-together with colleagues or try a random act of kindness. These practices will help you to connect and feel connected to others in meaningful ways.
I want to quit my job	Ex 3.5 Paper-pusher – origami (p.97) Ex 6.4 Discernment over reactivity (p.210) Ex 7.2 Times are a'changin' (p.252)	There are definitely days like these! Watch whether your inner critic is meddling with your judgements. Use these practices to try to skilfully discriminate between knee-jerk reactions and useful behaviours that are aligned with your values.

Quick reference guide for keeping mindful on the job

Work dilemma	Mindfulness practice	Benefits
I want to share/practise mindfulness with a colleague	Ex 1.1 Your starter for ten (p.3) 🎧 Ex 1.3 Mindfulness of breathing (p.15) 🎧 Ex 2.1 Take a chill pill (p.38) Ex 2.6 Body-focused attention training (p.65) 🎧 Ex 6.1 Take a moment (or two) (p.201)	Lovely! Try some simple, classic practices as these are usually the simplest to grasp. Hopefully your colleagues will find these practices simple and accessible to share with others too. Enjoy!
I'd like to enhance my well-being and happiness	Ex 3.7 Developing a profound sense of inner well-being (p.103) Ex 7.3 Making peace (p.258) Ex 7.7 Spreading the love and feeling good too (p.284) Ex 8.1 A breath of fresh air (p.295)	There is no time like the present for encouraging and cultivating a strong sense of well-being. These mindfulness practices will work wonders for increasing ease and contentment at work and in life.
My boss is being an arse	Ex 3.10 Enough is enough (p.112) 🎧 Ex 5.2 Hello and how are you? (mindful speech and listening) (p.160) Ex 5.5 Loving kindness for conflict (p.185) 🎧 Ex 6.4 Discernment over reactivity (p.210) Ex 7.7 Spreading the love and feeling good too (p.284)	Yes, possibly s/he is being tricky. Make space for your emotions. Take time before you act and take care of yourself. These practices will help you to manage your painful feelings and encourage you to reflect on whether you want to take action and, if so, help you to do this wisely.

Quick reference guide for keeping mindful on the job

Work dilemma	Mindfulness practice	Benefits
I feel good today—can I keep it up?	Ex 4.6 Here-ing sounds (p. 142) 🎧 Ex 6.1 Take a moment (or two) (p.201) Ex 7.2 Times are a'changin' (p. 252) 🎧 Ex 7.3 Making peace (p.258) Ex 7.7 Spreading the love and feeling good too (p.284)	Allow your sense of well-being to permeate your experience with these practices, but remember that clinging to it will not enhance ease and will probably cause unwanted stress; try to go with the flow: this paradoxically will increase the likelihood of feeling easeful.
Work dilemma	**Mindfulness practice**	**Benefits**
I feel vulnerable (sad, low, anxious, etc.)	Ex 3.1 Holding your nerve (p.78) Ex 3.7 Developing a reservoir of profound inner well-being (p. 103) Ex 3.10 Enough is enough (p.112) 🎧 Ex 5.4 Taming the mind (p.175) 🎧 Ex 7.2 Times are a'changin' (p. 252) 🎧	Be especially gentle with yourself. Allow the emotions to arise and keep track of self-judgements. Practise these exercises to help remain strong in the face of distress and remember that 'this too will pass'.

'appy mindfulness

If you don't know already (we're sure you've probably guessed anyway), there are several mindfulness-based apps on the market currently which you can download onto your mobile phone or tablet that will help you keep up with your mindfulness practice daily. A recent (2015) study carried out a review and evaluation of all the mindfulness-based apps that were on the market at that time (please see the Huffington Post article listed the 'Useful resources' section to find out more about this study and its findings). The top four rated apps identified in this study were:

1 Headspace
2 Smiling Mind
3 iMindfulness
4 Mindfulness Daily

You might find it useful to try out some of these apps for yourself. Along with many of them providing excellent audio guides to follow, they also serve as a great 'reminder' tool, so you don't forget to practise (which is easily done). Establishing any new habit is often a huge challenge at the best of times, let alone when you are inundated with pressing work demands, all day long. So get downloading and enjoy!

Now, despite all the guided practices, tips and advice contained within this book as well as all the other apps, books and materials out there to support your daily mindfulness practice, you may find that you still aren't getting much practice done. It's not uncommon for us to get in our own way when we first begin to practise mindfulness, and there are many excuses and obstacles that even the most experienced practitioners can come up against from time to time. Below we have listed five of the most common barriers that prevent us from practising, and offer some of our advice about what you can do about overcoming these (there really are no excuses!) if you experience them too.

Top five reasons/excuses for not practising (and what to do about it)

1 **Waa! I'm too tired:** Join the club of the most common reason 'not to'. But seriously, are you too tired to stand? Sit? Lie down? Breathe? Maybe you will nod off, so? There are a few reasons other than actually being really tired that you may experience tiredness as soon as you do a mindfulness practice and these are usually subtle(ish)

forms of avoiding difficult emotions, having a 'dull' mind, or habitual engagement in zoning out. Try:

► practising with your eyes open (very hard to fall asleep with your peepers open!);

► practising sitting on the very edge of your chair;

► practising standing up or walking (no, not sleep-walking);

► developing interest, curiosity and freshness;

► opening a window, going outside or having a walk around.

2 **I'm not interested enough:** Well, get interested! If this book wasn't inspiration enough, then there are literally hundreds of others that are available. Search on Google; you'll find loads of stimulating videos and other resources too. Again, you might find that your lack of interest or inspiration is a habitual tendency of yours, or you might discover that sometimes there really is no drama, no stimulation nor much occurring *in extremis*. Try:

► practising mindfulness doing something you love doing (i.e. playing sport, making love, eating spaghetti, drawing, writing, singing, listening to music!);

► getting some fresh air – enliven those little grey cells;

► cultivating interest by looking deeply and curiously into your experience as you practise mindfulness;

► practising acceptance of emotional neutrality – maybe nothing thrilling is going on right now; can you hang out here? Emotionally neutral spaces can be very restful, easeful and sustaining.

3 **I am too angry/upset/depressed/wired:** Remember that you don't need to be calm, peaceful or feeling fluffy. One mind state is not 'better' than another; each is just our emotional weather coming and going (yes, this will pass too). By attending to your emotions mindfully (curiously), you are actually making space to observe them without reacting habitually with defensiveness, distraction or dullness. Mindfulness is not about making your experience 'wrong' or trying to 'fix' an experience, but it is about gaining mastery and skill through acceptance and compassion. Try:

► having a bracing walk, which you may like to slow gradually as and if you start to feel less emotional;

► reminding yourself that 'this too shall pass';

► engaging with a short and simple breathing practice to allow yourself to contact the present moment and reminding yourself to desist from rumination, judgement or self- criticism;

▶ practising self-compassion. Painful emotions are hard, no need to make it worse – be kind to yourself.

4 **I'm doing it wrong/I am no good at it:** Oh, c'mon!!! We can safely assume that since you are reading this that somehow you figured out how to breathe when you arrived on the planet and that you have miraculously kept on doing it, so well done. Now just notice that. Great. Try:

▶ breathing (yes, you are doing it right now!) and noticing that you are; simple.

5 **I don't have time:** Yeah, we know, right!! So:

▶ try making time every day (5–10 minutes) to practise: make it your routine, maybe set specific time aside before you go to work, or as you commute, or practise as you wait for a meeting; walk to the deli or talk to colleagues;

▶ don't make mindfulness something 'special': it is ordinary; bring it to your everyday experience – you have an abundance of that!

▶ if you want to reap the rewards – practise, practise, practise;

▶ notice how much space there is in the day already in small ways, notice how impatience and scarcity in particular rob us from the sense of 'plenty';

▶ practise being generous with your time, by giving it to others;

▶ be kind: life might be hectic right now, so give yourself a break, be nice to number 1.

Farewell, friends

In this final chapter of the book we have:

▶ summarised some of the ongoing debate about the position of mindfulness in business and secular settings;

▶ given you a brief overview of the recent UK parliamentary comments on mindfulness at work;

▶ offered some useful tools for sustaining, maintaining and troubleshooting your mindfulness practice at work.

We hope that in reading this book you have recognised how mindfulness is relevant to our working lives today, maybe more so than ever. We hope that you have understood that in order to practise and benefit from it in your work, you do not need to carve out any extra time on top of everything else that you already have to do or join a temple and sit crossed-legged meditating for hours on end. No, the real mindfulness practice is to be embodied and brought to your actions and interaction at work each and every day and in doing so your experience and performance on the job is likely to significantly improve. The truth is that the reality of our working lives has changed dramatically over more recent years. Advancements in technology mean that we are now connected to one another in a way, and at a speed, that we have never known before. Of course this is excellent news for business as it brings with it seemingly endless possibilities for new and improved means to share information, and trade goods and services. However, we can also recognise how the expectations and pace of work have simultaneously increased exponentially, and how continuing to operate in old and habitual ways carries with it costs. Mindlessly running on autopilot in among this transforming work arena means that the functioning and well-being of an organisation, as well as that of its employees, will rapidly decline, which is then likely to be detrimental to that business's bottom line. Mindfulness offers us a much needed space within which to stand, from where we can gain a greater and wiser perspective and train ourselves to take more effective actions in our work. It provides us with the necessary tools to function and cope well in this rapidly changing and pressured global business environment. As we have seen, however, mindfulness is not just another technology to help us to de-stress and operate at our optimal level, it offers businesses and our day-to-day experience at work so much more besides. Implementing mindfulness into our places of work will also lay the foundations for a happier workforce and a healthier working culture which by nature will be more human, allowing us all to truly thrive. It seems that mindfulness really does have its place at work. It undoubtedly makes good sense for the future sustainability of business, as well as of our planet at large.

And now, alas, we find ourselves coming to the end of our time together and noticing an odd sensation of letting go after an intense literary journey. We would both love to sit down with you face to face to discuss any concerns, questions and unanswered queries, but of course this is impossible right now. However, we do invite you to be open to your experience – positive, negative or neutral – and to further your inquiry into this beautiful, abundant, beneficial and ever-evolving practice of mindfulness. Please do contact groups, teachers and internet communities and seek out further instruction where we may have omitted something in this book or you need further clarification. Above all, we really do hope that you have benefited from this book and wish you well on your journey and in all that you do in your work and life in general. We hope that with the wonderful practice of mindfulness you, your colleagues and your place of work will continue to flourish and find a deep sense of peace:

May you be well
May you be happy
May you find the heart's release

The breezes at dawn have secrets to tell you
Don't go back to sleep!
You must ask for what you really want.
Don't go back to sleep!
People are going back and forth across the doorsill where the two worlds touch,
The door is round and open
Don't go back to sleep!

Rumi

Useful resources

▶ Access to Insight (2013, November 30). *Right effort: samma vayamo* [from accesstoinsight.org]. Retrieved from: http://www.accesstoinsight.org/ptf/dhamma/sacca/sacca4/samma-vayamo/

▶ American Management Association. (2015, April 27). *Stress management and mindfulness in the workplace. Executive summary* [from amanet.org]. Retrieved from: http://www.amanet.org/training/articles/Stress-Management-and-Mindfulness-in-the-Workplace.aspx

► Boyce, B. (2015, September 26). *The good beneath the hype. Juicy stories sell. But when people oversell mindfulness its true value may be overlooked* [from mindful.org]. Retrieved from: http://www.mindful.org/the-good-beneath-the-hype/?utm_source=Mindful+Newsletter&utm_campaign=8945f9d108-August_2015_Issue_Mindful7_1_2015&utm_medium=email&utm_term=0_6d03e8c02c-8945f9d108-20962805

► Kabat-Zinn, J. (2015, October 20). *Mindfulness has huge health potential – but McMindfulness is no panacea* [from theguardian.com]. Retrieved from: http://www.theguardian.com/commentisfree/2015/oct/20/mindfulness-mental-health-potential-benefits-uk

► MAPPG. (2015, October 20). *Mindful Nation UK* [from themindfulnessinitiative.org.uk]. Retrieved from: http://themindfulnessinitiative.org.uk/images/reports/Mindfulness-APPG-Report_Mindful-Nation-UK_Oct2015.pdf

► Swami Jnaneshvara Bharati. (date unknown). *Modern yoga versus traditional yoga*. Retrieved from: http://www.swamij.com/traditional-yoga.htm

► Wei, M. (2015, August 24). *What mindfulness app is right for you?* [from huffingtonpost.com]. Retrieved from: http://www.huffingtonpost.com/marlynn-wei-md-jd/what-mindfulness-app-is-right-for-you_b_8026010.html

► Wilks, J. (2014). *Secular mindfulness; potential and pitfalls* [from bcbsdharma.org]. Retrieved from: http://www.bcbsdharma.org/article/secular-mindfulness-potential-pitfalls/

Notes and references

Chapter 1 – Using mindfulness at work

1 Wolever, R. Q., Bobinet, K. J., McCabe, K., Mackenzie, E. R., Fekete, E., Kusnick, C. A. and Baime, M. (2012). Effective and viable mind–body stress reduction in the workplace: A randomized controlled triaL. *Journal of Occupational Health Psychology*, 17(2), 246–258.

2 Duchemin, A. M., Steinberg, B. A., Marks, D. R., Vanover, K. and Klatt, M. (2015). A small randomized pilot study of a workplace mindfulness-based intervention for surgical intensive care unit personnel: Effects on salivary α-amylase levels. *Journal of Occupational and Environmental* Medicine, 57(4), 393–399.

3 Ismail, H. A. K., Coetzee, N., Du Toit, P., Rudolph, E. C. and Joubert, Y. T. (2013). Towards gaining a competitive advantage: the relationship between burnout, job satisfaction, social support and mindfulness. *Journal of Contemporary Management*, 10, 448–464.

4 Bond, F. W. and Bunce, D. (2000). Mediators of change in emotion-focused and problem focused worksite stress management interventions. *Journal of Occupational Health Psychology*, 5, 156–163.

5 Lloyd, J., Bond, F. W. and Flaxman, P. E. (2013). The value of psychological flexibility: Examining psychological mechanisms underpinning a cognitive behavioural therapy intervention for burnout. *Work Stress*, 27, 181–199.

6 Dane, E. and Brummel, B. J. (2014). Examining workplace mindfulness and its relations to job performance and turnover intention. *Human Relations*, 67, 105–128.

7 Condon, P., Desbordes, G., Miller, W. and DeSteno, D. (2013). Meditation increases compassionate responses to suffering. *Psychological Science*, 24, 2125–2127.

8 Jazaieri, H., Thupten Jinpa, G., McGonigal, K., Rosenberg, E. L., Finkelstein, J., Simon-Thomas, E. and Goldin, P. R. (2012). Enhancing compassion: A randomised controlled trial of a compassion cultivation program. *Journal of Happiness Studies*, 14(4), 1113–1126.

Chapter 2 – Improve focus and productivity

1 Ophir, E., Nass, C. and Wagner, A. D. (2009). Cognitive control in media multitaskers. *Proceedings of the National Academy of Sciences USA*, 106(37), 15583–15587.

2 Killingsworth, M. A. and Gilbert, D. T. (2010). A wandering mind is an unhappy mind. *Science*, 330, 932.

3 Maguire, E. A., Gadian, D. G., Johnsrude, I. S., Good, C. D., Ashburner, J., Frackowiak, R. S. J. and Frith, C. D. (2000). Navigation-related structural change in the hippocampi of taxi drivers. *Proceedings of the National Academy of Sciences USA*, 97, 4398–4403.

4 Fox, K. C., Nijeboer, S., Dixon, M. L., Floman, J. L., Ellamil, M., Rumak, S. P., Sedlmeier, P. and Christoff, K. (2014). Is meditation associated with altered brain structure? A systematic review and meta-analysis of morphometric neuroimaging in meditation practitioners. *Neuroscience & Biobehavioral Reviews*, 43, 48–73.

5 Moore, A. and Malinowski, P. (2009). Meditation, mindfulness and cognitive flexibility. *Consciousness and Cognition*, 18, 176–186.

6 Levy, D. M., Wobbrock, J. O., Kaszniak, A. W. and Ostergren, M. (2012). The effects of mindfulness meditation training on multitasking in a high stress information environment. *Proceedings of Graphics Interface Conference 2012*, 45–52.

7 Mrazek, M. D., Franklin, M. S., Phillips, D. T., Baird, B. and Schooler, J. W. (2013). Mindfulness training improves working memory capacity and GRE performance while reducing mind wandering. *Psychological Science*, 24(5), 776–781.

8 Lee, K. E., Williams, K. J. H., Sargent, L. D., Williams, N. S. G. and Johnson, K. A. (2015). 40-second green roof views sustain attention: The role of micro-breaks in attention restoration. *Journal of Environmental Psychology*, 42, 182–189.

9 Biron, M. and van Veldhoven, M. J. P. M. (2012). Emotional labor in service work: Psychological flexibility and emotion regulation. *Human Relations*, 65, 1259–1282.

10 Bond, F. W. and Flaxman, P. E. (2006). The ability of psychological flexibility and job control to predict learning, job performance and mental health. *Journal of Organizational Behavior Management*, 26, 113–130.

11 Hölzel, B. K., Carmody, J., Vangel, M., Congleton, C., Yerramsetti, S. M., Gard, T. and Lazar, S. W. (2011). Mindfulness practice leads to increases in regional brain gray matter density. *Psychiatry Research*, 191(1), 36–43.

Chapter 3 – Boost confidence

1 Goldin, P. R. and Gross, J. J. (2010). Effects of mindfulness-based stress reduction (MBSR) on emotion regulation in social anxiety disorder. *Emotion*, 10(1), 83–91.

2 Anderson, C., Brion, S., Moore, D. A. and Kennedy, J. A. (2012). A status-enhancement account of overconfidence. *Journal of Personality and Social Psychology*, 103(4), 718–735.

3 Amar, A. D., Hlupic, V. and Tamwatin, T. (in press) Effect of meditation on self-perception of leadership skills: a control study group study of CEOs. In: *74th Annual Meeting of the Academy of Management*, 1–5 Aug 2014, Philadelphia, PA.

4 Pepping, C. A., O'Donovan, A. and Davis, P. J. (2013). The positive effects of mindfulness on self-esteem. *The Journal of Positive Psychology*, 8(5), 376–386.

5 Breines, J. G. and Chen, S. (2012). Self-compassion increases self-improvement motivation. *Personality & Social Psychology Bulletin*, 38(9), 1133–1143.

6 Howell, A. J., Dopko, R. L., Turowski, J. B. and Buro, K. (2011). The disposition to apologize. *Personality and Individual Differences*, 51(4), 509–514.

7 Arimitsu, K. and S. G. (2015). Effects of compassion thinking on negative emotions. *Cognition and Emotions*. Retrieved from: http://dx.doi.org/10.1080/02699931.2015.1078292

Chapter 4 – Get creative

1 Baas, M., **Nevicka,** B. and Ten Velden, F. S. (2014). Specific mindfulness skills differentially predict creative performance. *Personality and Social Psychology Bulletin*, 40, 1092–1106.

2 Colzato, L. S., Ozturk, A. and Hommel, B. (2012). Meditate to create: the impact of focused-attention and open-monitoring training on convergent and divergent thinking. *Frontiers in Psychology*, 3, 116, 1–5.

3 Harmon-Jones, E., Gable, P. A. and Price, T. F. (2013). Does negative affect always narrow and positive affect always broaden the mind? Considering the influence of motivational intensity on cognitive scope. *Current Directions in Psychological Science*, 22(4), 301–307.

4 Fong, C. T. (2006). The effects of emotional ambivalence on creativity. *Academy of Management Journal*, 49(5), 1016–1030.

5 Ostafin, B. and Kassman, K. (2012). Stepping out of history: Mindfulness improves insight problem solving. *Consciousness and Cognition*, 21(2), 1031–1036.

6 Greenberg, J., Reiner, K. and Meiran, N. (2012). 'Mind the trap': Mindfulness practice reduces cognitive rigidity. *PLoS ONE*, 7(5): e36206. doi:10.1371/journaL.pone.0036206.

7 Porath, C. L. and Erez, A. (2007). Does rudeness matter? The effects of rude behavior on task performance and helpfulness. *Academy of Management Journal*, 50, 1181–1197.

8 Porath, C. L. and Erez, A. (2009). Overlooked but not untouched: How incivility reduces onlookers' performance on routine and creative tasks. *Organizational Behavior and Human Decision Processes*, 109, 29–44.

Chapter 5 – Succeed in teams

1 Holt-Lunstad, J., Smith, T. and Layton, B. (2010). Social relationships and mortality risk: A meta-analytic review. *PLoS Medicine*, 7(7), 1–19.

2 Hawkley, L. C. and Cacioppo, J. T. (2003). Loneliness and pathways to disease. *Brain, Behavior, and Immunity*, 17(1), 98–105.

3 Creswell, D., Irwin, M. R., Burklund, L. J., Lieberman, M. D., Arevalo, J. M. G., Ma, J. and Cole, S. W. (2012). Mindfulness-based stress reduction training reduces loneliness and pro-inflammatory gene expression in older adults: A small randomized controlled triaL. *Brain, Behavior, and Immunity*; 26 (7), 1095–1101.

4 Novembre, G., Zanon, M. and Silani, G. (2015). Empathy for social exclusion involves the sensory-discriminative component of pain: a within-subject fMRI study. *Social Cognitive & Affective Neuroscience*, 10(2), 153–164.

5 Lutz, A., Brefczynski-Lewis, J., Johnstone, T. and Davidson, R. J. (2008). Regulation of the neural circuitry of emotion by compassion meditation: effects of meditative expertise. *PLoS ONE*, 3(3): e1897. doi: 10.1371/journaL.pone.0001897.

6 Reb, J., Narayanan, J. and Chaturvedi, S. (2014). Leading mindfully: Two studies on the influence of supervisor trait mindfulness on employee well-being and performance. *Mindfulness*, 5(1), 36–45.

7 Schultz, P. P., Ryan, R. M., Niemiec, C. P., Legate, N. and Williams, G. C. (2014). Mindfulness, work climate, and psychological need satisfaction in employee well-being. *Mindfulness*, doi: 10.1007/s12671-014-0338-7.

8 Vianello, M., Galliani, E. M. and Haidt, J. (2010). Elevation at work: The organizational effects of leaders' moral excellence. *Journal of Positive Psychology*, 5, 390–411.

Chapter 6 – Maintain peak performance

1 Zeidan, F., Martucci, K. T., Kraft, R. A., Gordon, N. S., McHaffie, J. G. and Coghill, R. C. (2011). Brain mechanisms supporting the modulation of pain by mindfulness meditation. *The Journal of Neuroscience*, 31(14), 5540–5548.

2 Grant, J. A. and Rainville, P. (2009). Pain sensitivity and analgesic effects of mindful states in Zen meditators: A cross-sectional study. *Psychosomatic Medicine*, 7, 106–114.

3 Black, D. S., O'Reilly, G. A., Olmstead, R., Breen, E. C. and Irwin, M. R. (2015). Mindfulness meditation and improvement in sleep quality and daytime impairment among older adults with sleep disturbances: A randomized clinical triaL. *JAMA Internal Medicine*, 175(4), 494–501.

4 Luders, E., Kurth, F., Mayer, E. A., Toga, A. W., Narr, K. L. and Gaser, C. (2012). The unique brain anatomy of meditation practitioners: Alterations in cortical gyrification. *Frontiers in Human Neuroscience*, 6,(34). doi: 10.3389/fnhum.2012.00034.

5 Flaxman, P. E. and Bond, F. W. (2010). Worksite stress management training: Moderated effects and clinical significance. *Journal of Occupational Health Psychology*, 15, 347–358.

6 Astin, J., Pelletier, K. R., Levanovich, K., Baase, C. M., Park, Y. Y. and Bodnar, C. M. (2014). Mindfulness goes to work: Impact of an online workplace intervention. *Journal of Occupational and Environmental Medicine*, 56(7), 721–731.

7 Ly, K. H., Asplund, K. and Andersson, G. (2014). Stress management for middle managers via an acceptance and commitment-based smartphone application: A randomized controlled triaL. *Internet Interventions*, 1, 95–101.

8 Vlemincx, E., Van Diest, I., Lehrer, P. M., Aubert, A. E. and Van den Bergh, O. (2010). Respiratory variability preceding and following sighs: A resetter hypothesis. Biological *Psychology*, 84(1), 82–87.

9 Peters, J. R., Erisman, S. M., Upton, B. T., Baer, R. A. and Roemer, L. (2011). A preliminary investigation of the relationships between dispositional mindfulness and impulsivity. *Mindfulness*, 2(4), 228–235.

10 Windsor, T. D., Curtis, R. G. and Luszcz, M. A. (2015). Sense of purpose as a psychological resource for aging welL. *Developmental Psychology*, 51(7), 975–986.

Chapter 7 – Build a healthier business

1 Kahneman, D. and Deaton, A. (2010). High income improves evaluation of life but not emotional well-being. *Proceedings of the National Academy of Sciences*, 107 (38), 16489–16493.

2 Reid, E. (2015). Embracing, passing, revealing, and the ideal worker image: How people navigate expected and experienced professional identities. *Organization Science*, 26(4), doi: 10.1287/orsC.2015.0975.

3 Virtanen, M., Jokela, M., Nyberg, S. T., Madsen, I. E. H., Lallukka, T., Ahola, K. and Kivimaki, M. (2015). Long working hours and alcohol use: systematic review and meta-analysis of published studies and unpublished individual participant data. *BMJ* 2015; 350: g7772. doi:10.1136/bmJ.g7772.

4 Virtanen, M., Ferrie, J. E., Gimeno, D., Vahtera, J., Elovainio, M., Singh-Manoux, A. and Kivimäki, M. (2009). Long working hours and sleep disturbances: the Whitehall II prospective cohort study. *Sleep*, 32(6), 737–45.

5 Virtanen, M., Stansfeld, S. A., Fuhrer, R., Ferrie, J. E. and Kivimäki, M. (2012). Overtime work as a predictor of major depressive episode: a 5-year follow-up of the Whitehall II study. *PLoS ONE* 7(1): e30719. doi:10.1371/journaL.pone.0030719.

6 Kivimaki, M., Virtanen, M., Kawachi, I., Nyberg, S. T., Alfredsson, L., Batty, G. D. and Jokela, M. (2015). Long working hours, socioeconomic status, and the risk of incident type 2 diabetes: a meta-analysis of published and unpublished data from 222 120 individuals. *Lancet Diabetes Endocrinol*, 3(1), 27–34.

7 Virtanen, M., Heikkilä, K., Jokela, M., Ferrie, J. E., Batty, G. D., Vahtera, J. and Kivimäki, M. (2012). Long working hours and coronary heart disease: a systematic review and meta-analysis. *American Journal of Epidemiology*, 176(7), 586–596.

8 Virtanen, M., Singh-Manoux, A., Ferrie, J. E., Gimeno, D., Marmot, M. G., Elovainio, M. and Kivimäki, M. (2009). Long working hours and cognitive function: the Whitehall II study. *American Journal of Epidemiology*, 169(5), 596–605.

9 Kivimaki, M., Jokela, M., Nyberg, S. T., Singh-Manoux, A., Fransson, E. I., Alfredsson, L. and Virtanen, M. (2015). Long working hours and risk of coronary heart disease and stroke: a systematic review and meta-analysis of published and unpublished data for 603 838 individuals. *The Lancet.* Retrieved from: http://dx.doi.org/10.1016/S0140-6736(15)60295-1.

10 van der Helm, E., Gujar, N. and Walker, M. P. (2012). Sleep deprivation impairs the accurate recognition of human emotions. *Sleep,* 33(3), 335–342.

11 Gordon A. M. and Chen, S. (2014). The role of sleep in interpersonal conflict: Do sleepless nights mean worse fights? *Social Psychological and Personality Science,* 5, 168–175.

12 Killgore, W. D. S., Kahn-Greene, E. T., Lipizzi, E. L., Newman, R. A., Kamimori, G. H. and Balkin T. J. (2008). Sleep deprivation reduces perceived emotional intelligence and constructive thinking skills. *Sleep Medicine,* 9(5), 517–526.

13 Sonnentag, S., Binnewies, C. and Mojza, E. J. (2010). Staying well and engaged when demands are high: the role of psychological detachment. *Journal of Applied Psychology,* 95(5), 965–76.

14 **Mogilner,** C., Chance, Z. and Norton, M. (2012). Giving time gives you time. *Psychological Science,* 23, 1233–1238.

15 Melwani, S., Mueller, J. S. and Overbeck, J.R. (2012). Looking down: the influence of contempt and compassion on emergent leadership categorizations. *Journal of Applied Psychology,* 97(6), 1171–85.

16 Aknin, L., Hamlin, J. K. and Dunn, E. (2012). Giving leads to happiness in young children. *PLoS ONE,* 7(6).

17 Hamlin, J. K., Wynn, K., Bloom, P. and Mahajan, N. (2011). How infants and toddlers react to antisocial others. *Proceedings of the National Academy of Sciences,* 108, 19931–19936.

18 Hamlin, J. K. and Wynn, K. (2011). Young infants prefer prosocial to antisocial others. *Cognitive Development,* 26, 30–39.

19 Barsade, S. and O'Neill, O. A. (2014), What's love got to do with It? A longitudinal study of the culture of companionate love and employee and client outcomes in a long-term care setting, *Administrative Science Quarterly,* 59(4), 551–598.

20 Weng, H. Y., Fox, A. S., Shackman, A. J., Stodola, D. E., Caldwell, J. Z. K., Olson, M. C. and Davidson, R. J. (2013). Compassion training alters altruism and neural responses to suffering. *Psychological Science,* 24(7), 1171–1180.

21 Fredrickson, B. L., Cohn, M. A., Coffey, K. A., Pek, J. and Finkel, S. M. (2008). Open hearts build lives: Positive emotions, induced through loving-kindness meditation, build consequential personal resources. *Journal of Personality and Social Psychology*, 95, 1045–1062.

22 Fredrickson, B. L., Grewen, K. M., Coffey, K. A., Algoe, S. B., Firestine, A. M., Arevalo, J. M. G. and Cole, S. M. (2013). A functional genomic perspective on human well-being. *Proceedings of the National Academy of Sciences*, 110, 13684–13689.

Recommended reading

▶ Alidina, S. (2015). *The mindful way through stress: The proven 8-week path to health, happiness and wellbeing.* New York: The Guildford Press.

▶ Biglan, A. (2015). *The nurture effect: How the science of human behavior can improve our lives and our world.* Oakland, CA: Sage Publications.

▶ Bond, F. W., Flaxman, P. E. and Livheim, F. (2013). *The mindful and effective employee: An Acceptance and Commitment Therapy training manual for improving wellbeing and performance.* Oakland, CA US: New Harbinger Publications.

▶ Brach, T. (2003). *Radical acceptance: Embracing your life with the heart of a Buddha.* New York: Bantam.

▶ Brown, B. (2013). *Daring greatly: How the courage to be vulnerable transforms the way we live, love and lead.* London: Penguin Books.

▶ Burbea, R. (2014). *Seeing that frees: Meditations on emptiness and dependent arising.* Devon: Hermes Amara Publications.

▶ Dasa, G. P. (2013). *Urban monk: Exploring karma, consciousness and the divine.* New York: Conscious Living.

▶ Davidson, R. J. and Begley, S. (2012). *The emotional life of your brain: How its unique patterns affect the way you think, feel and live and how you can change them.* New York: Plume.

▶ Frankl, V. E. (2004). *Man's Search for meaning: The classic tribute to hope from the holocaust.* Rider.

▶ Fransella, F. and Dalton P. (2000). *Personal Construct Counselling in Action* (2nd edn). London: Sage Publications.

▶ Fredrickson, B. L. (2014). *Love 2.0: Finding happiness and health in moments of connection.* New York: Hudson Street Press.

▶ Gelles, D. (2015). *Mindful work: How meditation is changing business from the inside out.* London: Profile Books Ltd.

▶ Germer, C. (2009). *The mindful path to self-compassion: Freeing yourself from destructive thoughts and emotions.* New York: The Guildford Press.

▶ Gilbert, P. and Choden. (2015). *Mindful compassion: How the science of compassion can help you understand your emotions, live in the present and connect deeply with others.* Oakland, CA: New Harbinger.

▶ Goleman, D. (1996). *Emotional Intelligence: Why it can matter more than IQ.* London: Bloomsbury Publishing.

▶ Goleman, D. (1999). *Working with Emotional Intelligence*. New York: Bantam.

▶ Goleman, D. (2013). *Focus: The hidden driver of excellence*. London: Bloomsbury Publishing PlC.

▶ Goleman, D. (2015). *A force for good: The Dali Lama's vision for our world*. Bantam.

▶ Halliwell, E. (2015). *Mindfulness: How to live well by paying attention*. London: Hay House Publishing.

▶ Hanh, T. N. (2008). *The miracle of mindfulness: The classic guide to meditation by the world's most revered master*. Rider.

▶ Harris, R (2008). *The happiness trap. Based on ACT: A revolutionary mindfulness-based programme for overcoming stress, anxiety and depression*. London: Robinson.

▶ Harris, R (2012). *The reality slap: How to find fulfilment when life hurts*. London: Robinson.

▶ Hayes, S. C., Bond, F. W., Barnes-Holmes, D. and Austin, J. (2006). *Acceptance and mindfulness at work: Applying Acceptance and Commitment Therapy and Relational Frame Theory to organizational behavior management*. New York: The Haworth Press.

▶ Heaveredge, J. and Halliwell, E. (2012). *The mindfulness manifesto: How doing less and noticing more can help us thrive in a stressed-out world*. London: Hay House.

▶ Hougaard, R., Carter, J. C. and Coutts, G. (2015). *One second ahead: Enhance your performance at work with mindfulness*. Palgrave Macmillan.

▶ Huffington, A (2014). *Thrive: The third metric to redefining success and creating a happier life*. London: WH Allen.

▶ Juster, N. (2008). *The Phantom Tollbooth*. Harper Collins.

▶ Kabat-Zinn, J. (2011). *Full catastrophe living, revised edition: How to cope with stress, pain and illness using mindfulness meditation*. London: Piatkus.

▶ Kornfield, J. (1993). *A path with heart: A guide through the perils and promises of spiritual life*. New York: Bantam.

▶ Langer, E. (2005). *On becoming an artist: Reinventing yourself through mindful creativity*. New York: Ballantine Books.

▶ Langer, E. (2014). *Mindfulness: 25th anniversary edition*. Boston: Da Capo Press.

▶ Lewis, D. (2013). *The brain sell: When science meets shopping. How the new mind sciences and the persuasion industry are reading our thoughts, influencing our emotions, and stimulating us to shop.* London: Nicholas Brealey Publishing.

▶ Linehan, M. (2014). *DBT Skills Training Manual* (second edition). New York: Guildford Press.

▶ Marturano, J. (2014). *Finding the space to lead: A practical guide to mindful leadership.* New York: Bloomsbury Press.

▶ Neth, K. (2011). *Self compassion: Stop beating yourself up and leave insecurity behind.* New York: Harper Collins Publishers.

▶ Oliver, J., Hill, J. and Morris, E. (2015). *Activate your life: Using acceptance and mindfulness to build a life that is rich, fulfilling and fun.* London: Robinson.

▶ Penman, D. (2015). *Mindfulness for creativity: Adapt, create and thrive in a frantic world.* London: Piatkus.

▶ Peters, S. (2012). *The chimp paradox: The mind management programme to help you achieve success, confidence and happiness.* London: Vermilion.

▶ Ricard, M. (2015). *Altruism: The power of compassion to change yourself and the world.* London: Atlantic Books.

▶ Ricard, M. (2015). *Happiness: A guide to developing life's most important skill.* New York: Little, Brown and Company.

▶ Rock, D. (2009). *Your brain at work: Strategies for overcoming distraction, regaining focus, and working smarter all day long.* New York: Harper Business.

▶ Salzberg, S. (2002). *Loving kindness: The revolutionary art of happiness (shambhala classics).* Boston: Shambhala Publications.

▶ Salzberg, S. (2013). *Real happiness at work: Meditations for accomplishment, achievement and peace.* New York: Workman Publishing.

▶ Scott, V. (2009). *Conflict resolution at work for dummies.* New Jersey: John Wiley & Sons.

▶ Seldon, A. (2015). *Beyond happiness: The trap of happiness and how to find deeper meaning and joy.* London: Yellow Kite.

▶ Sinclair, M. (2010). *Fear and self-loathing in the City: A guide to keeping sane in the square mile.* London: Karnac Books.

▶ Sinclair, M. and Seydel, J. (2013). *Mindfulness for busy people: Turning frantic and frazzled into calm and composed.* Harlow, Essex UK: Pearson.

▶ Singer, T. and Ricard, M. (eds). (2015). *Caring economics: Conversations on altruism and compassion, between scientists, economists and the Dalai Lama.* New York: Picador.

▶ Smalley, S. and Winston, D. (2010). *Fully present: The science, art and practice of mindfulness.* Philadelphia: Da Capo Press.

▶ Southwick, S. M. and Charmey, D. S. (2012). *Resilience: The science of mastering life's greatest challenges.* Cambridge University Press.

▶ Tan, C. M. (2012). *Search inside yourself: The unexpected path to achieving success, happiness (and world peace).* New York: Harper Collins Publishers.

▶ Williams, M. and Penman, D. (2011). *Mindfulness: A practical guide to finding peace in a frantic world.* London: Piatkus.

Further useful resources

Online resources

▶ **Greater Good**: lots of articles including mentions of the latest research into mindfulness, compassion and happiness
http://greatergood.berkeley.edu/

▶ **Mindful**: full of articles and videos and updates from *Mindful Magazine*, relevant for mindfulness in everyday life and work, and other news relating to research and events on mindfulness and much, much more
http://www.mindful.org/

▶ **Wisdom 2.0**: jam packed full of free videos to watch of renowned mindfulness speakers and more, from the infamous Wisdom 2.0, the largest mindfulness conference in the world
http://www.wisdom2summit.com/

▶ **Action for Happiness**: lots of news, facts and resources and new initiatives/courses on happiness, mindfulness and much more
http://www.actionforhappiness.org/

▶ **The Mindfulness Initiative**: latest news from the UK-based advocacy project supporting the Mindfulness All Party Parliamentary Group. The initiative is aimed at increasing awareness of how mindfulness can benefit society and implementing it into UK services and institutions, including areas of education, work, health and the criminal justice system
http://www.themindfulnessinitiative.org.uk/

Further contacts for training, retreats and support

Below is a list of selected organisations (in no particular order) that offer further information and resources on mindfulness, some of which also include mindfulness-based therapy and coaching, formal training, courses and retreats:

▶ **Centre for Mindfulness, Research and Practice, Bangor University, UK**
http://www.bangor.ac.uk/mindfulness/

- **Oxford Mindfulness Centre, UK**
  http://www.oxfordmindfulness.org/
- **Be Mindful Online Mindfulness Course**
  http://www.bemindfulonline.com/the-course/
- **The London Centre for Mindfulness, UK**
  http://londoncentreformindfulness.com/
- **City Psychology Group, London, UK**
  http://citypsychology.com/
- **Institute for Mindful Leadership, Oakland, USA**
  http://instituteformindfulleadership.org/
- **Mindfulness in Schools Project, UK**
  http://mindfulnessinschools.org/
- **Breathworks, UK, Australia, USA**
  http://www.breathworks-mindfulness.org.uk/
- **Mindfulness at Work, UK**
  http://mindfulnessatwork.com/
- **The Mindfulness Project, London, UK**
  http://www.londonmindful.com/
- **London Insight Meditation, UK**
  http://www.londoninsight.org/about/about-us/
- **Gaia House, Devon, UK**
  http://gaiahouse.co.uk/
- **Spirit Rock, California, USA**
  http://www.spiritrock.org/
- **Shambhala Mountain Center, Colorado, USA**
  http://www.shambhalamountain.org/
- **The Center for Compassion and Altruism Research and Education, California, USA**
  http://ccare.stanford.edu/
- **Amaravati, Hertfordshire, UK**
  http://www.amaravati.org/
- **Plum Village, France**
  http://plumvillage.org/

▶ **Dhamma Dipa Vipassana Meditation Centre, Hereford, UK**
http://www.dipa.dhamma.org/

▶ **Sharpham House, Devon, UK**
http://www.sharphamtrust.org/

▶ **Moulin de Chaves, France**
http://www.moulindechaves.org/

▶ **The Mindfulness Institute, California, USA**
http://themindfulnessinstitute.com/

Index